Individualism and Collectivism

New Directions in Social Psychology
Richard E. Nisbett, Series Editor

Social psychology is moving in new directions as the root questions of culture, group structure, communication, collective representations, and societal conflict are being answered in innovative ways. The new social psychology not only employs the conceptual and methodological tools of social cognition but in asking broader questions often draws on sociology, political science, history, philosophy, and anthropology. By using this interdisciplinary approach, social psychologists are mapping out ways to understand the role groups play in influencing individual minds. New Directions in Social Psychology brings the best of this work together in an effort to shape and advance these emerging trends.

INDIVIDUALISM & COLLECTIVISM

Harry C. Triandis

Westview Press

Boulder • San Francisco • Oxford

New Directions in Social Psychology

Copyright © 1995 by Westview Press, Inc.

Published in 1995 in the United States of America by Westview Press, Inc., 5500 Central Avenue, Boulder, Colorado 80301-2877, and in the United Kingdom by Westview Press, 12 Hid's Copse Road, Cumnor Hill, Oxford OX2 9JJ

Library of Congress Cataloging-in-Publication Data
Triandis, Harry Charalambos, 1926–
    Individualism and collectivism / Harry C. Triandis.
       p.   cm. — (New directions in social psychology)
    Includes bibliographical references and index.
    ISBN 0-8133-1849-1 — ISBN 0-8133-1850-5 (pbk.)
    1. Individualism.   2. Collectivism.   I. Title.   II. Series.
HM136.T75   1995
302.5'4—dc20   94-46567
                                                                                                      CIP

Printed and bound in the United States of America

The paper used in this publication meets the requirements
of the American National Standard for Permanence of Paper
for Printed Library Materials Z39.48-1984.

10   9   8   7   6   5   4   3   2   1

Contents

Appendix: Measurement of Individualism
and Collectivism

Tables and Figures

Preface

I WAS RAISED IN GREECE, at a time when it was a traditional, collectivist culture. I came to North America to complete my undergraduate studies and did my Ph.D. at Cornell University. North America, north of the Rio Grande, contains largely individualist cultures. I have been fascinated by the two kinds of cultures and wrote about their differences early in my career (Triandis, 1972). Between 1980 and 1994 I did a good deal of empirical work exploring these constructs. Here I summarize this work, and I explore the rich literature produced by others that deals with this contrast.

Tendencies toward individualism and collectivism exist within every individual and in every society. Most people start by being collectivists, attached to their families. They become detached from them in different degrees and learn to be detached from collectives in different situations.

In collectivist cultures this detachment is minimal; people think of themselves as parts of their collectives and in most situations subordinate their personal goals to those of their collectives. People's social behavior is a consequence of norms, duties, and obligations. They do not give up relationships unless the relationship becomes extraordinarily costly. Such cultures are most stable. There is little change in social relationships. People do not leave their collectives; they live and die within them. When they get married, they link with another collective, and personal emotions are much less important than obligations and duties, so divorce is also rare. Children are brought up to be good members of the collective.

In individualistic cultures people are more detached from their collectives. They feel autonomous, and their social behavior maximizes enjoyment and depends on interpersonal contracts. If the goals of the collective do not match their personal goals, they think it is "obvious" that their personal goals have precedence. If the costs of relationships are greater than their enjoyments, they drop the relationships. They change relationships often, and when they get married, they do it on the basis of personal emotions, which often change over time, and thus divorce is frequent. They raise their children to be independent of their collectives. Freedom from the influence of the collective is a very important value.

Within any culture there are people who act more like collectivists or like individualists. The distributions of these attributes, however, are different.

In collectivist cultures people act like collectivists in most situations in which they are dealing with an ingroup, but they act like individualists, maximizing their benefits and outcomes, in most situations where they deal with outgroups. The switching of relationships from ingroup to outgroup and back to ingroup occurs with some regularity, and even kin can be placed in the position of being outgroup members if property or other important resources are to be divided. Thus, the maintenance of good relationships requires constant attention and the exchange of favors, gifts, and other resources. The important point is that people deal with each other not as individuals but as members of collectives, according to the roles they have in these groups, and put much effort into maintaining close relationships.

In individualist cultures people deal with each other as individuals and pay little attention to the group memberships of others. However, there are conventional ways of making group memberships salient. For example, race, religion, politics, or belief systems can function to create ingroups and outgroups, and then people in individualistic cultures act like collectivists. That makes social behavior complicated, which is why understanding the difference between individualism and collectivism is important.

This book was written to help the reader understand how the individualistic and collectivist patterns operate. They operate both across cultures and within any society and, in fact, within each human. There is a constant struggle between the collectivist and individualist elements within each human. It is useful to think of culture as a "tool kit" that contains elements that are individualistic or collectivist, which define a situation as *interpersonal* or *intergroup*. People sample elements from this tool kit to construct the meaning of situations, which determines their behavior. In cultures where most relationships are seen as *interpersonal*, we have individualism; in cultures where most situations are defined as *intergroup*, we have collectivism.

These definitions have important implications for political, social, religious, and economic life. They influence the way we perceive reality, and our philosophic views interact with these definitions, so we see the world through different lenses. In this book we will explore how the world looks through the two kinds of lenses.

In writing this book I was greatly helped by a Visiting Fellowship to the East-West Center in Honolulu, Hawaii. This was the ideal setting for writing this book because where East meets West, collectivism meets individualism. I profited greatly from discussions with Richard Brislin, who, like me, has been interested in this topic for many years. We talked every day as the book evolved, and he was especially helpful in suggesting how to start it and end it. I also received very useful, detailed comments on an early draft of the manuscript from Dharm Bawuk, Michele Gelfand, Bill Gudykunst,

Nancy Carlston, Yoshi Kashima, Uichol Kim, Richard Nisbett, and Ted Singelis. I thank all of them for taking the time to read and comment on the early versions of the manuscript.

Harry C. Triandis
Champaign, Illinois

1

*Introduction:
Two Constructs*

WHAT DO THE FOLLOWING incidents have in common?

1. In Brazil, a waiter brings one menu for four people and gives it to the "senior" member of the group, who orders the same food for all.

2. In France, each member of the group orders a different entree at a restaurant.

3. In India, a senior engineer is asked to move to New York, at a salary that is twenty-five times his salary in New Delhi, but he declines the opportunity.

4. In California, a senior engineer is asked to move to New York, at a salary that is 50 percent higher than his salary in Los Angeles, and he accepts.

5. On a street in Moscow, an older woman scolds a mother she does not know because she thinks the mother has not wrapped her child warmly enough.

6. In New York, a woman asks for help from passersby to escape from the beatings that her boyfriend is giving her, but no one helps.

7. In Japan, a supervisor knows a great deal about the personal life of each subordinate and arranges for one of his subordinates to meet a nice girl he can marry.

8. In England, a subordinate does not mention to his supervisor that his father has just died.

9. In Germany, a man walks on the grass in a public park and is reprimanded by several passersby.

10. In Illinois, a man marries a woman his parents disapprove of.

As we analyze episodes of this kind, we find that they can be explained by two constructs: collectivism and individualism. The odd-numbered episodes reflect an aspect of collectivism; the even-numbered ones an aspect of individualism. The fact that ten so diverse social behaviors can be explained by just two constructs indicates that the constructs are useful and powerful.

However, their wide applicability also represents a danger. Like the man with a hammer who uses it at every opportunity, if we do not sharpen their meaning, we can overuse the constructs.

The terms *individualism* and *collectivism* are used by many people in different parts of the world and are given various meanings. And because the terms are rather fuzzy, they are difficult to measure. Galileo Galilei said, "Science is measurement," meaning that if we are going to understand, classify, and predict events, we need to measure them. In recent years social psychologists have made numerous attempts to measure tendencies toward individualism and collectivism, and in doing so they discovered considerable complexity in what should be included in these constructs. They have also theorized about the causes and consequences of people's behaving in individualistic and collectivist ways and discovered that people are typically both individualists and collectivists. The optimal states of individual and societal health are linked to the balance between these tendencies. Many problems of modernity can be linked to too much individualism, whereas a lack of human rights can be attributed to too much collectivism. This book describes some of the studies that have led to these conclusions.

Collectivism may be initially defined as a social pattern consisting of closely linked individuals who see themselves as parts of one or more collectives (family, co-workers, tribe, nation); are primarily motivated by the norms of, and duties imposed by, those collectives; are willing to give priority to the goals of these collectives over their own personal goals; and emphasize their connectedness to members of these collectives. A preliminary definition of *individualism* is a social pattern that consists of loosely linked individuals who view themselves as independent of collectives; are primarily motivated by their own preferences, needs, rights, and the contracts they have established with others; give priority to their personal goals over the goals of others; and emphasize rational analyses of the advantages and disadvantages to associating with others.

The reader will want some explanation of why the ten behaviors mentioned above reflect these constructs. Brazil, India, Russia, and Japan are collectivist countries, though in different degrees. France, the United States, England, and Germany are individualistic countries, also in different degrees. Nevertheless, one can find both collectivist and individualistic elements in *all* these countries, in different combinations.

In Brazil, the waiter assumes that the senior member of the group will decide what to eat and that ultimately consuming the same food will intensify bonds among the members of the group, whereas in France, the waiter infers that each person has personal preferences that must be respected.

In India, the senior engineer feels he must stay close to his parents and that New York is simply too far. If his father were dying, it would be the engineer's duty to be at his bedside and facilitate his passage to the other state. Under similar conditions in the United States, it is more likely that the parent would be placed in a nursing home. The parent and his son have their own lives and are independent entities.

In Russia it is assumed that the whole community is responsible for child rearing. If the parent is not doing an adequate job, an older person is responsible for upholding community standards. "Putting one's nose in another person's business" is perfectly natural and expected.

One's supervisor in Japan is often like a father, one who is obliged to attend to the needs of his subordinates. Locating a suitable mate for a subordinate may be one of his duties. In England, where individualism is quite intense, the death of a parent may be private information not to be shared with a supervisor. U. Kim (1994b) did a national survey in Korea and asked a representative sample of firms whether they carry out specific acts in relation to their personnel. He found that 47 percent of Korean firms send condolences to employees whose grandparents died. No less than 79 percent congratulate employees when their children marry. Even school admission of an employee's child is cause for congratulation (15 percent of the firms); 31 percent congratulate employees for the birthday of one of their parents-in-law. No less than 40 percent send condolences for the death of a parent-in-law. Of course, all the firms congratulate employees on the birth of a child and the like. Services provided to employees include opportunities to go to picnics (89 percent) and to a library (44 percent).

Germany, though overall quite individualistic, is also collectivist in certain respects. The German episode is illustrative of collectivist behavior. Walking on hard-to-grow grassy areas is a community concern, and witnesses to such "deviant" behavior may take action. In most cultures, people try to marry a spouse that their parents find acceptable. However, in very individualistic cultures like the United States, it is assumed that people are independent entities and can marry someone regardless of parental disapproval. In individualist cultures marriage is an institution that only links two people and not their respective families. In collectivist cultures it links two families, in which case it is mandatory that the families find the mate acceptable.

Countries Versus Cultures

In the foregoing examples, I used the country as the equivalent of the culture. This equivalence is very approximate. Some estimates of the number of cultures that exist begin with 10,000. The UN had 186 countries at the time of this writing; thus it is obvious that each country includes many cultures. Most countries consist of hundreds of cultures and corresponding subcultures. For example, most occupational groups, corporations, or ethnic groups have fairly distinct cultures. A culture is usually linked to a language, a particular time period, and a place. English is widely used in different parts of the world, for example, India and Singapore, but that does not mean that all people who speak English possess the same culture. They may have more in common, of course, with other English speakers than with people who speak Chinese, but language on its own is insufficient to create a common culture. Historical period and geographic location are also needed to define a culture. The culture of British Columbia, Canada, is not identical to the culture of New South Wales, Australia. The culture of Illinois, 1950, is not the same as the culture of Illinois, 1990. Culture emerges in interaction. As people interact, some of their ways of thinking, feeling, and behaving are transmitted to each other and become automatic ways of reacting to specific situations. The shared beliefs, attitudes, norms, roles, and behaviors are aspects of culture.

Culture in the Examples

Culture is to society what memory is to individuals. It includes the things that have "worked" in the past. For example, one who invents a tool might tell his or her children about this tool. Others may pick up the idea and use it too. Soon, people come and go and the tool remains. The society uses the tool like a memory of what has worked in the past. Tools are parts of culture, just as are words, shared beliefs, attitudes, norms, roles, and values, which are called elements of "subjective culture" (Triandis, 1972).

One of culture's most important aspects is "unstated assumptions." The assumption that we are bound together into tight groups of interdependent individuals is fundamental to collectivism. The assumption that we are independent entities, different and distant from our groups, is fundamental to individualism. If we look at the ten examples, we see that such assumptions hold. The Brazilian waiter saw a group of interconnected individuals, with a "senior" member who would order the food. The French waiter saw individual preferences as unrelated to group influences. The Indian engineer saw himself linked to his parents; the American engineer saw his parents as having a life of their own. The elderly Russian woman saw herself linked to the mother passing by; the New Yorkers saw no ties to the woman asking for help. The Japanese supervisor saw himself linked to his subordinates and thus felt that it was his duty to take care of their personal problems. The English subordinate saw himself not linked at all to his supervisor, so the supervisor had no inherent right to obtain private information. The German citizens saw themselves linked to the community and felt a need to defend it from a person who broke the rules. The Illinois man saw himself as a discrete entity, only weakly linked to his parents.

Such basic unstated assumptions are so fundamental that we are unaware of them. It is not until we come into contact with people from another cultures that we realize that our assumptions are not universal. An interesting example is the case of a Japanese biologist by the name of Imanishi, discussed in detail by Dale (1986). Imanishi argued that it is not individuals who struggle for survival, as Darwin stated, but species. Darwin, as a Westerner, used the individual as the "obvious" unit of analysis. Imanishi, as a collectivist, used the species. Such a distinction is an interesting example of how our basic assumptions play themselves out in our purview of the world.

Individual Differences

We know that there are people in each of the countries that were mentioned in the examples who would have acted very differently. In every culture there are people who are *allocentric*, who believe, feel, and act very much like collectivists do around the world. There are also people who are *idiocentric*, who believe, feel, and act the way individualists do around the world. For example, we know Americans who would not hesitate to marry someone their parents dislike, but we also know Americans who would never do such a thing. In China those who press for human rights are likely to be idiocentric in a collectivist culture. In the United States, those who join communes are likely to be allocentric in an individualistic culture. Thus, in every culture we get the full distribution of both types.

If I claim that Americans eat red meat, that would be statistically correct because more than 85 percent of them do. Americans, in fact, eat more red meat than people in most other countries do. But there are vegetarians in the United States, and there are people who watch their cholesterol and eat only fish. Any generalization, therefore, is a statistical tendency.

Furthermore, what may be called "the situation" is very important. People who have been raised in collectivist cultures tend to "cognitively convert" situations into collectivist settings; people who have been raised in individualistic cultures tend to convert situations into individualistic settings. The Englishman who did not mention to his supervisor that his father had died may be more idiocentric than most Britons and also may have perceived the supervisor-subordinate situation as more distant, less interdependent, than is true of the perceptions of most Britons. In contrast, the trend in collectivist cultures is to perceive closeness between members of the group. Thus, for instance, after a meeting with a stranger, and after establishing what might become an ingroup relationship, the collectivist may ask, "How much money do you make per month?" The corresponding trend in individualistic cultures is to be idiocentric and convert most situations into social relationships of separateness. Thus, for instance, when individualists hear someone's calls for help, they may say to themselves, "That's not my problem."

Social Patterns

There are several factors to consider in ascertaining how a social pattern like collectivism or individualism operates. First, as mentioned earlier, language, historical period, and geographic region reflect specific "subjective cultures." Subjective culture may be defined as shared beliefs, attitudes, norms, roles, and values found among speakers of a particular language who live during the same historical period in a specified geographic region. These shared elements of subjective culture are usually transferred from generation to generation. Since communication requires language and occurs most readily among people who live in the same historic period and sufficiently close to each other to communicate easily, *language, time,* and *place* help define culture. Culture is superorganic (does not depend on the presence of particular individuals), and at some point in its history, it probably adopted the specific elements of subjective culture. Major changes in climate and ecology (e.g., methods of making a living, subsistence patterns), historical events (e.g., wars, conquests by another cultural group), and cultural diffusion (from migration or exposure to the products of other cultures) may drastically affect culture. For example, Weiss et al. (1993) showed how the Akkadians, a major civilization of the 3000 to 2200 B.C. period, collapsed as a society because of a significant climatic change. When the region to their north became exceedingly arid, there was mass migration to the Akkadians' area, which they were unable to stop in spite of building walls, and eventually they were overcome.

Frequently the elements of subjective culture become organized around a central theme. We then have a "cultural syndrome." With respect to individualism, the theme includes the idea that individuals are the units of analysis and are autonomous; in the case of collectivism, the theme incorporates the notion that groups are the units of analysis and individuals are tightly intertwined parts of these groups.

Gould and Kolb (1964) defined individualism as a belief that the individual is an end in herself and ought to realize the self and cultivate judgment, notwithstanding the weight of pervasive social pressure in the direction of conformity. Triandis (1990) relied on this definition to propose that collectivism includes (1) emphasis on the views, needs, and goals of the ingroup rather than on the self; (2) emphasis on behavior determined by social norms and duties rather than by pleasure or personal advantage; (3) common beliefs that are shared with the ingroup; and (4) willingness to cooperate with ingroup members.

In their important review of how the independent and interdependent self influences cognition, emotion, and motivation, Markus and Kitayama (1991b) used the terms *independent construal of the self, individualism, egocentric, separate, autonomous, idiocentric,* and *self-contained* as parallel. Similarly, they used the *interdependent construal of the self* as having the connotations of sociocentric, holistic, collective, allocentric, ensembled, constituitive, contextualist, connected, and relational. In short, many more or less equivalent terms can be found in the literature.

Gudykunst and San Antonio (1993) reported that the Japanese prefer "group-oriented" (*shudanshugi*) because "collectivism" (*zentaishugi*) has connotations suggesting dictatorial political systems. They reported preferred terms like *contextualist* and *interindividualism* and mentioned that individualism has negative connotations in Japan, where it is linked to "selfishness." In China also, individualism is a pejorative term. When I was in Beijing in 1988, I read in the local English-language press about an incident in which a student had clear symptoms of schizophrenia. He was initially deemed "too individualistic" but after becoming dangerous was diagnosed as mentally ill.

The terms *individualism* and *collectivism* have a history of about 300 years, which I will review in the next chapter, but I will outline some of the major points here. Durkheim (orig. 1893; retransl. 1984) drew a distinction between "mechanical solidarity," which occurs when members of a society are so similar that they relate to each other automatically without considering that any other option exists, and "organic solidarity," where there is functional specialization and people are interdependent because it is advantageous. The first pattern is similar to basic collectivism; the second to individualism.

The reader may have encountered other terms in the literature that overlap in meaning with collectivism and individualism. A sample of these follows: Toennies (1957) distinguished between *Gemeinschaft* (community) and *Gesellschaft* (society), which again correspond rather closely to the constructs of collectivism and individualism. F. Kluckhohn and Strodtbeck (1961) used the terms *collaterality* and *individualism;* Weber (1947, 1957), *communal* and *associative* social relations; Parsons (1949), the terms *collectivity* and *self-emphasis;* Bakan (1966), *community* and *agency;* Witkin and Berry (1975), *dependence* on the frame and *independence* from the frame; Weber (1930, 1958) and Inkeles and Smith (1974) used *traditionalism* and *modernity.* These constructs, although they do not match perfectly, include ideas that are largely overlapping.

Cultural Syndromes, Situations, and Behavior

In collectivist cultures people have more collectivist cognitive elements (e.g., my work group wants me to do this) and are more likely to sample these elements when they give meaning to social situations; in individualistic cultures people have more personal constructs (e.g., I am kind) and are more likely to sample such individualist elements (Triandis, 1989).

The same situation can be seen from different points of view, depending on which elements are sampled. In a given situation where, for instance, one is asked to contribute to a charity, some elements of the self will be sampled. An individualist is more likely to sample the individualist elements and think that being kind, responsible, and generous requires a contribution to the charity. A collectivist, in the same situation, may think that his family expects him to spend money on them as an aspect of being kind, and if he contributes to that charity, he may not be able to also contribute to his church, which would be consistent with the expectations of the other members of the church, and thus may decide not to give. In short, which elements are sampled is an important determinant of social behavior. Individuals have *both* individualistic and collectivist cognitive elements. Therefore, a person considered allocentric is one who is simply more likely than a person considered idiocentric to sample collectivist elements and use them to construct the meaning of a social situation.

In addition, in collectivist cultures, more situations are converted into collectivist ones. Consider the situation of buying a carpet for the house. Most individualists will shop around, will find one or two carpets that are within the price range they are willing to pay, and will consult one or two members of their family and buy the carpet. Most collectivists are likely to proceed in a more elaborate way. First, they are likely to establish a personal relationship with a storekeeper. Ideally, they will find a member of their kin group who sells carpets, or a friend of a member of the kinship group who does that. They will tell this person about their needs and give details of their income and family life. Having established trust with this merchant, they will examine the stock and find a number of carpets that may be suitable. They will then invite a large portion of their ingroup to view the carpets and express their opinions. Finally, after extensive consultations, they will purchase the carpet. Whereas the individualist primarily has an exchange relationship with the merchant—I pay my money and receive the carpet—the collectivist fosters a personal relationship, allowing the merchant to learn a great deal, in order to arrive at the best decision.

The consequence of such differences in behavior is that psychological variables operate somewhat differently in collectivist and individualistic cultures. The collectivist variables are likely to converge and form a cultural syndrome; the individualistic variables are likely to converge and form a different syndrome. For example, collectivists want their ingroups to be monolithic and homogeneous—with everyone thinking, feeling, and acting in the same way; they think that in such groups there will be harmony. They feel more comfortable than individualists in the presence of like-minded others.

Individualists emphasize harmony less and often think that an argument clears the air.

The importance of the situation can be seen in Moskowitz, Suh, and Desaulniers (1994), who monitored interpersonal behavior for twenty days, using an event-sampling strategy. The behaviors were classified as reflecting "agency" (similar to individualist behavior) or "communion" (collectivist behavior). They found that agency behaviors were more different when a person interacted with a supervisor or a subordinate than when men interacted with men or women with women; in contrast, communion behaviors were more frequent when women interacted with women than when men interacted with men. In sum, the situation is a major determinant of the behavior.

Ingroups and Outgroups

Ingroups are groups of individuals about whose welfare a person is concerned, with whom that person is willing to cooperate without demanding equitable returns, and separation from whom leads to anxiety (Triandis, 1988, p. 75). In Triandis, McCusker, et al. (1993), for instance, we found that our sample from Indonesia indicated that they feel anxious when they are not with their ingroup.

Ingroups are usually characterized by similarities among the members, and individuals have a sense of "common fate" with members of the ingroup. For example, those who live in the same village may have a sense of common fate linked to the ecology and climate of that locale. Belonging to the same group often has the effect of suggesting that one has the right to get involved in the affairs of fellow members. Clear outgroups are groups with which one has something to divide, perhaps unequally, or are harmful in some way, groups that disagree on valued attributes, or groups with which one is in conflict. There are also groups that are neither ingroups nor clear outgroups. In such ambiguous relationships collectivists and individualists are most likely to differ in their behavior. Collectivists are inclined to see ambiguous groups as outgroups; individualists tend to view groups characterized by such ambiguity as quasi-ingroups.

Each culture has its own important ingroups. The family is usually an ingroup, but depending on the culture, other groups, such as friends, political parties, civic organizations, social classes, religious groups, and educational, athletic, economic (e.g., the Mafia, corporations), artistic (e.g., an opera company), racial, tribal, caste, language (e.g., Quebec), or location (e.g., a village) collectives, may function as ingroups. J. K. Campbell (1964) described a culture in northern Greece in which the only ingroup is the kinship group. People do not make friends with those with whom they are not related. In this culture, despite intense conflict with outgroups, one must marry a member of the outgroup.

Even a member of the kin group can become an outgroup member if there are insults, improper behavior, or conflict over property. For example, in many collectivist cultures, "crimes of honor" involve a father or brother killing their daughter or sister who has broken an important taboo, such as having had premarital sexual relations. Among collectivists, who value homogeneity, when a relationship with another group is characterized by long-term conflict, ethnic cleansing can be seen as a "natural" consequence.

History is more important to collectivists than to individualists. Collectivists see themselves as links in a long chain that consists of ancestors and descendants. In fact, in collectivist cultures people usually can trace their lineage for hundreds, sometimes thousands of years. This rarely occurs among individualists. The individualist is in the center of the stage—what comes before and after is more or less irrelevant.

Brewer's Optimal Distinctiveness Theory

Brewer (1991) argued that individuals in all cultures wish to be both similar to an ingroup and different from an ingroup. If they feel included in the ingroup, their need for *assimilation* is minimal; if they feel excluded from the ingroup this need is maximal (see Figure 1.1). If they feel highly included, their need to be different is high. She called this need *differentiation*. If the individuals are not included, this need is minimal. As a result, the gradients of assimilation and differentiation are two lines that intersect at the *optimal distinctiveness* point. This is the point where people feel most comfortable. Brewer and Weber (1994) obtained impressive support for this conception in two experiments.

Extrapolating from Brewer's theory, I can state that in collectivist cultures the optimal distinctiveness point is close to the high-inclusiveness pole; in individualist cultures this point is near the low-inclusiveness pole. This conceptualization (Figure 1.1) also suggests that individualists have a sharp gradient for differentiation and a flat gradient for assimilation, and the opposite pattern holds for collectivists.

The Defining Attributes of the Constructs

Among individualists the self is defined independently of specific collectives. The autonomous individual, for example, thinks of herself as Ms. Ann Marie Elizabeth Smith, not "a mother," "a member of the X religion" or "of the Y tribe." In this social pattern one is not expected to get involved "in the business" of group members. Among collectivists the self includes many of the attributes of the groups a person belongs to.

FIGURE 1.1 Brewer's Theory and Individualism and Collectivism

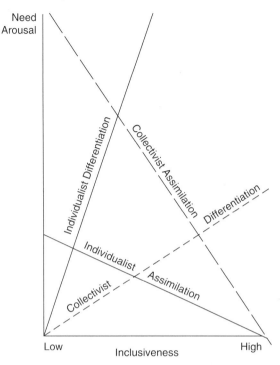

Collectivists are concerned with the goals of collectives and individuals. Such goals are consistent, so the individual does what the collective expects, asks, or demands, without opposing the will of the collective. Such individuals enjoy doing what is "right" from the perspective of the collective. Individualists, however, may have personal goals that are inconsistent with the goals of their ingroups. When conflict exists between the collective and the individual in individualistic cultures, it seems "natural" that the individual will attempt to reach her goals and ignore the goals of the ingroup. In collectivist cultures, in contrast, it is understood that the collective's goals override those of the individual.

A third defining attribute is that collectivists carry out their obligations and perform what is expected of them as specified by ingroup norms; individualists do what is enjoyable and required by contracts they have established with others. Although contracts carry a moral obligation similar to doing one's duty, collectivists are often socialized to *enjoy* doing their duty, even if that requires some sacrifices. Individualists do their duty only when their computations of the advantages and disadvantages suggest they would derive a clear benefit.

In order to understand interpersonal relationships in collectivist and individualist cultures, and in situations where people from these two kinds of cultures interact, we must learn about these constructs. Individualists are especially concerned with pleasure, and an aspect of this concern is an emphasis on high self-esteem.

The emphasis on high self-esteem may lead to narcissism, as discussed by Katz (1993). Based on observations in an affluent Midwestern suburban school, she reported on how individualism is generated in the United States. Working from copied pages prepared by the teacher, each student produced a booklet called "All About Me." The first page asked for basic information about the child's home and family. The second page was titled "what I like to eat," followed by other pages covering "what I like to watch on TV," "what I want for a present," "where I want to go on vacation," and so on. Katz observed that there were no pages on "what I want to know more about," "what I want to solve," or "what I want to make."

Collectivists would observe that there were no pages titled "what are my duties," "what am I expected to do for my mother," "what am I expected to do for my father," "what am I expected to do for my country." Individualists thus construct their self-concept by focusing on personal attributes; collectivists focus on collective attributes, linking them to other people and to collectives.

This link affects their view of relationships. Collectivists maintain established relationships even if it is not in their best interests to do so. Individualists rationally analyze the advantages and disadvantages of maintaining and fostering relationships. Collectivists may also make such computations, but their threshold for forfeiting relationships is much higher.

Cultural Clashes

The defining attributes combine to create different kinds of social behaviors in collectivist and individualist cultures. Such differences can be seen most clearly when people from a collectivist culture, like Japan, interact with people from an individualist culture, such as the United States. Nancy Sakamoto (1982), an American married to a Japanese, noted six underlying polite fictions that create problems for American-Japanese relationships. Whereas Americans assume that "you and I are equal," Japanese adopt the view that "you are my superior." In short, Japanese maintain good relationships by showing deference, especially to outsiders. Second, Americans assume that "you and I are close friends," whereas the Japanese take the view "I am in awe of you." For instance, a Japanese may say, "My wife's cooking is very poor" (implying that for such an exalted person as you, it is not good enough), and then produce a superb meal. Such apologies are used to lubricate relationships and create an ingroup with high solidarity.

Third, the American tends to take the position that "you and I are relaxed," whereas the Japanese takes the view "I am busy on your behalf." The American thinks that "hanging loose" is especially good for interpersonal relationships. However, the Japanese "stands at attention" to make sure that no one loses face. Fourth, the American assumes that "you and I are independent," and the Japanese assumes that "I depend on you." Assuming that people are independent, the American feels comfortable saying no, but the Japanese does not say no, since that might break the bond between the two. Fifth, the American assumes that "you and I are individuals," whereas the Japanese assumes that "you and I are members of groups." Any act has implications only for individuals in one case, but it usually has implications for groups in the other case. Sixth, the American takes the position that "you and I are unique," and the Japanese takes the position that "you and I feel/think alike." Thus, an American might look for original arguments to convince the Japanese, whereas the Japanese will tentatively sound out the American to find areas of agreement. Thus the American can be seen as confrontational and the Japanese as weak and indecisive. Silence is regarded as strength in Japan but is cold and negative in the United States. The American pattern thus reflects the underlying assumptions of individualism and the Japanese pattern those of collectivism.

The Utility of the Constructs

It is worth repeating that the fact that these constructs tie together very different behaviors in different parts of the world, as the examples that opened the chapter suggested, is one of their strengths. These constructs may be applied broadly, that is, to personal, business, and political interactions. A clash between these two opposing viewpoints could have international consequences. It is clear that following the cold war the major world conflicts are likely to be cultural and the difference between collectivist and individualist cultures may result in major cleavages (Huntington, 1993). The majority of the world, roughly 70 percent of the population, is collectivist, and many in these groups disagree with Western views. As they become more powerful (the economies of China and India are now among the top five), they will increasingly object to being "pushed around." For example, the individualistic emphasis on human rights does not necessarily suit all the leaders of collectivist countries.

The Asian point of view was expressed by Kausikan (1993, pp. 62–63), the representative of Singapore to the United Nations World Conference on Human Rights held in Vienna, Austria, in June 1993. He pointed out that Asia has become very strong economically and will not be ordered around and added:

Most Asians do not want to be considered good Westerners, even if they are friendly to the West. Many in Asia believe that the West's persistent economic problems stem from their emphasis on individual rights. Some suspect that attempts to foist Western interpretations of human rights on them may be intended to drag them down to the lowest common level.

Later on he stated:

Asia will insist on its own values and interests in the ongoing interpretation of international human rights. This will require genuine dialogue because most of Asia is now too strong to be coerced. Of course, cultural diversity should not be used to shield dictators. Murder is murder whether perpetrated in America or Asia. No nation claims torture as part of their cultural heritage. Everyone has the right to be recognized as a person before the law. And there are other such rights that must be enjoyed by all human beings everywhere in the civilized world. But the hard core of rights that is truly universal is smaller than the West maintained at Vienna and is less enamored with unlimited individual and press freedoms.

A concrete case was mentioned on National Public Radio several times in the spring of 1994. An American teenager sprayed paint on seventeen cars in Singapore. He was sentenced to receive six strikes with a cane, a process that is supposed to be so painful that individuals have been known to request lengthy prison sentences to avoid it. President Bill Clinton appealed to the Singapore government, arguing that the sentence was too severe. The sentence was reduced to four strikes but was carried out. The relevant magistrate in Singapore suggested to the U.S. critics that they should adopt the methods of Singapore to reduce crime in U.S. cities. The American position emphasizes sympathy with the individual, focusing on the pain that he will endure. The Singapore position recognizes that the society has been injured. This event is treated very differently through individualistic and collectivist glasses (i.e., the *Kulturbrille,* the "cultural glasses," of Ichheiser, 1970).

The issues raised here are complex. Granted, no culture considers torture desirable. But in any culture, torture may occur. In a collectivist culture, where the rights of the individual are less important than the rights of the state, when torture is convenient for the state, it will take place. Even in the United States, where the laws protect individuals as much as in any other country, police torture does occasionally take place. There is a tendency for the powerful to torture, as long as they can find a reasonable cover, such as serving God or the state. Thus, guarantees that torture is illegal are needed. At the same time, it is important for everyone to understand the difference between torture and appropriate punishment in specific cultures.

The case of the caning illustrates the fundamental difference in the perspective between individualists and collectivists, and it is my hope that in this book we will explore both points of view and by understanding them better facilitate the dialogue that Kausikan suggested is needed to reach a universal code of human rights.

Contact between individualists and collectivists is increasing, and a better understanding between the two is essential. A major factor leading to increased contact is that the West is generally rich and much of the world is generally poor. The gulf between the rich and the poor is becoming larger. In the eighteenth century the gross national product per capita (GNP/cap) of the rich was twice that of the poor; in 1950 this ratio had become 50 to 1; in 1990 it was 70 to 1. As the differences become larger and mass communication and easy transportation become available, mass migrations from the poor lands to the rich take place. Estimates that about 100,000 Chinese and 1 million Latin Americans are entering the United States illegally each year suggest that collectivists are increasingly more likely to interface with individualists.

In the formerly Communist countries, the shift toward market economies has much in common with the shift from collectivism to individualism in many parts of the world. The weakening of trade unions and the ascendancy of entrepreneurs who manage small companies worldwide, the shift from the Labor party to the Conservative party in Britain, and many other phenomena are not unrelated to these constructs.

At the same time, the globalization of economic activity in the world is characterized by a new tribalism (Kotkin, 1993). The Chinese of Hong Kong are investing with the Chinese of Singapore and Vancouver rather than with the Europeans; the Japanese form economic conglomerates (banks, manufacturing and trading companies) that channel economic activities among Japanese; the Jewish diaspora involves many exchanges among fellow Jews; the Greek shipowners trade with each other; and so on. Kotkin described the new tribes as cosmopolitans embedded in tribes who use one set of rules for the ingroup and a different one for the outgroup. This is a "classic" collectivist behavior pattern. The world is the stage of these cosmopolitans. They form unassimilated cultural pockets in larger communities, holding Calvinist values (puritan self-denial, Spartan private lives, opposition to the corrupt elites they compete with), and their major concern is economic success. They are scattered in both their origins and their destinations—Parses from India, Lebanese, Armenians, Ibos from Nigeria, Cubans in Florida, Koreans. As de Tocqueville (1985) observed, they never stop thinking about what they do not have. They are individualists in their motivational structure, yet collectivists in the way they relate to each other and their competitors.

If we are to understand each other fully, we must understand what individualism and collectivism are and how they operate in different situations. This book attempts to provide a better understanding of these views.

Outline of This Book

In Chapter 2, I review some of the uses of the terms *individualism* and *collectivism* from the eighteenth through the twentieth centuries. They were first used to discuss political systems but are now employed in anthropology, psychology, and sociology. Both Eastern and Western philosophers have had much to say on the issues central to the debate over individualism and collectivism. This discussion will illustrate that "pure" individualism or collectivism is undesirable and that a balanced mixture of the two social patterns is ideal. Some of these philosophers have proposed a "communitarian" agenda, which integrates the strengths of both individualism and collectivism. We will look briefly at these developments.

Chapter 3 provides an analysis of the attributes of individualism and collectivism and an examination of these constructs as "cultural syndromes." Individualism is defined by the attributes discussed above and is found mostly in Europe and North America, although some preliterate societies also have this cultural syndrome. Collectivism is organized around the centrality of the position of the collective and is found in most of the "rest" of the world. Thus, we usually have the contrast between "the West" and "the rest." Chapter 3 also presents the defining and culture-specific attributes of individualism and collectivism. There are more than a hundred attributes that appear related to these constructs in *some* culture. Thus, people in each culture behave in ways that reflect unique configurations of attributes, some collectivist and some individualist.

An analogy suggested by Triandis (1990), that collectivism is similar to water and individualism to ice, may help the student to understand the two constructs. Almost all cultures may be likened to lakes containing bits of floating ice. As cultures become more modern, complex, and dynamic, though, they become more individualist.

We know from the animal literature that infant primates thrive only when they have close relationships with others, which suggests the universal importance of collectives. Yet, as we enter the modern, impersonal, competitive world of large bureaucracies, we freeze many of our relationships and make them the subjects of intense analyses—should I invest time in this relationship or drop it? Will it pay to be nice to X? What are the costs of my relationship with Y? This view, then, shows that all of us are partly collectivists but are also more or less individualists. Some of us use very few collectivist elements; some of us use very few individualist elements.

In Chapter 4, I examine the probable antecedents of the constructs and focus on the geographic distribution of the cultural syndromes. We will see that although the West tends to be individualistic and much of the rest collectivist, there are many exceptions. Furthermore, in most societies, women tend to be more collectivist than men; the upper-class, urban, younger samples tend to be more individualistic than the lower-class, rural, and older samples. Other variables are also important antecedents of the cultural patterns and will be discussed in Chapter 4.

Chapter 5 focuses on the consequences of these cultural syndromes. It examines a number of phenomena that are apparently occurring in different patterns in collectivist and individualist cultures. For example, ingroups are perceived as more heterogeneous than outgroups in individualistic cultures, but this finding seems to be reversed in collectivist cultures. Perhaps the large social desirability of the concept of a homogeneous group among collectivists results in the perception of ingroups as more homogeneous than outgroups.

In Chapter 6, I present some applications of the theory concerning individualism and collectivism, including how we can help the two cultures adjust to each other. A valuable method of cross-cultural training is to present scenarios describing critical incidents involving members of two cultures. The trainee is asked to ascertain the cause of a certain behavior in the other group. Pretests establish what attributions people from the host culture generally make in such situations. When the trainee makes the incorrect attributions, she is told that another attribution is correct; when the correct attribution is selected, feedback is given that explains the key cultural features that result in that attribution's being correct. When members of the trainee's culture make many attributions that differ from the attributions made by members of the host culture, there is something to teach the trainee. Specifically, one shapes the attributions of the trainee to make them consistent (Triandis, 1975) with the attributions normally made in the host culture. Thus, the trainee learns to view the social environment in the way of the host. This increases the trainee's understanding and reduces culture shock.

Chapter 7 is an evaluation of the constructs. I examine the advantages and disadvantages of each cultural syndrome. "Pure" versions of each cultural pattern are seen as highly undesirable. Pure individualism means a Hobbesian "war of all against all," selfishness, narcissism, anomie, crime, high rates of divorce, and child abuse. Pure collectivism, under conditions of intergroup hostility, means ethnic cleansing, oppression of human rights, and exploitation of the ingroup's members for the benefit of the ingroup. In short, a healthy society uses both cultural patterns, perhaps in equal amounts, although this is subject to further research. However, although we may reject both pure individualism and collectivism, the reality is that pure versions continue to exist in some circumstances among many groups worldwide and must be studied and understood.

Finally, the Appendix presents what is known about the measurement of these constructs. Because there are upwards of twelve methods of measurement and because this information might not interest the average reader, it has been placed in a separate section. As we will see, multimethod measurement at the cultural level differs from that at the individual level.

2

Individualism and Collectivism in Philosophy and the Social Sciences

ENGLISH POLITICAL PHILOSOPHERS of the eighteenth and nineteenth centuries used the terms *individualism* and *collectivism* for the first time. Individualism was synonymous with liberalism and included the ideas of maximum freedom of the individual, the existence of voluntary groups that individuals can join or leave as they please, and equal participation of individuals in group activities. The term that contrasted with individualism was *authoritarianism*, which denied these freedoms of the individual and required individuals to submit to the will of an authority, such as the king. During that time a widely shared idea was that obedience to authority was essential to avoid lawlessness and anarchy.

In the eighteenth century the individualistic ideas of the American Revolution (all men are created equal, pursuit of happiness) and the French Revolution (liberty, equality) provoked reactions that were termed *collectivism*. The individualism of John Locke was countered by the collectivism of Jean-Jacques Rousseau, who in his *Social Contract* argued that the individual is free only by submitting to the general will. The general will was conceived as the common core of opinion that remains after private wills cancel each other out and that can be ascertained by majority voting. The general will is always right and tends to the public advantage (*Encyclopedia Britannica*, 1953 edition).

In economics the emphasis on laissez-faire individualism (e.g., Adam Smith in *The Wealth of Nations*) contrasted with the Marxist collectivist advocacy that the government should own the means of production. In politics there was the "as little government as possible" capitalism on the one hand and fascism on the other, where the leader embodied the will of the nation and all had to submit to that will. The positions of social democrats, socialists, and communists were divided between uncontrolled capitalism and fascism, becoming increasingly more collectivist in the order stated above.

Alexis de Tocqueville (originally translated in 1835 and 1840; reprinted in 1985), displeased with the regime of Louis Philippe in France, asked the Ministry of Justice, his employer, for permission to visit the United States to study the prison system. During the nine months in 1831–1832 he traveled throughout the country, he was impressed by the individualism that seemed to permeate this new society. His work inspired a modern study of individualism in America (Bellah et al., 1985).

Constructs very similar to individualism and collectivism have been used in philosophy and in all the social sciences. There is a large literature, which I can cover here only briefly; I will concentrate on those aspects that are most relevant to social psychology. The literature is large because the constructs touch on the central concerns of all the social sciences, and they appear to function as "bridges" between social psychological theories developed in the West and the realities of social life in East Asia, where a substantial number of social psychologists have become well known in recent years.

We will now review what philosophers, anthropologists, sociologists, political scientists, economists, and psychologists have contributed to the understanding of the constructs. It will become clear during this discussion that "pure" collectivism and individualism are quite undesirable social patterns, and what is needed is a mixture of the two. "Communitarians," in philosophy and other disciplines, have tried to define a social pattern that combines the best attributes of each of these cultural patterns. I will end the chapter by reviewing some of these conceptions.

Disciplinary Contributions

Philosophy

The Greek Sophists of the fifth century B.C. were among the first clearly individualist philosophers. They proclaimed, "In Crete do as the Cretans"; hence the *individual* can decide how to behave, without following the norms of her/his ingroup. Plato and Socrates opposed the Sophists because they did not have "standards of what is good and proper." Their reputation in the West has been poor because of this opposition. The word "sophistry" suggests this. However, the Sophists' purpose was to teach their pupils to be successful in the courts, in debate, and in politics. Individual success is a key idea of individualism. The social organization of Athens, with its democracy, debates, and so on, made such skills valuable, and in fact the Sophists were financially very successful.

According to the Sophists any means to success was "good." Socrates and Plato thought this idea immoral and that one should stick to the "truth" even if that means not succeeding. Protagoras, a major Sophist philosopher, trained young men to succeed and charged high fees, through which he became rich. Plato provided a model of civic life that included philosopher kings, not unlike the authorities of the ingroup that one finds in collectivist cultures. Certainly, his *Republic* was a collectivist, paternalistic document.

In the East, in approximately the same period, Confucius emphasized the importance of virtue. This view is implicit also in most of the Eastern religions, such as Hinduism, Buddhism, Taoism, and Shintoism. In those religions, the most important consideration is given to virtue—defined as traditionally "proper" behavior—rather than to what is revealed in a "great book" (the Truth).

Hofstede (1991) argued that the Eastern ideologies emphasize the importance of virtuous action and the need to carry out the prescribed rituals, whereas the religions of the Levantine region emphasize the correct "belief." Thus, the West is more concerned with belief, logic, analysis, and theory; the East with ethical behavior, self-improvement, ritual, meditation, and the correct way of living. In the East, ideas such as harmony with others, tolerance of differences of opinions, filial piety (obedience to parents, respect for parents, honoring ancestors, financial support of parents), chastity of women, and patriotism are more important than belief in a particular deity. In the West, faith in the appropriate "prophet" or deity is crucial. In the East, the individual is a link in a chain between ancestors and descendants. In the West, the individual "stands alone before his creator."

Hofstede's summary of the Confucian tradition (1991, p. 165) included the following points:

1. The stability of society is based on unequal relations between people. Relationships are based on mutual and complementary obligations.

2. The family is the prototype of all social organizations. Saving face is all-important.

3. Virtuous behavior toward others consists of not treating others as one would not like to be treated oneself (the negative version of the Golden Rule).

4. Virtue with regard to one's tasks in life consists of trying to acquire skills and education, working hard, not spending more than necessary, and being patient and persevering. It is remarkable how well these values come through in empirical studies of the modern Chinese (Chinese Cultural Connection, 1987; Triandis, Bontempo, et al., 1990).

At the same time, when reading Confucius (1915), one is struck by the extent to which some of his statements urged people to be individualists. For example, unlike the tendency of most collectivists (which we will review in Chapter 3) to pay more attention to the context and the situation than to internal processes, Confucius advocated that "the superior man can find himself in no position in which he is not himself. In a high situation he does not treat with contempt his inferiors, in a low situation he does not court the favour of his superiors" (Doctrine of the Mean, Confucius, 1915, pp. 105–106). In short, the individual's attributes are steady, regardless of who the other is. Similarly, Confucius advocated direct speech and honesty, but modern collectivists often engage in indirect speech and use white lies very often. Confucius's emphasis on duty was coupled with an emphasis on self-development. In short, his positions were more complex and balanced than the attributes developed by his followers.

The Chinese tradition (deBary, in preparation) includes prescriptions such as: "Be loyal to your sovereign, filial to your parents, friendly to your younger brothers, and brotherly to your older brothers." It specifies in great detail how many good deeds are necessary (1,200 to become an immortal of heaven, 300 to become an immortal of earth), what not to do (swear to seek vindication, love liquor, be angry with relatives, be an unfaithful husband, boast and brag, disobey commands of superiors, be disloyal, leap over food that is on the floor, etc.), and what to do (be gentle, obedient).

For example, good deeds are to aid your relatives, teachers, or friends; save good people from calamities; save people from falling into debt or crime or from becoming separated from their families. Helping the poor, travelers, and the seriously sick are also mentioned as good deeds. Most of the good deeds promote both collectivist goals and the general public good (e.g., in winter give bedding to the poor). The collectivism is clear: Do not ignore your own relatives and treat others as if they were your kin; do not let what you hear from servants and slaves cause you to turn against your relatives and friends.

The concreteness of the proscriptions is especially noteworthy. For instance, one must not dance on the last day of the month; weep, spit, or urinate facing north; point at a rainbow; kill tortoises or snakes. These concrete proscriptions are mixed together with very general ones, such as not killing men unjustly or wrongly seizing another's property. There are also specifications of what behavior is appropriate for office helpers, physicians, monks, women, rich men, household slaves, farmers and peasants, dealers and merchants, craftsmen, fishermen, and wine sellers. For example, scholars are told that they must be loyal to the emperor and filial to their parents, must teach decorum and duty, and must defend their relatives.

However, one should not assume that the collectivist pattern is the only one found in the Chinese tradition. DeBary (1979) showed that during the late Ming period in China a number of philosophers emphasized individual self-fulfillment and self-realization. However, much opposition developed to these views, and they were rejected. The rejection of individualism was accomplished by "reasserting the objective authority of the classics and the social character of the Way" (deBary, 1979, pp. 153–154).

In the West, individualism and collectivism were at the center of much thought and debate. John Locke's and Rousseau's views about the relationship of the citizen to the state have already been mentioned. The former emphasized the individual; the latter focused on the collective. The meaning of the term *individualism* was significantly changed by the French intellectual de Tocqueville (1835, 1840; 1985), who used the word in connection with democracy in America and contrasted the American social structure with the structures found in the aristocratic European tradition. De Tocqueville was the first to present individualism at the individual level as more than just egoism, although he feared that egoism would become its final phase.

Although many philosophers in the nineteenth century explored ideas related to individualism and collectivism, we must concentrate here on the twentieth century. Dewey (1930), for instance, discussed the old and new individualism. The old included liberation from legal and religious restrictions; the new focused on self-cultivation.

Kateb (1992) saw a strong link between individualism and the democratic culture. He criticized Rousseau as dealing with a community that was small, simple, and static, which no longer describe modern societies. According to Kateb, individualism is essential in modern societies.

Dumont (1986) saw individualism as a consequence of Protestantism (humans do not have to go through the church to communicate with God), political developments (social contract, emphasis on equality and liberty), and economic developments (such as affluence). Elias (1991) saw individualism as starting with Descartes ("Cogito, ergo sum").

A major recent development in philosophy is the exploration of the possibilities of communitarian societies, in which some of the desirable attributes of both individualism and collectivism are combined. Taylor (1989) argued that there is a need for both a core morality that can be imposed by the society and certain nonnegotiable rights for the individual, such as life, liberty, free speech, and due process. Though the postmodern philosophers (e.g., Jacques Derrida and Michel Foucault) are currently fashionable in the humanities, Taylor rejected them as superindividualists. He also did not agree with the view held by many anthropologists that all cultures are of equal value.

There is vigorous debate in contemporary philosophy around the constructs of liberalism and communitarianism. However, this is not directly relevant to our subject because it stops within the cultural confines of the West. A broader view is provided by anthropologists, who view the topic from an Eastern perspective as well.

Behind these philosophic discussions there is a more fundamental difference in worldviews, which emerges in analyses of myths. Joseph Campbell, the most esteemed researcher of myths, thought that myths are basically similar all over the world, but he saw a large difference between the myths of the West and East. He drew the line between East and West in Iran (Segal, 1987). Campbell linked the West with primitive hunters and the East with primitive planters. He argued that the hunters are individualists and the planters collectivists. The hunters strive to conquer the world, and they help others only incidentally; the planters see the individual absorbed in the whole and subordinate to the whole.

In Volumes 2 and 3 of his *Masks of God*, Campbell was most sympathetic to the East and denigrated the divisive, self-centered, futile strivings of the individualists of the West. But after visiting India, where he saw how individuals are ignored and expected to serve the group, he changed his mind. Collectivism, he realized, often requires conformity to ingroup authorities and even totalitarian political systems. It oppresses women. Thus, in Volume 4 he praised the creativity of the West and the freedom of the individual from the conformity imposed by the group, which often benefits only the men or only the leaders of the group. He also, at that time, rejected the totalitarianism that was then so frequently found in the Third World.

Campbell observed that a major shift from collectivism to individualism occurred in the West after the Middle Ages with the myths of *Tristan* and *Parzifal*, because for the first time in human history "love" became the basis of the union of men and women, as opposed to considerations that served the group. This particular individualism emerged in the northern and western regions of Europe and eventually led to a secular individualism that is very different from the religious collectivism of the "Levantine East" (Jews, Christians, and Muslims). The basis of human understanding of the world became *experience* instead of *authority*. Many of the fundamental attitudes of the modern world are consequences of the view that experience has priority when it conflicts with authority. If the authorities say that the world is flat, and if we see the ships' masts rising on the horizon and have other such experiences that indicate that the world is round, we simply reject the views of the authorities.

This situation is similar to the one developed by Asch (1956) to study conformity. He arranged for several confederates to look at a set of lines and report that one was "the longest," whereas the naive subject saw that line as not being the longest. Thus, he set up a conflict between social reality and perceived reality. About a third of the American samples conformed to social reality by agreeing with the majority that gave the false report. We can think of these people as allocentric. They centered their view of the world on the way other people saw it.

The "secular spirituality" of the West resulted in self-responsible individuals acting, *not* in terms of laws from the outside, but in terms of a developing realization of self-worth. Most of the peoples of the West are characterized by individualism in everyday life and religious collectivism in their understanding of the world.

History

A major attempt to understand English individualism was made by Macfarlane (1978). He provided evidence that there was individualism in Britain as early as A.D. 1200. He paid much attention to the institution of primogeniture. The oldest son inherited the land so that property would not be divided. The other sons had to make their way as well as they could in society, and since they had learned about the good life, they struggled hard through various entrepreneurial activities to become rich. The presence of tin and other resources as well as opportunities for commerce made affluence possible. Affluence leads to individualism. Also the system resulted in a good deal of immigration to the colonies, and immigrants tend to be more individualistic, since they leave their ingroups behind.

Another historical view is that individualism is born when rapid social change, including much social strife, results in the destruction of existing groups, making it necessary for individuals to act alone. Similarly, when there is much social mobility, individuals do not conform to groups. An especially interesting view along these lines was provided by Schooler (1990a, 1990b), who saw individualism as typical of hunting societies, where the immediate return from one's efforts and no possibility of food accumulation leads to equality. There is little property; dwellings are not fixed; there is little authority and much geographic mobility—all of which lead to individualism. Schooler reviewed the work of Macfarlane and pointed out that individualism emerges when property rights are attached to individuals rather than to groups. But his most interesting point was about Japan. He argued that in the sixteenth century, Japan suffered under the influence of several conflicting tendencies. Influences from China and the West clashed and resulted in a breaking down of social controls. It was a period when Japan was militaristic and expansionist (invading Korea twice), technologically able to produce high-quality goods (even first-rate copies of European weapons), which resulted in high social mobility. The boundaries between the samurai and merchants were much less clear during that period than during later periods. Mobility leads to individualism. Moreover, producing high-quality goods through individual action (craftsmen) means working alone, and such work leads to individualism. Thus, according to Schooler, Japan had an individualistic period in the sixteenth century. In this study we will not be able to explore why Japan became more collectivist at a later time.

Anthropology

C. Kluckhohn (1956) argued that certain binary oppositions can be found in the way people around the world conceptualize values. One of these oppositions was whether the relationship between individuals and groups places the individual or the group at the center of things. Should the individual be autonomous or dependent, active or accepting, and so forth? F. Kluckhohn and Strodtbeck (1961) used these ideas in developing their linear (e.g., submission to elders), collateral (e.g., agreement with group norms), and individualistic (e.g., doing what self-conceptions dictate) orientations.

Redfield (1956) provided a useful discussion of peasant societies. According to him, this kind of society is characterized by intense attachment to the soil, reverence toward ancestral ways, restraint on individual self-seeking in favor of family and community, suspiciousness of outsiders, and a sober and earthy ethic, such as support for marriages that are economically desirable. This pattern clearly has a major overlap with the collectivist patterns.

Margaret Mead (1967) examined cooperation and competition among primitive peoples by reviewing thirteen ethnographies. She identified the Manus, Kwakiutl, and Ifagao as competitive; the Bachiga, Ojibwa, Eskimo, and Arapesh as individualist; and the Iroquois, Samoa, Zuni, Bathonga, Dakota, and Maori as cooperative. Triandis (1988) used the notions of subordination of the individual goals to group goals and of achievement aimed at improving the position of the ingroup more than personal achievement as clues to categorize these same cultures as individualistic and collectivist. He made hierarchies (from least to most) for both kinds of cultures. For the individualistic ones the hierarchy was Manus, Bachiga, Ifagao, Dakota, Kwakiutl, Ojibwa, Eskimo. For the collectivist cultures it was Maori, Arapesh, Bathonga, Iroquois, Samoa, Zuni.

Mead had classified her societies on other attributes, so it was possible to examine the above individualist-collectivist dichotomy against the attributes she had used. Triandis (1988) did statistical analyses on Mead's data and found that individualistic societies tend to be hunting, gathering, fishing, and foraging, and collectivist societies are usually agricultural; individualists engage in trade with other tribes, and collectivists do not; individualists prod their children to become adults as soon as possible, and collectivists want them to become adults when they are "ready."

The individualistic cultures emphasized goals like self-sufficiency and self-glorification; the collectivist cultures emphasized the good of the ingroup. Among individualists, power was desired and often achieved, whereas the collectivists were less status conscious. The individualistic cultures had a view of the universe that included a struggle between individuals and gods, whereas the collectivists expected that if they did their duty, everything would be all right.

An important conclusion from this study was that no society is "purely" individualist or collectivist. The cultural pattern is situation specific. For example, the Kwakiutl are individualists when they are relating to other chiefs but collectivists when they relate to their family. Nevertheless, the individualism-collectivism template can be used to identify the conditions and situations under which each cultural syndrome is likely to operate in each culture.

I suggested above that individualism and collectivism are situation specific. That is, an individual may be very individualistic at work and quite collectivist in the extended family. The situation specificity of the constructs inspired Hui (1984, 1988) to develop separate individualism-collectivism scales for family, friends, neighbors, and so forth. Triandis (1990) suggested that one might use a German philosopher's (Spranger, 1928) six value types—social, economic, political, truth, religious, and aesthetic—to define six types of situations. Mao's China specified that the collective (the state) has a role in all six situations and thus was a most collectivist culture for a short period of time. Muslim societies impose their standards on the social (family life), economic (no usury), truth (does it agree with Qur'an?), religious, and aesthetic (no human figures allowed) domains but do relatively little with politics (even in Iran elections are allowed).

In most individualist cultures almost none of these areas is the domain of the state. In social life, many family types (single parents, etc.) are tolerated; in economics, there is much freedom (though price controls are permitted during emergencies); in politics and religion, there are many choices; in the truth domain, freedom of the press assures no control by collectives; finally, in aesthetics, there is clearly much freedom, though some collectivist U.S. senators attempt occasionally to dictate what is socially acceptable and the type of artistic expression that can be supported by grants from the National Endowment for the Humanities.

Gross and Rayner (1985) proposed two kinds of cultures: those that emphasize the "grid" (relationships such as worker-boss, adult-child) and those that emphasize the "group" (behavior depends on membership in a definable group). The former has a faint resemblance to individualism and the latter to collectivism. They suggested five measures of the importance of the group: (1) the proportion of time spent in the group, relative to the total time that could have been spent; (2) the frequency of meetings; (3) the closeness of links and the interlocking character of such links; (4) the proportion of shared over the unshared links; and (5) the strength of the group boundary, making admission to the group easy or difficult. These criteria are quite different from the ones used by most researchers to identify collectivism. However, some researchers (e.g., Yoshi Kashima, personal communication, 1993) have used multimethod measurements that included the closeness of links, but they have found no relationship to other measures of collectivism. Clearly, there is a need for research to link these kinds of ideas with the other ideas about collectivism.

The most important contribution by an anthropologist to this topic was made by Hsu (1983). He compared at depth Chinese and Japanese cultures on the one hand and American culture on the other and saw China as the prototypic collectivist culture, able to ignore the outside world and functioning on the basis of the Confucian "proper action" (*li*) between lord and citizen, father and son, older and younger brother, friend and friend, and husband and wife. He emphasized the importance of harmony within the ingroup and noted less crime, fewer hospital admissions (possibly because home care is more available), and less drug abuse among collectivists than individualists. He also noted more scientific achievements, democratic institutions, conquests of new frontiers, domination of things (owning objects) and animals (pets), and attempts to proselytize among individualists. Hsu was very emphatic about the link between individualism and competition. This link was supported by Triandis, Bontempo, et al. (1988) in a study that identified, through factor analysis of attitude items, a factor called *self-reliance with competition,* which accounted for more variance than any other factor. According to Hsu, the link of individualism and competition results in aggressive creativity and large military expenditures and increases prejudice toward racial and religious groups as the dominant group puts down minorities in order to boost its self-concept. But in this case, Hsu neglected to mention that in collectivist cultures people are more likely to mistreat outgroups, and many of the great massacres of history (the Nazi Holocaust in 1940–1945, the rape of Nanjing, China, by the Japanese in 1937, ethnic cleansing in Bosnia in 1991–1994) occurred during the collectivist phases of the relevant cultures. In short, both extreme individualism and collectivism are likely to result in poor intergroup relations.

Anthropologists generally approve of the cultures they study, and thus collectivism is often approved by them. But as with all generalizations, there are exceptions, and anthropologist G. M. Erchak (1992) admitted that individualism has many advantages. He cautioned that the determinants of individualism and other cultural patterns are complex and include history, ethnic tradition, microecology, and sociobiology among the factors that shape cultural patterns. Thus we should not be looking for simple explanations of the origins of these patterns.

Sociology

Parsons (1949) recognized the contrast between collectivity and self-emphasis. Riesman, Glazer, and Denney (1961) developed the typology of the tradition-, inner-, and outer-directed humans. The tradition-directed type has much in common with the collectivist, since that type conforms to norms, emphasizes the importance of relationships, accepts rigid discipline, and feels a sense of belonging to groups. The inner-directed type emerged after the Renaissance and is characterized by mobility, production, colonization, and the tendency to decide among many choices and to fight the barriers of the material environment. The outer-directed type finds that the great barriers are people and engages in service rather than manufacture. This type is shallow, free with his/her money, friendly, but uncertain of her or his own values. The inner- and outer-directed types overlap with the individualist, though the former is more typical of the early part of the twentieth century and the latter of the last part of this century.

Lukes (1973) included the following in his discussion of the concept of individualism: the dignity of man; autonomy; privacy; self-development; and political, economic, religious, ethical, epistemological, and methodological individualism.

According to epistemological and methodological individualism, only individuals are the bases of any analyses of societies and the data must be individual data. In short, there are no cultural-level or societal-level phenomena to be explained by cultural-level variables. For example, one would explain suicide rates, a clear societal-level phenomenon, with processes leading individuals to commit suicide and not consider societal-level variables such as the rate of unemployment or GNP/cap. O'Neill (1976) edited a book that examined the controversies centered around epistemological and methodological individualism.

Lukes explained how the first three elements on his list result in equality and liberty. Freedom means that the individual is able to realize all human potentialities. To the extent that this is not possible (e.g., the poor in the United States), the individual is not free.

Some sociologists have considered British sociology individualist and French sociology collectivist. Social exchange theory, according to Ekeh (1974), included both the individualist and collectivist sociological traditions, and modern theory is a wedding of the two traditions. A most individualistic sociologist was George Homans (1961), who derived his sociological propositions from animal and Skinnerian psychology.

A major study by Bellah et al. (1988) expressed concern that individualism is becoming cancerous in American life. Individualism was seen as emphasizing hedonism, competition, self-reliance, utilitarian pursuits, and open communication with the community only if it serves the person. Most important, it emphasizes freedom, equality and equity, participation, trust of others, competence, exchanges, fairness, independence and separation from family, loneliness, self-improvement, and the desire to be distinguished. The independence from home, church, work, and from rigid standards results in loneliness and sometimes alienation. The standard is no longer "what is good?" but "does it feel good?" These scholars saw a crisis in the relating of personal and community goals and noted that therapy is thought of as an answer to any problem.

Bellah et al. (1988) also identified several kinds of individualism: religious, utilitarian, and expressive. For example, according to the biblical individualist, the individual relates directly to God; the utilitarian emphasizes exchanges that maximize returns for the individual. Expressive individualists emphasize having fun. The self is the only reality that really matters. However, individualism is compatible with conformity, since people who do not know what is right have to depend on social comparisons to guide their life. Keeping up with the Joneses is the central motto of life among these individualists. Since members of the upper class pay attention to traditions and social norms that secure their comfortable positions in society, and members of the lower class have to do their duty in order to keep their jobs, individualism is maximal in the middle class. This view is inconsistent with Daab's (1991) findings in Poland, and further research is needed. Bellah et al. (1988) provided readings from de Tocqueville and others that illustrate the main points of their thesis. They stressed that individualists have little connection with their own history, are intensely concerned with being unique, and are quite utilitarian, which results in ceaseless productivity.

Thomson (1989) analyzed seventy-nine articles, sixty from the 1920s and nineteen from the 1970s. Most of the articles were critical of extreme individualism. But the meaning of individualism was different during the two time periods. The main focus of the 1920s articles was that individualism includes self-expression but involves the absence of self-control. The main focus of the 1970s articles was that individualism includes self-absorption and the quest for self-development.

Psychology

Hofstede (1980) analyzed about 117,000 protocols that IBM had collected from its own employees, concerning their value preferences. After summing the responses of individuals in each country, he obtained a set of numbers that included the sums of the answers to the various questions, for each country. A factor analysis based on the correlations among the answers to the questions, across countries, revealed four factors: *power distance, uncertainty avoidance, individualism,* and *masculinity.* Relevant to our discussion are power distance and individualism, which correlated approximately −.70. Power distance refers to people seeing that those at the top of the social structure are very different from those at the bottom. It is characteristic of societies where people in power are arrogantly dominant and where that is expected and acceptable. The negative correlation between power distance and individualism suggests that acceptance of hierarchy is low in individualistic cultures. However, the generality of this relationship is not yet established because although this relationship is very clear in Hofstede's data, it was not found in the data of preliterate societies (e.g., see the discussion of the work of Margaret Mead, above), and one can find cultures that are collectivist and egalitarian (e.g., the Israeli kibbutz; two cultures studied by Billings, 1989).

Hofstede's individualism-collectivism factor was quite similar to the contrasts identified by Triandis (1972) when studying traditional Greeks and Americans. The Greeks were collectivists; the Americans were individualists. In addition, in studies of Hispanics and others, the data fell into place when this contrast was used (e.g., Marin and Triandis, 1985). Hui (1984, 1988) developed a scale to measure the constructs, emphasizing that some people "do their own thing" and others share their problems and joys and are greatly concerned with the fate of their ingroups. He argued that in collectivist cultures the ingroup is the unit of survival, and thus people feel emotionally dependent on others. As might be expected, interaction with ingroup members is high and privacy is low. Hui and Triandis (1986) surveyed social scientists located on all populated continents and asked them if certain attributes were consistent with their understanding of the constructs of individualism and collectivism. They found that these social scientists believed that collectivists are high in their consideration of the implications of their actions for others, tend to share material and nonmaterial resources, feel susceptible to social influence, are very concerned with their self-presentation and saving face, share their outcomes with others, and feel that their lives are involved in the lives of others. Among collectivists, concern about the ingroup was a central theme.

Various researchers have developed scales to measure the constructs at the individual level (Hui, 1984, 1988; Triandis, Leung, et al., 1985), and cross-culturally (Triandis, Bontempo, et al., 1988; Triandis, McCusker, and Hui, 1990). A broad literature corresponding to these constructs was reviewed by Triandis (1988, 1990). The measurements showed that individualism included ideas such as "independence and self-reliance," "distance from ingroups," "competition," and "hedonism"; collectivism included ideas such as "interdependence," "sociability," and "family integrity" (e.g., children should live at home until they get married; old parents should live with their children until they die). A confirmatory factor analysis reported by Triandis, Chan, et al. (submitted) showed that the data did fit this seven-factor pattern.

Other work suggested that there are a large number of different types of collectivism and individualism (Triandis, 1994), so the constructs must be defined polythetically (Triandis, 1990). That is, the constructs should be defined as is done in zoology, where each phylum is specified by some combination of "defining attributes" and each species is defined by several additional attributes. Thus, the phylum is clearly specified as long as the defining attributes are present (e.g., feathers and wings equals birds) and each species has many additional attributes. In short, a general construct such as collectivism is specified by its defining attributes. Different types of the construct, such as Japanese collectivism, require the addition of culture-specific attributes. In Chapter 3 I will discuss the defining attributes of individualism and collectivism in considerable detail. In this chapter I will present them only briefly.

A View from Japan. Tanaka (1983), in response to questions I asked in a letter, argued that people may act in an individualist or collectivist way depending on their location in a hierarchy, as well as their demographic attributes. Tanaka said, "In Japan women do not influence men on religious, philosophical, and political issues, but men do influence other men." He also indicated that public action is much more important than what a person does that is not known to significant others. For example, actions that are inappropriate (such as visiting a brothel) do not worry most Japanese unless the perpetrator is found out and there is public dishonor. There is more difference between the "private" and the "public" settings in collectivist cultures than there is in individualist cultures. This point has been emphasized also by others, including Lebra in Gudykunst (1993). One way to think about a transgression is that it is seen as an action of little importance, as long as the behavior does not threaten the ingroup. But if it becomes public, then it does threaten the ingroup's honor, and it is therefore of very great importance.

Thus, individualists may see those acts as immoral regardless of whether they have public consequences, whereas some collectivists may see them as immoral only if they do have public consequences. This difference also reflects the relative importance of guilt and shame. Collectivists are more sensitive to shame, individualists to guilt. Another way to think about it is that individualists pay attention to internal processes (e.g., see Newman, 1993), such as principles, and collectivists pay attention to the situation (public/private) and to saving face. These points must be seen in context: Many modern Japanese have absorbed Western value systems and have become individualistic in their assessment of the actions of others. We see within Japan severe disagreements on whether certain actions (e.g., obtaining political contributions in exchange for favorable judgments by government officials) are acceptable. Such disagreements probably reflect a division between the traditional collectivist morality and the modern individualistic morality that parallels the Japanese generational division.

Furthermore, collectivists often find themselves in a dilemma when they have to communicate an unpleasant message. Although they value honesty, they value even more keeping relationships. If telling the truth means damaging a relationship, they would rather tell a white lie. Thus, they may be seen as "dishonest" by individualists, who care much less about preserving good relationships.

Tanaka's point corresponds to observations by Trilling (1972), who argued that the concept of "sincerity" is a modern idea and did not exist prior to the sixteenth century. Up to that time, he said, deception was widely practiced. He pointed to the advice that Machiavelli gave to the prince: Deceive and maximize your outcomes. But as people realized that they have a choice concerning who they want to be, the idea of "authenticity" emerged, and one had to act consistently with one's own self-concept even if the action would never be found out by others. Thus, Trilling's analysis suggests a link between individualism and the emphasis on the Western concept of sincerity and authenticity that contrasts with the collectivist concern for proper action as defined by others.

The meaning of "success" can vary with culture. Tanaka argued that money does not mean success in Japan. It is the achievement of high status that signifies success. High status may be achieved in social, economic, political, bureaucratic, or educational settings.

Triandis's (1988) Analysis of Individualism and Collectivism. Triandis (1988) examined the individualism-collectivism contrast with the help of Deutsch's (1949, 1962) analyses of interdependence. When there is *promotive* interdependence (goals of self and group are compatible), one has collectivism; when there is *contrient* interdependence (goals are negatively correlated), one has conflict. When there is no relationship between personal and collective goals, one has individualism.

Triandis (1988) attempted to trace the development of collectivism to the training to obey authority figures necessary for the construction of major public works. An exhibit in China from about the year 10,000 B.C. suggested the origin of collectivism: A village was reconstructed, near Xian, and around that village there was a large trench that protected the village from wild animals during the night. The guide said that the volume of earth that was removed to build that trench was the equivalent of 123 truckloads. Obviously, success in such a project, using the primitive tools available, required extreme cooperation and coordination of action.

At the National Museum in Beijing, one can see pictures of the development of the Chinese canal system. This elaborate system required the coordination of 100,000 workers at one time. Similarly, the Great Wall, which is the only structure on earth that can be seen from the moon, was an enormous undertaking, one that only a collectivist culture could have produced at that time.

There is evidence that national constitutions (Massimini and Calegari, 1979) reflect the cultures of their countries. For example, the Chinese constitution mentions labor, instruction, and participation in decisions much more frequently than the Italian constitution does, and the Italian one mentions finances and individual values more frequently than the Chinese constitution.

Triandis (1988) noted that certain social movements such as fascism were rejections of individualism. That was precisely the way that Fromm, in *Escape from Freedom*, analyzed the emergence of Nazism. Triandis (1988) noted that individualists are socialized to be self-sufficient and independent, whereas collectivists are socialized to be conforming and dependent. In situations of economic crises, such as that created by the Weimar Republic in Germany, self-sufficiency was not possible. Then individuals voluntarily submitted to a collectivist dictator.

Triandis (1988) reported on a Thai psychologist's (Wichiarajote, 1975) view of his country in relation to the United States. He saw individualism versus collectivism in terms of achievement versus affiliation, self-assertion versus respectfulness, equalitarian versus hierarchical organization, peer versus parental influences, free versus constrained expression of ideas, self-orientation versus other orientation, autonomy versus mutual dependence, fear of failure versus fear of rejection, principle-centeredness versus person-centeredness, organizational loyalty versus small group loyalty, encouragement of evaluation versus fear of evaluation, achieved versus ascribed criteria for promotion, fairness versus sacrifice, frankness versus not telling what one feels, future versus present orientation, self-importance versus self-effacement, being creative versus conforming, material versus spiritual, and valuing efficiency versus peace of mind.

Triandis (1988) noted that Waterman (1984) defended individualism, and M. B. Smith (1978), Hogan (1975), Lasch (1978), and Sampson (1977) criticized it, and that various types of individualism were proposed in the literature, many approaching communitarianism, that is, combining the strong points of both individualism and collectivism (e.g., Kanfer, 1979; Rotenburg, 1977; Rakoff, 1978).

Triandis (1988) also attempted to identify types of collectivism by noting that in some cultures collectives make broad demands, insisting on conformity in many different areas of life, including marriage, language, friendship, education, religion, politics, and occupation. In other cultures, collectives do not specify any of the above. The depth (intensity) of attachment to a collective can vary and the consequences of ignoring ingroup norms may be serious or of little consequence, depending on the specific culture. Ignoring the norms of the collective may result in much or little internal conflict for the individual. Theocracies, including the Amish and Dukhobors, are influenced broadly and in depth by their collectives. Elias (1991) described the Hutterites of Canada as a society where social life is not changing. They wear the costumes and speak the language of their ancestors;

there is no contact with the mass media; a council of elders controls social life; strict and kind child rearing ensures obedience and loyalty.

Furthermore, according to Triandis's (1988) explorations of different kinds of collectivism, the ingroup can vary: The patriot is attached to the country, the familist to the family, the party member to the party, and so on. Thus, the type of ingroup results in different kinds of collectivism.

Ho and Chiu's Analysis of Individualism-Collectivism. Ho and Chiu (1994) discussed the "component ideas" of individualism and collectivism, with special reference to Chinese culture. In China, individualism connotes selfishness, placing self-interests above those of the group, lack of concern for others, and aversion to group discipline. Collectivism, in contrast, has positive connotations, affirming the solidarity of the group. Ho and Chiu contrasted this with the Western view, which sees individualism as affirming the uniqueness, autonomy, freedom, and intrinsic worth of the individual, while insisting on personal responsibility for one's own conduct, well-being, and salvation. They stated that collectivism has appeared in varied forms— in tribal societies, ancient empires, the communism of early Christians, and in communes, the kibbutzim, and experiments in communal living. Common to these forms is the emphasis on interdependence and the insistence that the interests of the group or collective take priority over those of the individual. They argued that collectives are organized on the basis of two fundamental principles: (1) the priority of collective interests, governing the vertical individual-collective relationship; and (2) the reciprocity of responsibilities and obligations, governing both vertical and horizontal interpersonal relationships within the collective. Collectives are based on blood and marriage ties, tribal or ethnic origin, caste, institutional affiliation, and nationality. Both reference and membership groups can function as ingroups. Of course, there are complications arising out of the fact that individuals belong to several ingroups simultaneously.

Ho and Chiu proposed a dialectic view in which the individual and the group derive their meaning from coexistence with each other. As an analog they used the symphony orchestra, in which the individuality of the members is subjugated to the common good. They reported, then, a content analysis of Chinese sayings that indicates that the number affirming individuality (thirty-four) and self-reliance (forty-one) is substantial. However, there are even more sayings that stress collectivist themes, such as group efforts, the consequences of one's actions, conformity, cooperation, and affiliation. Overall they found more collectivist than individualistic sayings.

The Cultural and Individual Levels of Analysis. The contrast between the individualism and collectivism behavioral domains also appears in the area of individual differences. Triandis, Leung, et al. (1985) pointed out that in every society there are individuals who are countercultural. Thus, in collectivist societies there are *idiocentrics*, who look for the earliest opportunity to escape the "oppression" of their ingroups, and in individualistic societies there are *allocentrics*, who reject individual pursuits and join gangs, clubs, communes, and other collectives. The idiocentrics reject conformity to the ingroup and are most likely to leave their culture and seek membership in individualistic cultures. They are also very likely to criticize and object to their culture.

It is important to keep the cultural and individual levels of analysis separate and not assume that the correlation between the two levels will be 1.0. In some cases (e.g., S. H. Schwartz, 1994) it is around .8, but it could be much lower (Hofstede, Bond, and Luk, 1993).

One might have assumed that people who support collectivist political regimes are allocentric, but this apparently is not the case. Georgas (personal communication, 1992), in a study of politics and allocentrism-idiocentrism constructs in Greece, found that Greek Communists were idiocentric. That may be an important observation because it shows that the assumption that support for political systems corresponds to idiocentrism-allocentrism is not valid. It seems likely that all revolutionaries are idiocentric. If this observation also holds for the former Soviet Union, it explains a phenomenon widely reported in the press: It is the former Communists who are the new Russian entrepreneurs! A study that located the modal positions of members of the current Russian political parties, as well as Russian entrepreneurs, on the typology we are discussing would be fascinating.

Wiggins (1991) used Bakan's concepts of agency (high A+) or (low A−) and communion (C+) versus (C−) and identified four types of people. Those who were C+ focused on intimacy, union, and solidarity; those who were C− displayed remoteness, hostility, and disaffection; those who were A+ were concerned with power, mastery, and assertion; those who were A− displayed weakness, failure, submission. Wiggins pointed to correspondences between agency and communion on the one hand and various other concepts on the other. For example, agency corresponds to the Confucian utilitarian sphere and communion to the Confucian moral sphere. Several other concepts show similar contrasts, such as striving for superiority versus social interest, need for power versus need for tenderness, self-assertion versus expressiveness, emphasis on status versus emphasis on love, and surgency (arrogance) versus agreeableness.

Culture-Specific and Culture-General Definitions. In this book I attempt to provide a view of collectivism and individualism that can be used throughout the world. It seems to be supported by studies of beliefs, attitudes, and values (e.g., Triandis, Bontempo, Betancourt, et al., 1986; Triandis, Bontempo, Villareal, et al., 1988; Triandis, McCusker, Hui, 1990;

Schwartz, 1994) carried out in many cultures. However, there are also studies that attempt to derive the structure of values emically (from a culture-specific context), such as the Chinese Cultural Connection (1987) or Hamaguchi's (1985) analysis of Japanese "contextualism," which is probably a description of Japanese collectivism. I do not think that this difference in point of view is very great (Bond, in preparation). In any case, this issue links with the debate about "universalistic" and "indigenous psychology" (Berry et al., 1992, pp. 380–384; Heelas and Lock, 1981; U. Kim and Berry, 1993) and would take us too far from our current focus.

The Individualism-Collectivism 1990 Conference. A conference organized by Uichol Kim in Korea, in July 1990, brought together scholars interested in individualism and collectivism. Some of the papers from this conference appeared in U. Kim et al. (1994). The introduction to that volume quoted Hofstede (1991), who defined individualism as that which is found in societies where the ties between individuals are loose and people are expected to look after themselves, and collectivism as that which is found in societies where people are integrated in cohesive ingroups that protect them in exchange for unquestioned loyalty.

U. Kim et al. rejected both methodological individualism (i.e., individuals are the only elements to be used to understand the functioning of societies) and methodological collectivism (i.e., collectives determine and explain the psychological makeup of individuals). They argued that both are too narrow, and that it is better to consider two levels of analysis and their interactions. They presented multidimensional and multifaceted models in their book.

The issue of the mix between the collectivist and individualist elements in both individuals and cultures is one of the important themes we will review in the chapters that follow. One way of thinking about these constructs is that we are all collectivists but some of us are also individualists. In any society there are some people who are extreme individualists because they have suppressed all collectivist elements within their psychological functioning. In short, we all start by being dependent on some adults who raise us, and most of us feel close to some set of such providers of security and sustenance. However, in individualistic cultures children are encouraged to become detached from such caregivers, and as they become detached they may find rewards associated with acting based on their own desires, which detaches them further. In many cases doing what they please and doing what is required by a group clash, and then these individuals suppress their collectivism. Conversely, in collectivist cultures children who do as they wish are scolded, and they learn to suppress their individualistic tendencies, and when they do what is expected by their group they are praised. Thus those who are raised in collectivist cultures have an augmented set of collectivist elements and a diminished set of individualist elements; those raised in individualist cultures have a diminished set of collectivist elements and an augmented set of individualist elements. In sum, all of us have both collectivist and individualist elements in our cognitive systems, but in different mixtures. When we are in social situations we sample these elements differentially, and thus social behavior is different across cultures.

At the political level liberalism represents a moral-political philosophy and way of life that rejects the traditional, ascribed, communal, and medieval social orders. Within any country there are people who are more individualistic (the middle and upper classes rather than the lower classes) and others who are more collectivist (e.g., rural, older samples, those who have traveled very little).

The conference papers included debates about the most "defining" attributes of the constructs. Thus, Kagitcibasi favored separation from ingroups and human relatedness as the defining attributes of individualism and collectivism respectively. She argued that both tendencies may be found in individuals and suggested that in some societies, such as Turkey, there is independence on the material dimension and interdependence along the socio-emotional dimension. Reykowski thought that the defining attribute is the kind of self (socially embedded or not) that is found in a culture. This is similar to the position of Markus and Kitayama (1991b). Triandis thought that goal structure (are individual and collective goals compatible?) and self-definition (I am a part of my group) are the key defining attributes. Kim saw individualism as characterized by emphasis on internal attributes, a discrete boundary between the self and others, self-actualization, freedom, and a decontextualized conception of the self. By contrast, collectivism is characterized by large dependence on context in communication and information processing, shifts in behavior depending on the situation (e.g., am I interacting with an ingroup or an outgroup member), sensitivity to hierarchy, internal constraints, other focus (e.g., paying attention to the needs of the other person), and emphasis on harmony within the ingroup.

Communitarianism

Communitarianism has been completely interdisciplinary, with philosophers (e.g., Taylor, 1985; Kymlicka, 1989), sociologists (e.g., Etzioni, 1988), and others making a contribution. Etzioni (1988) proposed that individuals (I) and collectives (We) are both essential elements and have the same basic conceptual and moral standing. The "I" and the "We" are in perpetual creative conflict. The individual is a product of the community but also influences the community. All decisions should consider both individual pleasure and the moral standing of the decision. Moral standing refers to the internalized norms concerning proper action. When people violate their moral commitment to increase their pleasure they activate defense mechanisms. Thus it is most desirable that actions balance pleasure and the moral dimension.

Fowers and Tredinnick (mimeo, n.d.) provided a useful summary of the contrast between individualism, collectivism, and the communitarian view. They argued that the self-other boundary of individualists is firmly drawn at one's body; in the case of collectivists it is fluid, with close affiliation within the ingroup and firm boundaries with outgroups. Communitarians see the boundary at the individual's skin, with ties of rights and duties between persons and various collectives, the larger community included. Locus of control among individualists is internal (e.g., behavior depends on attitudes, personality); among collectivists, external (behavior depends on traditions, norms); and among communitarians the individual's aims are important, but they are framed within the traditions and needs of the group. Identity is self-defined among individualists, is based on the individual's status and roles in the group among collectivists, and is assumed to develop within a culture and becomes elaborated on the basis of the individual's abilities and the group's needs among the communitarians.

They argued further that the locus of evaluation is the individual's preferences, the group's norms and leaders, and the individual in light of community moral standards, in these three patterns respectively. Fulfillment is defined by the individual in individualism, is based on good role performance for the benefit of the group in collectivism, and occurs when there is both private satisfaction and fulfillment of public duties among communitarians. Conflict resolution uses negotiation and confrontation and is based on cost-benefit analyses or the expression of the individual's needs among individualists, occurs when high-status leaders resolve disputes among collectivists, and is sensitive to both the individual's needs and duties and community standards among communitarians.

Thus, communitarians attempt to discover social orders that combine the most desirable attributes of both individualism and collectivism. Communitarians do not agree among themselves, and there is considerable debate. There are also critics of this position. For example, Buchanan (1989) argued that liberalism neglects community, undervalues political life, understresses obligations and commitments, neglects the embedded self, and overstates the importance of justice. Nevertheless the argument of Buchanan's article does not favor the communitarian agenda. Sandel (1982) noted that totalitarian regimes emerge when traditional communities are destroyed. He argued that justice may be overemphasized in liberalism, but this is a consequence of not having community or a shared moral perspective. He said that a community that puts justice first is a community of strangers.

Walzer (1990) offered a communitarian critique of liberalism, noting that there are two arguments against liberalism, each of which is only partially valid. Furthermore, to the extent that one argument is valid, it undercuts the other argument. (1) Total atomism leads to meaninglessness. The consequences include high rates of divorce, political apathy, and a fragmented society. (2) There is no such thing as total atomism. People have parents, spouses, children. They do have ties. The essence of any community is collectivist interdependence. Walzer asserted that each critique is partially correct. He agreed that there is much geographic and social mobility, marital and political shifting of loyalties, and we know each other less well than in stable cultures. But we can still talk to each other and relate. Nevertheless, it would be desirable to teach children to do more sharing, more team work. Walzer believed that we should not overemphasize the extent to which people act in voluntary ways, since the data do not support that view (e.g., most people have the same religion as their parents).

Selznick (1992) believed that liberalism can embrace both political and economic realism. We must have personal autonomy but also work for the common good. It is important to find a common core of values, such as pragmatism, and direct people to be autonomous while participating in effective communities. Thus, the basic values of communitarians are autonomy, fairness, rationality, law, and love. Although it is clear that societies have changed from status to contract and from mutuality, intimacy, and little mobility to choice, rationality, and utilitarianism, most aspects of John Locke's individualism are still valid. The autonomous individual, Locke argued, forms the state, but the state exists only if the individuals consent to it, and political power exists only if individuals consent to it. Unfortunately, in my opinion, these views are too idealistic. Having experienced the German occupation during World War II, I do not remember much consent of the citizens, and unfortunately there are many regimes analogous to that of the German occupation in the modern world.

Thus the communitarian debate is primarily philosophical and attempts to define a desirable social order. I am very sympathetic to their goals, but I see serious limitations to this perspective because it is prescriptive rather than responsive to what ordinary people do. In this book, I try to examine the way that individualism and collectivism actually operate in societies.

°   °   °

It is clear from this review that those who have used the concepts of individualism and collectivism had different definitions, conceptions, associations, antecedents, and consequences in mind. For example, Charles Eliot (1910), a president emeritus of Harvard, defined collectivism as objecting to individual initiatives that override the interests of the many, and when the two are in conflict the interests of the many should prevail. This view is rather different from the definitions that we reviewed here and shows how much divergence there is in the meaning of the concepts. However, there is overlap among the various conceptions. Eliot's view is similar to the criterion about goal consistency that I proposed above. Thus, it is important to identify defining and culture-specific attributes, measure them, and determine empirically, in each culture, which attributes need to be used to define the prevailing social pattern of that culture. I will do this in the next chapter, which will also outline a theory of individualism and collectivism.

3

Attributes of Individualism and Collectivism

T HIS CHAPTER WILL PROVIDE an overview of the defining characteristics and some of the specific cultural manifestations of individualism and
collectivism, known as cultural syndromes. A cultural syndrome is a pattern
characterized by shared beliefs, attitudes, norms, roles, and values that are
organized around a theme and that can be found in certain geographic regions during a particular historic period.

Although more research needs to be done, results so far indicate that on a
number of tests the different methods of measuring the construct converge
(Triandis, McCusker, and Hui, 1990; Triandis, Chan, et al., submitted),
showing that individualism and collectivism are cultural syndromes. They
are made up of more-basic cultural syndromes and show up at the individual level. The particular shape they take is influenced by a number of experiential and situational factors.

Four universal dimensions of the constructs follow: 1. The definition of
the self is interdependent in collectivism and independent in individualism
(Markus and Kitayama, 1991b; Reykowski, 1994). This is reflected in various aspects of daily life, including the extent to which individuals share resources with group members and conform to the norms of the group. Scales
for the measurement of this aspect have been developed by Singelis (1994)
and by Gudykunst, Matsumoto, et al. (1994).

2. Personal and communal goals are closely aligned in collectivism and
not at all aligned in individualism. One can identify collectivism when group
goals have priority and individualism when personal goals have priority.
When ingroup and personal goals are compatible, one has collectivism;
when they are not, individualism is the result (Triandis, 1988, 1990; S. H.
Schwartz, 1990, 1994). For example, DeVos (quoted in Gudykunst, 1993, p.
130) stressed the subordination of individual needs to family and group

needs in Japan. A scale for the measurement of this aspect was developed by Yamaguchi (1994).

3. Cognitions that focus on norms, obligations, and duties guide much of social behavior in collectivist cultures. Those that focus on attitudes, personal needs, rights, and contracts (Miller, 1994) guide social behavior in individualistic cultures (Davidson et al., 1976).

Bontempo and Rivero (1992) correlated the Hofstede (1980) individualism score of the country with the relative importance of norms and attitudes as determined in studies that utilized the Fishbein and Ajzen (1975) theory of reasoned action in that country. The more individualistic the country, the more attitudes rather than norms predicted the behavioral intentions of subjects, with respect to a variety of behaviors. The correlation was .73, $p <$ .001.

4. An emphasis on relationships, even when they are disadvantageous, is common in collectivist cultures. In individualist cultures, the emphasis is on rational analyses of the advantages and disadvantages of maintaining a relationship (U. Kim et al., 1994). The Kim conception is parallel to the conception of Mills and Clark (1982).

The four aspects can be measured independently, and they have been found (Triandis, Chan, et al., submitted) to correlate about .40. This correlation is substantial because the reliabilities of these measures tend to be low (around .70), so correlations above .49 are impossible. The importance of this point is that individualism and collectivism are "real" in the sense that the measurements of the four aspects do converge. Individualism and collectivism are not just intuitive, theoretical entities. With these four themes in mind, we may examine the different kinds of individualism and collectivism.

Horizontal Versus Vertical

There are four kinds of self: independent or interdependent (Markus and Kitayama, 1991b) and same or different. The combinations of these four types can be categorized as horizontal individualism (independent/same) and horizontal collectivism (interdependent/same), vertical individualism (independent/different) and vertical collectivism (interdependent/different). In collectivist cultures, horizontal includes a sense of social cohesion and of oneness with members of the ingroup. Vertical includes a sense of serving the ingroup and sacrificing for the benefit of the ingroup and doing one's duty. In both individualist and collectivist cultures, the vertical dimension accepts inequality, and rank has its privileges. This is reflective of the "different self." In contrast, the horizontal dimension emphasizes that people should be similar on most attributes, especially status. This reflects the "same self," which does not want to stand out.

This typology accounts for data reported by Chen, Meindl, and Hunt (submitted) and Daun (1991, 1992). Working with Chinese data, Chen, Meindl, and Hunt (submitted) proposed a distinction between horizontal and vertical collectivism. Although these data did not establish two distinct kinds of collectivism, Chen and Meindl (submitted) did show some meaningful patterns of intercorrelations with outside variables. For example, they found that Chinese who were vertical collectivists supported reforms introduced by the Communist party, whereas the horizontal collectivists were opposed to these reforms. Presumably, the verticals are more sensitive than the horizontals to cues coming from authorities and are more willing to sacrifice themselves. The horizontals, in contrast, have fundamentally Confucian values of cohesion and thus see the reforms as creating competition and weakening solidarity. Furthermore, horizontal collectivism correlated $-.13$ $(p < .05)$ with preference for differential rules for compensation in an organization. This makes sense: If one has a sense of oneness with fellow employees, one would not be enthusiastic about differential compensation. Vertical collectivism did not show any relationship with this outside variable. Vertical collectivism, though, correlated significantly with age, having a managerial role, and degree of seniority in an organization. Presumably, those who have power favor the tendency of group members to do what the organization wants them to do, because those who have power benefit from such behavior. Although this study does not definitively establish the distinction between horizontal and vertical collectivism, it is sufficiently strong to lead us to accept the distinction (until further research shows that it is unnecessary).

The research by Daun (1991, 1992) suggested that Sweden has a horizontal individualist culture. In contrast, data from the upper-middle class in the United States (reviewed by Markus and Kitayama, 1991b) suggested that in North America there is considerable vertical individualism, at least among some samples and in certain situations, including business transactions. We can see the distinctions by comparing the findings in specific cultures in more detail.

Daun's data showed that Swedes are extremely self-reliant. If they ask for a cigarette, they are likely to insist on paying for it on the spot. The elderly do not live with their children, and living by oneself is highly valued. If one is to stay overnight at a friend's house, one takes one's own sheets. And 87 percent of Swedes indicate that they would like to live "as [they] please."

The Swedes obtained high scores on individualism in Hofstede's (1980) survey, but they do not like people who "stick out." They do not like to be unique and conspicuous, which contrasts with other kinds of individualists, such as the North Americans, English, French, or Germans. For example, high social status is desired by only 2 percent of the Swedish population, compared with 7 percent of Americans and 25 percent of Germans, in comparable polls. Whether the difference between 2 and 7 percent is sufficient to call the United States vertical remains in question. We still do not know what the average percentage across all individualistic cultures is. For example, if it is 3 percent, then 7 percent would make the United States a vertical individualist culture.

Furthermore, consistent with the discussion in Chapter 1, the constructs are situation specific. The United States is undoubtedly horizontal in social situations but vertical in situations of taxation for the purposes of income redistribution or acceptance of inequality of income.

We do know that collectivism is correlated with power distance (Hofstede, 1980) about .67, which suggests that vertical collectivism and horizontal individualism are the "typical" patterns around the world. However, some individualist cultures, like Australia and Sweden, are more horizontal than others. In this context, then, the United States is more vertical than the average individualistic culture and thus might be called a vertical individualistic culture. But it should be understood that even vertical individualistic cultures are rather horizontal, because all individualistic cultures, relative to collectivist cultures, are horizontal.

My suggestion that middle- and upper-class Americans tend toward vertical individualism derives from the observation that they are often offended if an experimenter suggests to them that they are "average" (Weldon, 1984; Markus and Kitayama, 1991a). They want to be distinguished and to "stick out," and they behave in ways that tend to make them distinct. Faced with large inequalities in their societies, with slums and hunger among 15 percent of the population, they are not especially aroused, and unlike the Swedes, are unwilling to pay taxes at the 70 percent top rate in order to redistribute wealth and foster equality. Furthermore, about 65 percent of the people tested in Milgram's (1974) famous experiments obeyed highly distasteful instructions. In Australia, Kilham and Mann (1974) obtained only 40 percent rates of conformity.

On the positive side, being vertical is consistent with the emphasis on "being the best." That may be a factor in many American inventions—such as the electric light, computers, and VCRs—that collectivists then perfect.

The members of Israeli kibbutzim would have an interdependent, "same self," or they would be horizontal collectivists. They neither want to stand out nor to dominate others in their group, and they value community needs more than individual desires.

The Indians, with their great concern for standing out (see Triandis, 1972), which is consistent with the caste system, must have a different self. However, until they become old and are allowed to withdraw from life's duties, they have many family obligations and duties and are quite interdependent, and thus may be considered vertical collectivists.

It may be useful to make further distinctions, for example, by considering different kinds of vertical relationships. Differentiation among individuals may occur in different domains. Kashima and Callan (1994), discussing the Japanese work group, argued that the Japanese differentiate structural roles (who is in charge), but not functional roles (who is to do what), more than do Americans, whereas Americans do the opposite. It would be too complicated to describe cultures by taking into account the vertical-horizontal dimensions in every domain, but a complete analysis would probably require such complexity.

One way to measure these tendencies is to create multiple-choice-format scenarios that describe different situations and ask the individual to select one of four answers, with each answer reflecting one of the four patterns. For example, one can ask: If you had to describe yourself to another person, which of the following descriptions would you choose?

1. achievement oriented (vertical individualism)
2. cooperative (horizontal collectivism)
3. dutiful (vertical collectivism)
4. unique (horizontal individualism)

By asking individuals to give their first and second choices, it is possible to obtain an individual's profile of behavior across situations. Of course, the sample of situations for this test is crucial, and we have not yet determined the best sample. If Hofstede's (1980) finding of a correlation between power distance and collectivism is used as a guide, it may be that most collectivist cultures are vertical and most individualist cultures are horizontal. In that case, a vertical individualistic culture, such as the United States, may have a profile such as this one: horizontal individualism, 40 percent; vertical individualism, 30 percent; horizontal collectivism, 20 percent; and vertical collectivism, 10 percent. Sweden's profile may be 50, 20, 20, 10, respectively. Britain might have a 20, 50, 10, 20 profile; Germany a 20, 40, 10, 30; France and northern Italy 30, 40, 10, 20, and southern Italy might have a 10, 30, 20, 40 profile. These numbers are hypotheses, but they suggest that future research using such scenarios, tapping a representative sample of situations in each culture, may prove quite informative.

Japan might have a profile such as 20 percent horizontal individualism, 5 percent vertical individualism, 25 percent horizontal collectivism, and 50 percent vertical collectivism. I suggest that horizontal collectivism may be relatively high because sticking out is an embarrassment in Japan, where the term for "different" (*chigau*) is synonymous with "wrong" (Markus and Kitayama, 1991b). Vertical collectivism would be very high because the Japanese also have a strong sense of hierarchy, which is reflected in the specific required language forms for each type of status relationship and in other social norms.

Fiske's Four Kinds of Sociality

The typology I have just described matches very closely with Fiske's (1990, 1992) theory of sociality. Fiske identified four basic forms of social behavior. These forms occur in every culture, although the specific manifestation of the form can vary across cultures. The main ideas of the four forms are *sharing, hierarchy, equality,* and *proportionality.* If we focus on how resources should be distributed, the first pattern dictates to do so "according to need," the second "according to status," the third "equally," and the fourth "according to contribution" (i.e., equity).

The first is called communal sharing (CS) and is the sort of behavior that goes on in most families. Resources are divided according to need. People take what they need and no one keeps a record. There are cultures where the land is owned by everyone. Fiske described a culture in which he did his fieldwork (the Moose, in Burkina Faso, West Africa) where land is owned in this way. Even in modern cultures, a city park is a common property. Thus CS is characterized by need-based responding among all in the group. In addition, there is a strong sense of belonging to the group, the self is relational and includes the group's identity, most thinking is in terms of "we" and "they" rather than "I" and "you." There are fears of isolation and loneliness. Relationships are conceived as being "eternal," and gifts are given even when they are not reciprocated. Work is shared and is a collective responsibility. Land belongs to all and is sacred. Decisions are made through consensus. There is much emphasis on intimacy, nurturance, altruism, caring, selflessness, generosity, sharing, and concern for others. However, there is also strong ingroup favoritism and hostility toward outgroups, which can be linked to racism, genocide, and supernationalism.

The second form is called authority ranking (AR). In this pattern, resources are divided according to rank. For example, in the traditional Chinese family, the grandfather eats first, selecting the pieces he likes best, then the oldest son, then the other sons, eat according to age. After the sons have made their choices, the oldest female can choose, followed by the other females in descending order of age. If the resource is "attention" (Derber, 1979), the president of the United States gets a lot more than the secretaries of the departments, who get more than the managers, and so on. The janitors may get little or no attention, unless they go on strike! In this pattern the self is either exalted or humble and inequality is "natural." There is emphasis on precedence in walking and seating arrangements, and a high-status person is expected to give large gifts and has many obligations for the protection of the lower-status members of the group. Authority ranking leads to a focus on respect, deference, loyalty, and obedience, and the impertinent are punished. Land belongs to the king or the equivalent. There is identification with the leader, and some followers are ready to die for the leader. Wars extend the authority of the leader, but misfortunes cause the leader to lose the "mandate of heaven."

The third form is equality matching (EM), where resources must be distributed equally. One person cuts the cake and the other selects the piece. Total equality is the essence of this pattern. The history of the United States has many examples of EM, including "one man, one vote" and the distribution of absolutely equal parcels of land to settlers in the West. In this pattern gift giving must be comparable, justice means equality, and reciprocity is very important. Work is shared equally, and the self is like every other self. Misfortunes should be equally distributed, and revenge is an appropriate way to deal with enemies.

The fourth form is called market pricing (MP). Each person receives resources commensurate with her contributions—the more you give, the more you get. If you spend twice as many years studying, your salary should be twice as large. For example, in the United States, college graduates earn about 70 percent more than high school graduates. In this pattern social relations are analyzed according to "profit" and "loss," gifts are given according to previous contributions to the relationship, and achievement is very important. There is a tendency toward quantification of everything in this type of scheme, so people compute percentages (e.g., taxes, interests), work in units of time, see land as an investment, and allow the market to decide most things. The self in MP is defined by one's occupation, and politically people believe that their decisions should lead to the greatest good for the greatest number. Despite this belief, there are wars to gain or preserve economic benefits, and one sees exploitation of workers and computation of "kill ratios," both of which suggest that market value is more important than social or personal value.

Fiske argued that these basic patterns of interpersonal relationships are found everywhere. But the specific content of each pattern is different in each culture. For example, in one culture MP is done with money, in another with cows, and in a third one with curved-tooth pigs. People construct their social behavior by combining these four patterns. In general, in collectivist cultures people use CS and in individualistic cultures they are more likely to use MP. Horizontal cultures tend to use EM and vertical cultures to use AR.

Fiske (1993) showed that social errors of Bengalis, Koreans, Chinese, and Vai (Liberia and Sierra Leone) residing in the United States, such as calling someone they know by the wrong name, misremembering with whom they had done something, or mistakenly directing an action at an inappropriate person, involve persons with whom the actor is in the same one of the four relationships. In short, if I have a CS relationship with A and B, and A does something, I might remember that B did it. These findings support the hypothesis that the four universal patterns of sociality underlie everyday social cognition.

Returning to the typology now, it is clear that vertical collectivism is CS + AR; vertical individualism is MP + AR; horizontal collectivism is CS + EM; and horizontal individualism is MP + EM.

Culture and Politics

It would seem plausible that the type of culture predisposes a particular political system. It so happens that a typology of values and political systems developed by Rokeach (1973) matches our typology. Rokeach asked people to rank-order eighteen values, like *freedom* and *equality*. He identified people who (1) placed both of these values among their top four or five values, (2) placed both of these values among their bottom four or five values, (3) emphasized freedom and de-emphasized equality, and (4) emphasized equality and de-emphasized freedom.

He then discovered that these four types of people favored different political systems. Namely, those who were high on freedom and equality were social democrats of the Swedish variety; those who emphasized freedom and placed equality low were Reagan-type free-market democrats; those who emphasized equality and de-emphasized freedom favored communism; and those who gave both freedom and equality a low rank were fascists. He did content analyses of speeches made by leaders, including Hitler, Lenin, and U.S. presidents, and found support for his argument. Specifically, Lenin rarely used the word *freedom* but employed the word *equality* frequently; Hitler used neither word much; U.S. presidents typically used *freedom* frequently and *equality* rarely; and Swedish prime ministers used both words often.

Rokeach's typology is strictly "Western," but we might generalize it, the way it appears in Table 3.1. The table indicates how vertical and horizontal collectivism and individualism correspond to different combinations of the kind of self, Fiske orientation, Rokeach values, and different political systems.

We have already discussed horizontal individualism in Sweden, and we might add the British Labor party and other socialist movements as examples. The link of horizontal collectivism and the Israeli kibbutz has been mentioned. Vertical individualism and market democracies have been discussed above. The only political system we have not covered is the one that corresponds to vertical collectivism. Here, rather than use the harsh Rokeach label of "fascism," I use "communalism," with an understanding that in many of these societies the village chiefs or tribal chiefs have many dictatorial attributes, but since they are a "collective of elders," there is no cult of personality such as that found in fascism. Examples of traditional

TABLE 3.1   Culture, Self, Orientation, and Politics

	Vertical		Horizontal	
	Collectivism	*Individualism*	*Collectivism*	*Individualism*
Kind of self	Interdependent Different from others	Independent Different from others	Interdependent Same as others	Independent Same as others
Fiske orientation	Communal sharing Authority ranking	Market pricing Authority ranking	Communal sharing Equality matching	Market pricing Equality matching
Rokeach values	Low equality Low freedom	Low equality High freedom	High equality Low freedom	High equality High freedom
Political system	Communalism (e.g., Indian village)	Market democracy (e.g., U.S., France)	Communal living (e.g., Israeli kibbutz)	Democratic socialism (e.g., Sweden, British Labor party)

societies with dictators can be found, and perhaps the most extreme is the nineteenth-century African King Shaka Zulu (see Edgerton, 1985, pp. 228–229). He executed as many as one million people because he believed that the only way to rule is through terror.

Chiefs take different forms in different cultures. For example, in traditional Greece, the rich landowners controlled local politics in ways that I witnessed when I was the interpreter for the international observers of the referendum that brought back the king in 1946. In Africa the tribal chief, in India the panchayat (village council), in the Pacific "the big men," control much of village life. There is evidence that the greater the differences in wealth in a society, the greater the authoritarianism of the rulers (for a review, see Edgerton, 1985, p. 229). In most religions, the controlling authorities, such as the pope and the cardinals, the mullahs of Iran, play similar controlling roles.

Gelfand, Triandis, and Chan (in preparation) asked Illinois students to make similarity judgments among sentences that represented individualism (e.g., do my own thing), collectivism (e.g., do what my group wants me to do), and authoritarianism (e.g., obedience to authority). The researchers submitted these judgments to multidimensional scaling and found that these subjects saw individualism and authoritarianism as opposites; collectivism was orthogonal (unrelated) to that dimension. Thus, in the natural cognitions of American undergraduates at least, individualism and collectivism are orthogonal and the opposite of individualism is authoritarianism. Whether that is also true of the natural cognitions of people in collectivist countries requires further research.

In any case, this study suggests some complexities in the analysis of politics. According to Table 3.1 we associate vertical collectivism with authoritarian regimes. If collectivism and authoritarianism are really different, as the Gelfand, Triandis, and Chan study suggested, then the presentation in Table 3.1 needs to be modified, and additional complexities must be introduced.

Factors Conducive to Individualism and Collectivism

The degree of individualism or collectivism in any given culture is influenced by certain factors, including two specific cultural syndromes: cultural tightness versus looseness, and cultural complexity versus simplicity. Individualism is most often a consequence of looseness and cultural complexity; collectivism is most often a consequence of tightness and cultural simplicity.

Tightness Versus Looseness

Tightness (Pelto, 1968) refers to the extent members of a culture (1) agree about what constitutes correct action; (2) must behave exactly according to the norms of the culture; and (3) suffer or offer severe criticism for even slight deviations from norms. We can see these syndromes in contrasting cultures. The United States is a relatively loose culture; Japan is a tight culture. An example was offered by Naito (1994) concerning the acceptability of chewing gum in class. In the United States only 12 percent of the second-grade and 0 percent of the fourth-grade children indicated that it was unacceptable to do that. The equivalent data from Japan were 92 percent for both grades. This supports (1) above. In tight cultures there are few appropriate ways to respond to a particular situation. The members of the culture have clear ideas about what to do (e.g., Do you want sexual relations? Get married). As suggested by (2) above, everyone is expected to follow the norms.

Although modern Japan is much looser, Japanese history, specifically during the Tokugawa period (1603–1867), provides many examples of extreme tightness. Edgerton (1985, p. 174) quoted an American who became a Japanese naturalized citizen at the end of the nineteenth century, as follows: "The individual was completely and pitilessly sacrificed to the community. Even now the only safe rule of conduct in a Japanese settlement is to act in all things according to local custom; for the slightest divergence from rule will be observed with disfavor." During the Tokugawa period there were hundreds of rules. Hundreds of commandments, rather than Western religion's ten, were regarded as sacred and observed with compulsive attention. There were laws that specified precisely how men, women, and children were required to work, build their houses, dress, stand, walk, sit, rise, speak, breath, eat, drink, and smile, and all were enforced collectively. Consistent with (3) above, the community faced collective punishment if it failed in its duty to enforce them. Furthermore, the rules were so strongly internalized that they were "followed without any expression of difficulty or reluctance in doing so" (Edgerton, 1985, p. 176). A person's honor and self-esteem depended on following the rules, and failure to do so shamed not only the individual but also the whole group.

Tightness occurs in homogeneous cultures that are relatively isolated from other cultures. There is often a high population density, and these cultures are not especially dynamic. They have typically had an agricultural base that rewarded people for paying attention to what others were doing. In preliterate societies tightness is associated with communal control of property, corporate control of stored food and production power, strong religious leaders, hereditary recruitment into priesthood, and high levels of taxation (Pelto, 1968).

Loose cultures, in contrast, have multiple, sometimes conflicting, norms about what to do (e.g., Do you want sexual relations? Get married, go to a bar, find a steady lover, and so on). Those who deviate from norms are not necessarily punished. Looseness occurs in heterogeneous societies, where people get rewarded for independent action and there is little population density. In addition, there is a high probability that cultures that are located at the intersections of major other cultures (e.g., Thailand at the intersection of India and China) will be loose, because people are aware that there are many ways to respond to a situation.

Very hot climates tend toward loose cultures, and colder climates press toward tight ones (Robbins, de Walt, and Pelto, 1972). One interpretation is that in warm climates, where the earliest humans lived, people did not have to "control themselves" to conquer the environment. As they moved to more and more unfavorable and unnaturally cold environments, they had to act in a certain way in order to survive. In very cold climates (e.g., the Arctic), undisciplined behavior can result in frostbite and even death. Greater control of self may result in tightness and also in high suicide rates, whereas looseness may contribute to high homicide rates (Robbins, de Walt, and Pelto, 1972).

Both tightness and looseness are situation-specific. A culture may be tight in social and political situations and loose in economic or religious situations. Thus when we state that a culture is tight (or loose), we mean that tightness (or looseness) is characteristic across many, but not all, situations.

Examples of Tight Cultures. Members of collectivist cultures tend to be very tight. Turkish immigrants to Western Europe, especially if they are of lower-social-class background, are especially tight because they are trying to preserve their culture. The importance of conformity to norms is made particularly obvious when the tight culture conflicts with a looser culture. A dispatch from France relates an incident that occurred in Colmar, where a conflict between generations and cultures resulted in parents' killing their daughter (*L'Express*, French weekly newspaper published in Toronto, Canada, August 24–30, 1993, p. 7). The girl, age fifteen, of Turkish ethnic background, was accused by her family of being "too integrated into French culture." Her desire to live like a French girl of her age infuriated her parents and the rest of her family. The girl asked to be placed with foster parents, which a judge agreed to do. However, when she visited her family on August 15, it was the last time she was seen alive. An investigation revealed that the decision "to execute" her had been made by the entire family.

Japan is considered a tight, though complex, culture, and people are socialized to act properly. Sanger (1993) provided an example by telling the story of Yuhei Komoda, age 13, who died on January 13, 1993. He was bullied by a jeering crowd of classmates and shoved around as dozens of other students watched. He was later found suffocated in a closet. Although it is not known whether he provoked his classmates, it is worth noting that this bullying, called *ijime*, occurs when a person does not "fit in." In nineteenth-century Japan, the samurai were permitted to kill anyone of lower status whose behavior was "unexpected" (Edgerton, 1985, p. 175). *Ijime* takes many forms, such as beatings, exclusion from the group, and desecration of uniforms. Yuhei's "crimes" consisted of speaking standard Japanese instead of the local dialect, coming from a wealthy home, and not being part of the group in a society that demands conformity. "They had lived here only seventeen years," said the reporter of the regional newspaper, referring to the family. The father had studied in Tokyo, and that set him apart, which was another "explanation." Interestingly, the town focused on the boys who committed the crime, feeling sorry for them.

Iwao (1993) pointed out that conformity to age-appropriate norms is very high in Japan because such conformity is the safest protection from criticism. It eliminates the need to make personal adjustments. Criticism is dreaded in tight cultures. Of course, in a pressure cooker atmosphere, once in a while there is a deviation from the ideal. The 22,000 cases of bullying reported every year to the Japanese Ministry of Education are relatively few for a nation with 15,000 high schools and is a relatively minor problem if compared with the violence in American schools. Nevertheless, it does reflect tightness.

Because correct action is so important in tight cultures, people are given a lot of practice in controlling themselves. The traditional Japanese tea ceremony affords excellent training in appropriate behavior and self-control. A group of six to eight people (usually men) sit Japanese style (uncomfortable for those who are unaccustomed to this position) for an hour or so while the ceremony takes place. Sitting in this way for a long time requires considerable self-control. (Westerners might have to control the urge to stretch their legs and act in a loose manner during such ceremonies.) The seating arrangement reflects a hierarchy. The assembled face a beautiful object and are seated so the person with the highest status is closest to the object, and the person with the least status is seated furthest away from that object.

The dark green, bitter tea is poured while the participants listen to the sound of hot and cold water falling (which make very distinct sounds). The participants admire the beautiful object and enjoy the sounds of the pouring water. The bowl is first presented to the person with the highest status, who initially declines it, but it is offered again until he accepts it. Then he passes it on to the host, who refills it and offers it to the next person, who again declines but is ultimately persuaded to drink. There is precision in accepting and declining the tea, and the use of the same cup is symbolic of group solidarity. For at least one hour every move is as specified in the book of traditional Japanese etiquette. If one learns to behave according to the book for one hour, one may be able to behave virtuously for a lifetime.

However, many young contemporary Japanese have never participated in a tea ceremony. In fact, I have found that a number of my Japanese friends are not at all interested in traditional Japan. The shift toward individualism, clear in Hayashi's data (1992a, 1992b), seems to play a part in rejection of tradition.

Examples of Loose Cultures. The Thais are a prototypical loose culture. There is very little concern with work norms and etiquette. If an employee decides to leave his or her place of employment because of homesickness, or any other reason, he or she may leave without giving a formal resignation (Phillips, 1965). After the employee leaves, no one comments. The Thais are heterogeneous, and there is relatively little pressure to act interdependently. There are many accepted ways to behave in a given situation.

Correlates of Tightness and Looseness. Tightness seems associated with precision in manufacturing and law and order. Crime rates in general are lower in tight cultures. Perhaps the difference between the United States and Japan is most interesting because both countries are industrial and wealthy. The homicide rates in the United States are 9.1 times higher than in Japan; among males age fifteen to twenty-four, the U.S. rate is 75 times that of Japan; in the case of violent crime, the U.S. rate is 361 times the Japanese rate; motor vehicle thefts are 22 times higher in the United States; incarceration rates are 11 times higher in the United States (*USA Today*, March 29, 1994, p. 2). Although North America is more heterogeneous than Japan, these differences may be traced to cultural differences. One theory of criminal behavior (Gottfredson and Hirschi, 1990) is based on the concept of self-control. It is very probable that impulse control is stressed in a tight culture.

Looseness seems to be associated with creativity and surprise. For example, in speech, surprising and impressing a listener with clever combinations of words is approved in loose cultures. Studies of the meaning of words in some thirty countries, conducted by Osgood and his associates and described by Triandis (1994, pp. 97–100), showed that in tight cultures, such as traditional Greece and Japan, the concepts of "duty" and "discipline" have very clear meanings: They are "good," "powerful," and "active." However, in Western countries, these words have ambiguous meanings, and their "conflict index" (a measurement of the amount of disagreement) among members of the culture in judging their meaning was high. Looseness reflects a culture in which deviance is tolerated, norms are expressed in many ways, and group organization, formality, durability, and solidarity are not as often fostered.

Measurement of Tightness and Looseness. At the present time a number of researchers are working on developing methods for the measurement of tightness, but until several converging methods are found, definitive suggestions cannot be offered. However, as a provisional method until this work is completed, tightness may be gauged by determining the percentage of people who are left-handed. This works well because in all cultures the right hand is considered the correct one, but in cultures that are tight there is pressure for those who are naturally left-handed to become right-handed. When pressure to conform is absent, around 14 percent of the population is left-handed (Dawson, 1974), and when there is extreme pressure, the percentage drops to as low as .28 percent (Bakare, 1974). Dawson has developed highly reliable methods of obtaining the relevant data. For example, he interviewed people and asked them to hold various objects in the "usual way you use them," such as a pencil, toothbrush, and scissors, and observed which hand they used.

A scenario method may also be useful in measuring tightness and looseness. A study by Kurowski (1993) used scenarios with situations in which the protagonist's desires, needs, perceived rights, or point of view were different from the norms of respected other people. The respondents were asked to indicate what advice they would give to a person in that situation. In addition, the researcher measured the level of collectivism and individualism of the respondents. She found that collectivists advised that conformity should be obtained by talking to the protagonist. Individualists saw behavior that deviates from norms as acceptable. In short, individualism is linked to looseness and collectivism to tightness.

Cultural Complexity

To obtain a crude index of cultural complexity in a given country we can use the gross national product per capita (GNP/cap). Affluent cultures are more complex than less affluent ones in that there is more differentiation in the various domains of life. For example, there are 250,000 job descriptions in the *Dictionary of Occupational Titles*. In hunting, gathering, or foraging cultures there are fewer than a dozen "jobs" in the form of distinct roles. Several other measures may reflect cultural complexity. For example, Berry (1994) argued that the size of the community is a good index.

Cultural complexity may be the most important dimension that discriminates among cultures (R. A. C. Stewart, 1971; Ember and Levinson, 1991). It tends to be related to looseness, whereas cultural simplicity is generally correlated with tightness. Thus the factors that are mentioned below as relevant for complexity-simplicity are also relevant for looseness-tightness.

Factors Contributing to Tightness and Complexity

Certain factors are especially important in shaping complex and simple cultures, including the homogeneity of the members of the culture and the distribution of traits and attributes. The homogeneity of the members of the culture is related to both tightness and complexity. Members of a culture can agree on the norms that must be imposed when they are homogeneous, and there is also likely to be greater cultural simplicity. Thus, homogeneity predisposes a culture toward collectivism. The more homogeneous the culture, the more beliefs, attitudes, norms, roles, and values are shared. When a deviation from norms occurs, it is very clear that it has occurred and people feel they must do something about it. Homogeneity thus leads to tightness and collectivism. When there is much sharing of beliefs and values, but a distinct hierarchy, the probability of vertical collectivism is high.

If the distribution of most traits and attributes in a culture is narrow, in other words, if most people are more or less alike, there is a tendency for people to fit in and thus to develop a "same self." Then, horizontal collectivism is more probable. Uniqueness is not valued. For example, when everyone is short, being tall is "bad." When I was in high school in Greece, my being six feet, four inches, tall was a distinct disadvantage, and I was often ridiculed for my "abnormal" size.

In contrast, if the distribution is wide, there is usually some value placed on one end of the distribution and there is rejection of the other end of the distribution. In that case, people try to be on the socially valued side of the distribution. Often that means cultivating a "different self" that is distinct and unique.

Of special importance is the distribution of resources. If everyone has more or less the same resources, as is typical in hunting and gathering societies, equality is greatly valued and widely practiced. Because the distribution of strength between men and women is nevertheless present, there is more status given to men than to women, but even in that case the differences are not large (Duley and Edwards, 1986). When men engage in occupations that are much more dangerous than the activities of women, that provides an additional factor in status differentiation between men and women (Nisbett, 1990).

In short, when the distribution of resources is relatively even, that increases the probability of horizontal forms of the culture. When distribution of resources is very wide and there are large differences in income between the top and bottom 10 percent of the distribution, as one finds in Latin America, then inequality becomes a major aspect of the culture and we see vertical forms of the culture. Members of the society see those at the top as very different from those at the bottom of the distribution, that is, there is much power distance (Hofstede, 1980).

Membership Characteristics of the Culture

Rate of Change. Clearly, if members come and go and new members keep coming in, there will be more heterogeneity of point of view and more complexity, which results in a more individualistic culture. Ziller (1965) reviewed experimental social psychology studies on open (changing membership) and closed (constant membership) groups. In reviewing his results, I found (Triandis, 1990) that the attributes of these groups were parallel to the attributes of individualistic and collectivist cultures. Specifically, open groups show less time perspective and less reciprocity of action than closed groups; they see relationships as transitory; they do not identify with the group very much; they are more creative; members can join such groups easily and are easily assimilated. In closed groups, group members show much reciprocity and are less likely to maximize individual gains by taking advantage of other group members; but people have great difficulties becoming assimilated in such groups. Thus, the greater the rate of change of group membership, the greater the individualism.

Lalonde and Silverman (1994) examined how people in open or closed groups respond to a social injustice, under conditions when their social identity is salient (as happens in collectivist cultures) or not salient. The study has relevance to the social issue of how a member of a minority group deals with an injustice. Will a person try to deal with the injustice as an individual, or will that person try to get the minority group to deal with it? They found that an individualistic response was preferred to a collective response in the open groups, but not in the closed groups. Closed groups with highly salient social identities behaved in these laboratory situations like collectivists.

Density. When the number of people per unit of area is large, people have to develop many rules for social behavior to reduce the probability of conflict. In addition to the norms and rules of social behavior, they develop institutions such as courts, voting, adjudicators, and mediators to deal with conflicts that arise. In small societies (say, fewer than 10,000 people), the greater the density, the greater the collectivism. However, in large societies, it is possible to achieve conflict reduction through an elaborate bureaucracy. Thus in small, dense societies we can expect collectivism; in large, dense societies we can expect to find elaborate bureaucracies.

Number of Choices. In complex environments, such as modern information societies, people have a large number of choices. In most preliterate cultures there are few choices. Also, among the poor, underprivileged segments of even the most modern societies, the number of choices is small. As affluence and complexity increase, the number of choices also increases. In information societies the data banks include information of enormous complexity. The significance of the number of choices is that it implies that individuals may arrive at different decisions depending on how the information is processed. The individual is conscious of a decision's personal nature. People make their own decisions and may be labeled individualists.

Number of Ingroups

If only one ingroup is present, it dominates social life. It provides the only source of norms, identity, and social support. Collectivists may have relatively few ingroups, but they identify very strongly with them. The ingroups of collectivists provide social insurance, protection, and a relaxing atmosphere.

The presence of many ingroups encourages individualism. For example, the separation of church and state in the United States automatically creates more than one ingroup and is a premise upon which multiculturalism and democracy are based. It is also the foundation for social movements because each ingroup can potentially become a social movement.

Multiple ingroups are especially important in large urban centers, where the social controls of small ingroups are often weak. The social structures of these communities are loose, and several of the factors we have discussed converge to put more emphasis on personal responsibility and less on norms. With more ingroups and looseness there is an increase in social diversity, tolerance for deviance, and multiculturalism. Thus the factors that make cultures loose and allow many choices favor individualism. Conversely, collectivism is maximal in tight cultures, where there are few choices.

Tightness, Cultural Complexity, and Individualism-Collectivism

The hypothesized relationships among tightness, cultural complexity, and individualism-collectivism are presented in Figure 3.1. The cultures are placed in this figure on the basis of a reading of the relevant ethnographies,

FIGURE 3.1   Relationship of Tightness, Cultural Complexity, and Individualism-Collectivism

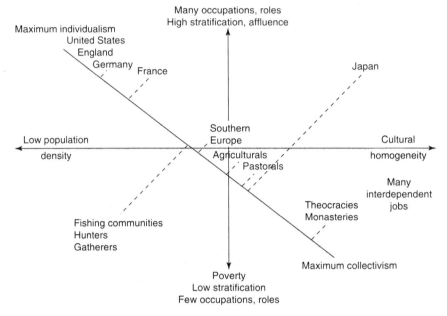

Source: H.C. Triandis, *Culture and Social Behavior* (New York: McGraw-Hill, 1994). Reprinted with permission.

a matter of judgment. For example, in many agricultural cultures one sees ethnographic descriptions such as found in D. Lee (1976), who described the Arapesh. In this culture, people plant seeds in the gardens of their neighbors and enjoy mostly the food planted by others. The Arapesh may have six isolated plots, which, from the point of view of efficiency, should be cultivated by six persons working alone. But they prefer to work together and move as a team from one plot to the other. The wasted motion of six people moving among the plots is a price they are willing to pay. Independent action in this case is looked upon disdainfully.

As one can see from Figure 3.1, overall collectivism is maximal in tight, simpler cultures. The kibbutz in Israel and the Mennonites, Dukhabors, and Amish in North America provide examples of such cultures. Conversely, individualism is maximal in loose, complex cultures. Large cities in the West would be good examples of such cultures. But remember that all humans have both tendencies in some mixture. Narcissists may use collectivist cognitions rarely, whereas those in theocracies may seldom use individualist cognitions. Once we perfect our tests of these tendencies, it would be interesting to measure key samples in many cultures and validate Figure 3.1.

The Individual in Individualist and Collectivist Cultures

Humans are evolved primates, and primates require groups to survive. And yet as we adjust to our environment, we also become individualists, although our individualism may take different forms. We might emphasize self-reliance, hedonism, or simply emotional distance from our ingroups. We might become extremely or not so extremely competitive. Thus collectivism is a more coherent reality for all of us, whereas individualism is a bit more nebulous and depends on the social environments in which we were raised, our successes and failures in life, and the specific rewards we have gained from individualistic behaviors.

Humans are aware of both the individualist and the collectivist themes that follow. But in some cultures they are more likely to sample the individualist or collectivist themes in constructing their social behavior. Thus, when we say that some individual is a collectivist, we simply mean that in the case of this particular individual the sampling of collectivist themes is more probable and will occur in more situations.

Empirical research in many collectivist cultures (e.g., Korea: Cha, 1994; China: Ho and Chiu, 1994) has shown that popular sayings include both individualistic and collectivist themes. The number of collectivist sayings, however, is larger than the number of individualist ones.

Lew (1994) interviewed various Chinese samples and asked them to discuss their values. I did a content analysis of his list of values and found that about 40 percent of the values were horizontal collectivist (HC), 30 percent vertical collectivist (VC), 15 percent vertical individualist (VI), and 15 percent horizontal individualist (HI). Lew also examined their goals, and a similar analysis on my part showed that 50 percent were VC, 30 percent HC, 18 percent VI, and 2 percent HI. In short, there is no doubt that both kinds of values and goals can be found. Similarly, Avrahami and Dar (1993) identified a blend of individualistic and collectivist orientations among kibbutz high school graduates in Israel.

In every culture there are some horizontal and some vertical individualists and some horizontal and some vertical collectivists. But in each culture there is a modal pattern with a characteristic distribution of individuals among the four types.

Factors That Influence Personal Tendencies

There are several factors that increase a person's proclivity toward either individualism or collectivism. These factors can influence particular individuals within the two different types of cultures, partly accounting for the variety within the culture.

Age

The older one is, the more social relations one is likely to have established. There is evidence (Noricks et al., 1987) that people become more collectivist with age. Noricks et al. replicated Shweder and Bourne's (1982) study in which Americans, when making judgments about a person's attributes (e.g., "he is intelligent when dealing with his mother-in-law" versus "he is intelligent"), used context less and were context free more often than Oriyas from India. Noricks et al. studied a large sample from Chico, California. The context-free responses reported by Shweder and Bourne were 72 percent for Chicago and 50 percent for the Oriyas; Chico gave 65 percent, essentially replicating the previous findings. However, that percentage was different for those age fifty and over, who were more like the Oriyas (57 percent), while those under age fifty provided 68 percent context-free responses. In short, as people age, they become more embedded in a mobile society, establish more networks, and have more opportunities to describe people in context. Replication of this study in a collectivist culture would be desirable to see if the 50 percent of the average Oriyas becomes even smaller for aged collectivists or stays the same.

A parallel finding was obtained by Triandis, Bontempo, Villareal, et al. (1988), evaluating Japanese students who were individualists and their parents who were collectivists. However, students in Japan are an unusual sample. They work very hard to get admitted to a university, and while they are students they have a few years of "freedom" to do their own thing before becoming "slaves of the corporation," as some Japanese women call them (Iwao, 1993). Also, there is a confound: The parents came from the generation that was born soon after World War II and had experienced the privations of that period, which unquestionably provided a sense of common fate with other Japanese. The students did not have that experience. Thus, although the results of these two studies are consistent, we still need more research to be sure.

Studies of child-rearing attitudes of Japanese and Americans in some cases found the older samples more collectivist than the younger samples in both cultures. Therefore, the age difference was more important than the national difference (for a review, see Gudykunst, 1993, p. 131).

Social Class

In all societies the upper social classes are likely to be relatively more individualistic than the lower social classes (Daab, 1991). In a sample of 883 Australian eleven-year-olds, Marjoribanks (1991) found that upper-social-status parents pressed toward individualism more than lower-social-status parents. A greater emphasis on obedience is also found in the lower social classes in modern, complex societies, whereas the upper classes emphasize creativity and self-reliance (Kohn, 1969). It is more useful for a worker than for a professional to be obedient, so the child-rearing pattern matches the likely future occupations of the child, based on social class.

Child Rearing

Adamopoulos and Bontempo (1984) argued that child-rearing patterns around the world can be described by using two dimensions: acceptance-rejection (see also Rohner, 1986) and independence-dependence. The latter is especially relevant for individualism and collectivism. Individualists tend to use acceptance/independence, which leads to high self-confidence. The evidence that individualists have unusually positive self-esteem and show self-enhancement is strong and has been reviewed by Markus and Kitayama (1991b). Collectivists tend to use acceptance/dependence, which leads to conformity. The evidence that collectivists are high in conformity is fairly strong. They conform more often to ingroup authorities, such as parents, than do individualists.

The independence-dependence dimension is a crucial discriminator of the child rearing of individualist and collectivist cultures. In individualistic cultures independence is expected and valued, and self-actualization is encouraged. Mother and child are distinct and the child is encouraged to leave the nest. In collectivist cultures dependence is expected and valued. The underlying assumption is that mother and child are one and can be "the same." Doumanis (1983) noted that collectivism emphasizes social relations and individualism emphasizes achievement.

In collectivist cultures, child rearing is sometimes very intrusive (Guthrie, 1961). Breaking the will of the child to make her totally obedient is sometimes evident. Dependence of the child on the parents is often encouraged. Collectivists control their children by providing high rates of interaction, guidance, and consultation. Consequently, their children become dependent on teachers and other adults for help in making important decisions. As a faculty member for thirty-six years, I have had many requests for advice about personal decisions (e.g., should I marry so and so?) from students from collectivist cultures, but never from students from individualist cultures.

It is important to realize that parental control tends to have a different meaning in collectivist and individualistic cultures. In collectivist cultures it is often perceived as "love" because it is part of the effort of the parents to make the child a useful member of the ingroup or the society; in individualistic cultures it is often perceived as "overcontrol" and generates negative affect.

Children learn the dominant pattern of the culture first and other skills later. Thus children in collectivist cultures learn to be good ingroup members and may or may not learn to also be self-reliant, independent, achieving, and so on. In contrast, children in individualistic cultures learn to be independent and self-reliant, but they may not learn how to be good team players (Rosenthal and Bornholt, 1988).

The parent-child bond is especially strong in collectivist cultures, and the spouse-spouse bond is less strong. The reverse is the case in individualistic cultures. The data on role perceptions (Triandis, 1972) show this difference rather sharply.

Chinese Child-Rearing as an Example of Collectivist Socialization.
Wu (1985) illustrated how collectivist cultures, like China, create collectivist personalities. In Chinese culture, children and adults do most activities together; they do not lead separate lives, as is typical in individualistic cultures. When children are less than five years old, their mother is in close proximity, day and night. With such closeness as children, it is natural for adults to want to live with their old parents. If this is not possible, they will visit them as often as they can. Children are indulged not only by parents but also by the whole extended family. After a child is scolded or punished, the parent is affectionate to reestablish the closeness. Such strong acceptance of the child results in a personality that is optimistic, trusting, and sociable (Rohner, 1986). Dependence of the child on others is viewed as natural and desirable.

In societies that emphasize individualism, children are urged to become self-reliant and independent and dependence is considered undesirable. Conflicts develop when children raised by collectivist parents must interact with children raised by individualist parents. Wu (1985) discussed the case of Chinese and Australians. The Chinese are distressed when a child is told by Australian teachers to solve the problem of an attack by fighting back himself. The Chinese elders are likely to ask that the attack be reported to them so that they can discipline the attacker. The confusion in this case is eliminated by developing this rule: "If the attacker is Chinese, do not hit back and report the attack to the elders; if the attacker is not Chinese, deal with the situation yourself by hitting back."

Russian Child Rearing. Pearson's (1990) description of Russian socialization practices provided a parallel with Wu's. Just like the Chinese involvement of all adults who happen to be present in the raising of children, many Russians get involved (called *vospitanie*) in raising children, which, as pointed out earlier, can take the form of a Muscovite passerby's criticizing a mother for not wrapping up her child sufficiently well.

The scolding and interference by any adult who happens to be present is in striking contrast with a lack of intervention prevalent in individualistic societies. Pearson (1990, pp. 52–58) provided an extensive description of collectivist child rearing, which she claimed has been traditional in Russia and is greatly valued. Such child rearing stresses that the interest of the individual and society are the same; it encourages sharing of toys; it includes collective activities, such as collective cleaning of the playroom; it encourages belonging to several collectives, each of which has strict norms that must be followed.

Collectivist child rearing results in what Pearson claimed is remarkable coordination when tasks must be shared, which she did not find in other countries (her husband was ambassador in France and Mexico as well), for example, when a reception for several hundred people had to be prepared. However, she pointed out that close supervision is essential because the collective assumes that there will be close supervision.

Traditional Greek Child Rearing. Triandis and Vassiliou (1972) discussed traditional Greek child rearing. The description has many common elements with Chinese and Russian child rearing. Having analyzed data about role perceptions, they concluded that traditional Greeks show more positive affect and intimacy within family roles than is found among Americans, with the only exception occurring in the husband-wife role, where the reverse was observed. In traditional Greece, emotions are channeled into the parent-child roles, especially the mother-son one, which is characterized by extreme interdependence. The researchers noted the conflict between dependence and achievement and saw the minority that does achieve as able to break the bonds of overdependence and extreme interdependence.

When completing sentences, Greek subjects mentioned "good conduct" as linked to *love, trust,* and *respect* much more frequently than did American subjects. This is consistent with the collectivist emphasis on virtuous action.

General Consideration of Collectivist Child Rearing. In general, collectivist child rearing is warmer and also more controlling than individualist child rearing. For example, Bronfenbrenner (1970) noted that Russian children are hugged, kissed, and cuddled more than American children, but they are also not allowed much freedom of movement. Aggression is less common in the extended families' collectivist cultures, partly because children are strongly discouraged from displaying this emotion. Since children play with their relatives, it would disrupt the entire ingroup if they were to fight (Minturn and Lambert, 1964).

In extended families, collectivism is more likely because children cannot receive special treatment. More uniformity is used in child rearing, and there is consensus about how to raise children. The ideal child is one that obeys. In nuclear families individualism is more probable because children may be treated specially. For example, parents might prepare the favorite food of one child, but if there are many children, this is usually impossible.

Travel, Education, and Occupation

Traveling and living abroad increase the probability of having to decide on one's own about lifestyle, and this leads to individualism. Those who travel a lot become exposed to different viewpoints, and experiences such as these encourage individualism. But there is also the possibility that an individualist living in a collectivist society may become acculturated.

Education generally leads to greater exposure to cultural diversity and tends toward individualism. However, the more traditionally educated (Sunday School, Qur'anic School, language of own ethnic group) a person is, the more collectivist the person becomes. In a study (Triandis and Singelis, submitted) where education and eleven other variables of subjective collectivism were used among American students, education was the most important (had the highest beta weight).

The particular occupation and job that a person engages in may result in working in teams or solitude. The more teamwork one does, the more one learns to pay attention to the needs of others, and thus the more one moves toward collectivism.

Other Hypotheses

When an individual is faced with a social situation, the situation causes a particular behavioral pattern. The behavior that is warranted is sometimes clear-cut but other times may be ambiguous. For example, if the ingroup is under attack by an outgroup, the probability that the vertical collectivism pattern will be activated is very high. At a funeral, the probability that horizontal collectivism will become activated is high all over the world. If the situation demands that a person write a unique book, the probability of vertical individualism emerging is high. If the situation calls for a member of an underrepresented group to be on a committee, a horizontal individualistic schema is most likely (the member is like all other members being represented and is a self-reliant and independent member of the committee).

But situations are often ambiguous. For example, suppose the situation involves a person who wants to take a trip that will inconvenience many other people. In that case, a person from a modal pattern of vertical collectivism will activate themes of duties that cannot be performed during the trip and may decide not to take the trip; an individual from the horizontal collectivism pattern may think about the social support that s/he will not be able to give during the trip and may cancel the trip. But both kinds of individualists suppress such themes and feel emotionally detached from the ingroup and thus will be able to take the trip. Thus, in this kind of ambiguous situation, the behavior of members of a culture "matches" the modal pattern of that culture. Overall, collectivists tend to change themselves to fit into situations (Diaz-Guerrero, 1979, 1991; Diaz-Guerrero and Diaz-Loving, 1990); individualists try to change the situation to fit themselves.

Similarly, the same-self versus different-self schemata may become activated under different circumstances. A clear situation may be that of cutting a birthday cake, where everybody is expected to have an equal piece—unless someone requests a low-calorie slice. In this situation, a same-self schema is very likely to be activated. However, when one gives a lecture, the different-self schema has a high probability of being activated.

Examples of ambiguous situations include a man's deciding how to dress. He can dress like everyone else (the Tokyo subway is remarkable in that most men wear a white shirt and a dark tie) or choose to wear something that will be conspicuous. This decision ultimately depends on the kind of self that is activated.

In other words, there is a strong situation-predisposition interaction. This is shown rather clearly by Caudill and Scarr's (1962) study conducted in Japan. They used the scenarios from the F. Kluckhohn and Strodtbeck (1961) questionnaire that measured collaterality (paying attention to peers), linearity (paying attention to those in authority), and individualism (paying attention to one's own internal needs and views), for which the symbols C, L, and I were used respectively. These scenarios describe different situations, and people were asked to indicate what they, and most people in their culture, would do in these situations. Most situations produced a $C > L > I$ or $L > C > I$ pattern, although there were situations with an $I > L > C$ and other patterns.

The important point to remember is that people who frequently use a particular cultural pattern, like vertical collectivism, are most comfortable doing what that pattern implies. They develop beliefs and attitudes and select norms and values that fit that pattern; they behave according to that pattern and thus develop habits (automatic behaviors carried out without thinking) that are consistent with that pattern. When they are in a new social situation, to the extent that this is possible, they try to use that cultural pattern. In short, they have developed a "structure of habits" (Triandis, 1980) that fits that pattern and will try to use that pattern in most situations. If the person is an individualist, to override the individualist structure of habits requires hard cognitive work. That is, the person must instruct himself to suppress individualistic tendencies in situations that require collectivist behaviors. People avoid such hard work, so they are most likely to use their habitual behavior patterns.

Thus, for instance, people in the kibbutz use horizontal collectivism when possible; in the United States people use vertical individualism, if that is possible; in India people seek situations in which they can use vertical collectivism. In sum, in each culture people overlearn a particular pattern that has worked for them in the past, and they use it out of habit, without thinking.

However, the probability that the collectivist cognitive system will be activated is increased if factors such as the following obtain:

1. The individual knows that most other people in that particular situation are collectivists, which makes the collectivist norm salient.
2. The individual is in a collective, such as the family.
3. The situation emphasizes that people are in the same collective (e.g., the wearing of the same uniform).
4. The task is cooperative.

Individual Attributes That Reflect Individualism and Collectivism

There are a variety of attributes that indicate whether a particular person is an individualist or a collectivist. In a collectivist culture many, but not all, of the collectivist attributes presented below are found. Similarly, for an individualist culture, some, but not all, of the individualist attributes are present. These attributes are culture specific. That is, each species of collectivism is constructed by some combination of the collectivist attributes; each individualist culture is characterized by a combination of the individualist attributes. For example, one type of collectivism may consist of the basic collectivist attributes presented in the beginning of the chapter and some combination of the collectivist attributes presented below. People in that culture, however, may also use some of the individualistic attributes presented below. That is why we call these "culture-specific" attributes.

Self-Perception

The collectivists use groups as the basic units of social perception; the individualists find it natural to use individuals as the basic units of social perception. In traditional Greece, a visitor from Athens is likely to be referred to as "the Athenian" even when people know her name. In Indonesia many people do not use personal names, though such names are given, but instead use *teknonyms* (Geertz, 1983), which refer to the order of birth within a family (e.g., the equivalent of the "second son of the Smith family"). By contrast, Margaret Thatcher, a classic individualist, made this statement to an audience of women: "There is no society; there are only individuals and their families" (National Public Radio, 1993).

Lebra (in Gudykunst, 1993, p. 53) pointed out that there is no Japanese equivalent for the English "I." Different words are used to refer to the self, depending on the social situation, the speaker's gender, age, and other social attributes relative to the listener. The terms reflect status differences, and the speaker usually attempts to elevate the status of the other, while reducing his or her own status, by choosing the correct wording. Similarly, "you" changes wording, depending on the social context. The complexity of such choices explains why Japanese bilinguals often prefer to talk to each other in English.

Social perception among collectivists consists of a set of relationships organized around an individual. Among individualists the focus is on an individual who does have relationships. This point is made clear in the work of Lebra (1984), who mentioned that when she interviewed Japanese women, she learned much about their relationships and almost nothing about themselves, whereas when she interviewed American women, she learned almost nothing about their relationships but a great deal about them.

Collectivists frequently have realistic self-perceptions about their abilities, and individualists frequently have flattering self-perceptions. For example, Markus and Kitayama (1991b) reported that when various populations (e.g., college students) were asked questions such as "what percent of this population (e.g., college students) is higher than you are on X?" when X was an ability, American men showed a self-enhancement bias. That is, their judgments did not average 50 percent, as they should have, but only 36 percent. In short, they admitted that on the average only about a third of the relevant population was higher than they were on this socially desirable trait. American women showed less bias. Their answers averaged 47 percent. Japanese men showed even less bias; their answers averaged 49 percent. Japanese women showed a modesty bias; their answers averaged 58 percent. In other words, Japanese women college students, on the average, indicated that they were below average in ability.

On the trait "independence" only 33 percent of American men and 34 percent of American women saw others as higher than they were, whereas the Japanese percentages were 46 and 54 respectively. In short, as presented by Markus and Kitayama (1991b), Americans have a strong sense of "false uniqueness."

Markus and Kitayama (1991b) also reviewed studies showing more self-serving bias among individualists than collectivists. For example, a national survey of American students found that 70 percent of students believed that they were above average in leadership ability compared to other students.

None thought they were below average, and 25 percent of them thought they were at the top 1 percent of the distribution.

The ideal American of the middle and upper class is "distinguished," that is, has had great accomplishments. In Japan the ideal person is the one with a large number of successful relationships with others (Kitayama, 1993).

Kitayama (1993) reported a study in which positive and negative attributes were presented to subjects in the United States and Japan who were then asked: Do they apply to you? Do they apply to your friend? Will your friend say that they apply to you? The frequency of saying "yes, they do apply" to the positive attributes was higher in the United States than in Japan; the frequency of saying "yes, they do apply" to the negative attributes was lower in the United States than in Japan. In short, relative to Japanese, Americans see themselves as having more positive and fewer negative attributes, which results in higher self-esteem. This tendency was also found in studies of reaction time. The U.S. reaction times were shorter than the Japanese times, when people were asked, "Do you have this attribute?" because the Japanese are not comfortable with such decontextualized abstractions. Furthermore, the Americans were quick to see positive attributes attached to them and negative attributes not attached to them.

Kitayama also presented 400 situations to American and Japanese samples. Two hundred were success and 200 were failure situations; 100 of each kind were generated in Japan and 100 of each kind were generated in the United States. The subjects were asked whether their self-esteem would be affected if they were in each situation. The success situations were rated by Americans as more likely to affect them (thus boosting their self-esteem) than was the case with the Japanese; the failure situations did not show a cultural difference. Situations generated by Americans had especially self-enhancing effects for Americans. In short, Americans are more sensitive to success situations than are Japanese and thus increase their self-esteem by success; Japanese decrease their self-esteem because of failure more often than the other cultural group (see the parallel findings in Kashima and Triandis, 1986).

If one assumes that the two groups have an equal number of successes and failures, one can say that this mechanism seems to explain the cultural differences in self-esteem. It also explains the consistently puzzling finding that Japanese workers report very low job satisfaction, though they work hard and are loyal to their corporations. If they focus on their failures, they will be less satisfied with their work than if they focus on their successes.

Why do Americans focus on success and Japanese focus on failure? I argue that it is related to the looseness-tightness dimension. In loose cultures, in any situation a person is allowed much freedom to pick different behaviors. If the behaviors prove unsuccessful, the person tries some other behaviors, and when the behaviors are successful, people praise the performance and note the success. It is assumed that if one tries ten behaviors, eight will be failures, but so what? The important thing is to have two successes. In tight cultures, in any situation a person must do one or two things correctly. Failure to do these things correctly results in criticism. People fear criticism and focus on failures because these failures are the cause of much distress for them. Thus, more generally, individualists focus on the positive and collectivists focus on the negative consequences of their behavior, and this may be one explanation of the empirical findings (Chao and Seligman, manuscript) that Americans are more optimistic than the Chinese.

Radford et al. (1993) reported that Japanese subjects have lower decisional self-esteem, that is, feel less confident when making decisions, than Australians. The Japanese reported complacency (I put little effort into making decisions), avoidance (I avoid making decisions), and hypervigilance (I panic if I have to make decisions quickly) more frequently than did the Australians, although the Japanese indicated they did not take as much care before making a choice as did the Australians. The Japanese also reported more stress when they had to make a decision without consultation.

J. D. Campbell (1990) found that the self-concepts of low-self-esteem individuals are less certain than those of high-self-esteem individuals. The lows use less extremity and self-reported confidence when rating themselves on bipolar adjective scales, which may explain the Japanese response set of using the middle positions on rating scales and their avoidance of the extreme positions on such scales (see Triandis, 1972).

This difference may be traceable to an even more fundamental mechanism: Americans solicit and receive information that confirms desirable internal attributes; Japanese seek to find their deviance from norms. This may reflect American individualism and Japanese tightness. Tightness, as we have seen, includes greater sensitivity to deviation from norms.

Attributions

Fundamental elements in providing meaning to events are the attributions that people make. Individualists attribute events to internal individual causes more frequently than collectivists, who tend to attribute them to external causes (Morris and Peng, submitted; Newman, 1993). Thus individualists make the "fundamental attribution error" of stressing internal rather than external causes more frequently than do collectivists (P. B. Smith and Bond, 1994).

Identity and Emotions

Identity among collectivists is defined by relationships and group memberships. Individualists base identity on what they own and their experiences. Not surprisingly, the emotions of collectivists tend to be other-focused (e.g., empathy) and of short duration (they last as long as the collectivists are in a situation). The emotions of individualists are ego-focused (e.g., anger) and of long duration (do not necessarily change with the situation). Markus and Kitayama (1991b) described the rich vocabulary of the Japanese language for other-focused emotions, such as *amae* (hope-expectation of someone's indulgence and favor). Matsumoto (1989) found that collectivists identify sadness more easily than individualists, and individualists are more likely to perceive happiness than collectivists. Americans are more likely than Japanese to seek "fun" situations, and Japanese are more likely than Americans to seek situations that produce harmonious interpersonal atmospheres. East Asian collectivists try to display only positive emotions toward acquaintances and tend to control negative emotions (Gudykunst, 1993, p. 153).

Cognitions

Collectivists think often about the needs of their ingroup. Individualists tend to focus on personal needs, rights, capacities, and the contracts they have made.

Markus and Kitayama (1991b) reviewed evidence that collectivists find it more difficult to think in a counterfactual manner. Because they are embedded in their social environment, they are more disturbed when unrealistic situations are described to them. Individualists, in contrast, do not feel their selves violated by such situations and are able to react to them without hesitation.

There is less concern for cognitive consistency in collectivist cultures. The attitude-behavior links are weaker in collectivist cultures and relatively strong in individualistic cultures (Y. Kashima et al., 1992). In Japan, proper behavior rather than attitude is important (Iwao and Triandis, 1993).

Motivation

The motive structure of collectivists reflects receptivity and adjustment to the needs of others. The basic motive structure of individualists reflects their internal needs, rights, and capacities, including the ability to withstand social pressures (Markus and Kitayama, 1991b). Bond (1986) found that the Chinese show a relatively high need for abasement, socially oriented achievement, endurance, nurturance, and order and not much need for individual achievement, aggression, and exhibition. Achievement motivation is socially oriented among collectivists and individually oriented among individualists. Yu and Yang (1994) developed separate scales for these two kinds of motivation and showed that these scales are uncorrelated ($r = .02$). Those who score high in socially oriented motivation prefer jobs that provide extensive family benefits to jobs that are enjoyable but do not provide such benefits.

Many Americans, as we have already seen, have a tendency toward false uniqueness. It is likely that individualists are motivated to prove to themselves that they have socially desirable attributes. That would pressure them toward high personal achievement. However, with respect to motivation, it is also relevant that attributions made by collectivists tend to emphasize *effort* as a determinant of performance, whereas individualists tend to use *abilities* as the major determinant.

Collectivists do not use the Performance = Ability × Effort formulation common among individualists (Singh, 1981). They use a Performance = Ability + Effort formulation. Since individualists see performance as a personal quality, if the person has no ability or expends no effort, his performance is considered to be poor. Collectivists see performance as a group quality, and thus it is possible to succeed if one member of the group has ability and the others expend effort.

Ronen (1994) organized the literature on differences in motivation across countries. He found challenging jobs, autonomy, advancement, recognition, and earnings emphasized in individualist countries. Among collectivist countries the emphasis is placed on various forms of security and social relationships (with managers and co-workers).

Attitudes

Collectivists favor attitudes that reflect sociability (e.g., I like to live close to my good friends), interdependence (e.g., I can depend on my relatives for financial support if I need it), and family integrity (e.g., old parents should live with their children until they die). Individualists believe in self-reliance (e.g., when a group is slowing me down, I do the job alone), hedonism (e.g., I value the good life), competition (e.g., I want to be the best), and emotional detachment from ingroups (e.g., if my brother fails in school, it is not my concern). Holding an opinion that disagrees with that of the collectivist ingroup is a sure sign of bad character (Hofstede, 1982). Attitudes are paramount among individualists, and norms are relegated to secondary importance (Bontempo and Rivero, 1992).

Norms

In collectivist cultures there is more consensus concerning the roles of men and women than in individualistic cultures (Williams and Best, 1990). Collectivists use equality or need as the basis for allocating resources to ingroup members, and equity (to each according to his/her contribution) as the basis for allocation to outgroup members (P. B. Smith and Bond, 1994). The latter is especially the case if it is unlikely that there will be future interaction with the outgroup (Han and Park, 1990). Many collectivists feel that when a kin member is rich he must distribute much of what he owns to the ingroup members (Hofstede, 1982). Among Samoans in Hawaii, it is common for all relatives to have access to one's bank book (Brislin, 1993a).

Values

The values of collectivists include security, good social relationships, ingroup harmony, and personalized relationships (see Triandis, McCusker, and Hui, 1990; S. H. Schwartz, 1994). East Asian collectivists are also very high in insisting on "virtuous action" (Hofstede, 1991); they value "persistence" more than Western samples (Blinco, 1992; Triandis, Bontempo, Leung, and Hui, 1990). In a large study of 200 teachers and 200 "others" from more than forty countries, S. H. Schwartz (1994) identified two collectivist clusters of values that he called "conservation" and "harmony" and two individualist clusters that he called "intellectual autonomy" and "affective autonomy." The contrasting collectivist values (family security, social order, respect for tradition, honoring parents and elders, security, and politeness) and individualist values (being curious, broadminded, and creative and having an exciting and varied life, full of pleasures) were obtained in every country. Orthogonal to the previous dimension was power versus universalism. Universalism included *equality* as a value. Thus, our typology is present in Schwartz's values data, for example, collectivist with power values corresponds to vertical collectivism. Engel (1988) studied the work values of 220 American and 368 Japanese fully employed men. He found that the former placed the highest values on individualism, independence, and self-sufficiency; the latter on group involvement and loyalty to the employer and the country.

Social Behavior

Collectivists shift their behavior depending on context more than do individualists. This is seen clearly when we study social behavior toward ingroup and outgroup members. As Hwang (1987) put it, the first thing that a Chinese does in a social situation is to ask: "What is the *guanxi* (relationship) between us?" "How strong is our *guanxi*?" (p. 949). Social behavior is very different when a collectivist is interacting with an ingroup than when she is interacting with an outgroup member; it is only slightly different in the case of individualists (see Triandis, 1972; Gudykunst, Yoon, and Nishida, 1987; Bond, 1988; Chan, 1991; Iwata, 1992).

More generally, collectivists behave somewhat differently toward each relative, co-worker, neighbor, and acquaintance (Hui, 1984; Chiu, 1990), and more or less uniformly only with strangers. This means that personality is less evident in collectivist than it is in individualist cultures, because the situation is such a powerful determinant of social behavior. That observation is consistent with the finding that collectivists communicate with strangers less than individualists do (Gudykunst, 1993; Wheeler, Reis, and Bond, 1989).

Triandis, McCusker, and Hui (1990) found that subjects from the People's Republic of China (PRC) made more distinctions between ingroup and outgroup members than did subjects from the United States. The Chinese showed more intimacy and subordination in ingroups and more formality and superordination toward outgroups than did American samples. Collectivists are often more intimate with same-sex close friends than with their different-sex friends or spouse; individualists often show the reverse pattern (Gudykunst, 1993, pp. 161, 292). Collectivists, also, are more likely than individualists to be embarrassed in social situations (Singelis and Sharkey, in press). Suh (1994) found in samples from China and Korea large differences in the level of positive emotions depending on whether the situation included a friend or a stranger; U.S. samples did not show such differences.

The behavior of collectivists differs more in private versus public settings than does the behavior of individualists (U. Kim, 1994b). Lebra (1984) explained the Japanese terms *uchi* (in) and *soto* (out), *omote* (front) and *ura* (back), which are used to describe the appropriateness of social behavior. In-back is associated with intimate behaviors; in-front requires meeting obligations; out-back is anomic behavior, such as insulting the other; out-front is ritualistic behavior. This typology might be translated as: Ingroup/private is intimate; ingroup/public requires impression management; outgroup/private is anomic; outgroup/public is ritualistic (Barlund, 1975).

Collectivists expect social situations to be pleasant. Triandis, Marin, Lisansky, and Betancourt (1984) examined data from Hispanic and non-Hispanic samples and found that Hispanics anticipated higher probabilities of positive behaviors and lower probabilities of negative behaviors occurring in most social situations. They called this the *simpatia* cultural script. A person tries to be *simpatico*, that is, agreeable, pleasant, attractive, and noncritical. The same phenomenon has been found among East Asian collectivists, who emphasize ingroup harmony and acceptance of hierarchy in social behavior.

Collectivists have fewer skills than individualists in dealing with new groups and strangers (Cohen, 1991), but once a relationship is established, it tends to become more intimate and long lasting than the relationships of individualists (Gudykunst, 1983; Verma, 1992).

Conformity to ingroup norms not only is more common among collectivists but is also internalized to such an extent that it is automatic, and people enjoy doing what is expected of them (Bontempo, Lobel, and Triandis, 1990; Gudykunst, 1993, p. 140). But conformity to outgroups is rare (according to Williams and Sogon, quoted by Gudykunst, 1993, p. 322).

Collectivists often use the concept of "limited good" (Foster, 1965), which assumes that "good" is limited, and thus if an outgroup gets it, that is a threat to the ingroup. Even a random event, such as winning a lottery, that favors the outgroup is resented by the ingroup. Thus, hostile social behaviors toward outgroups might be generated by random events.

Social behavior, especially during leisure time, occurs in small groups with greater frequency among collectivists. Individualists prefer socializing in couples. For example, Korean skiers often ski in groups, whereas Americans tend to ski alone or in couples (Brandt, 1974). Similarly, collectivists are more likely to eat in large groups (Triandis, 1990; Levine, 1992). Most interaction among collectivists is individual-group, and most interaction among individualists occurs between two individuals (Wheeler, Reis, and Bond, 1989).

Attitudes Toward Privacy

Collectivists hold that one's business is also the business of the group—friends should be concerned with each other's personal matters. The collective is entitled to know, even regulate, what individuals do and think in private (Ho and Chiu, 1994). Individualists hold that people should mind their own business, privacy should be respected, people should be able to think freely. Space, too, is treated differently: Collectivists use few partitions and often use the same space for different purposes at different times of the day. Individualists use more partitions and designate spaces for specific purposes, such as bedroom and living room.

Communication

Collectivists are likely to say "what is mine is yours," whereas individualists are likely to maintain that "what is mine is not to be used without my permission." In speech, collectivists employ "we" often and they depend on context (tone of voice, gestures, posture, etc.) to convey meaning. Individualists tend to use "I" and emphasize content. Silence, too, is perceived differently in that it is embarrassing to individualists and a signal of strength for collectivists (Iwao, 1993). Collectivists are expected to "read the other's mind" during communication, so the message is quite indirect, dependent on hints, the use of the eyes, distance between bodies, and so on. Individualists say what is on their minds, even if it risks damaging the relationship. The Japanese are known to avoid saying no directly, and in fact Ueda (1974) has identified sixteen ways to say no.

Collectivist communication emphasizes context and concern for the feelings of the other and avoids the devaluation of ingroup others; individualist communication emphasizes clarity (M-S. Kim, Sharkey, and Singelis, 1994;

Triandis, 1994). Collectivists tend to use duty and obligation arguments to persuade others, and individualists tend to use arguments that point to unfavorable consequences, such as threats to the individual (Gudykunst, 1993, pp. 169, 170, 228). Gudykunst (in press) has developed a theory consisting of ninety-four axioms that link aspects of individualism and collectivism to communication.

Conflict Resolution

Trubisky, Ting-Toomey, and Lin (1991) compared Taiwan and U.S. respondents and found that in conflict situations the former were more likely than the latter to use obliging, avoiding, integrating, and compromising styles of conflict resolution. Similarly, Ohbuchi and Takahashi (1993) studied 94 Japanese and 98 American students and asked them to report on conflicts they had recently experienced. The researchers collected 475 episodes, which they submitted to a content analysis.

They found that the Japanese were motivated to preserve the relationship. The findings were interpreted as being consistent with theoretical notions about collectivism (Triandis, 1989) and interdependence (Markus and Kitayama, 1991b). However, once the relationship is clearly hostile, as occurs when the other group is clearly an outgroup, collectivists tend to be more outspoken than individualists (Moghaddam, Taylor, and Wright, 1993) and more likely to commit atrocities.

Morality

Morality among collectivists is more contextual and the supreme value is the welfare of the collective. Ma (1988) provided a Chinese perspective, and Miller (1994) an Indian perspective, on moral judgment. These perspectives are different from the individualistic and androcentric perspective of Kohlberg (1981).

Kohlberg's perspective emphasized abstract principles and rights as the most "mature" stage of moral development. The Eastern perspective, like that of Confucius, emphasizes social cohesion. Concern for others starts with concern for the family and gradually extends to wider circles. However, Confucius did not see these circles extending to include all humans, whereas Gandhi did. Thus the most abstract morality is to make humankind one's own ingroup. The question remains whether any human is capable of universal concern.

Morality in collectivist cultures is linked to an adherence to many rules. They can be quite specific (Naito, 1994), such as to dictate that students knock at the door before entering a teacher's room. If most behavior is compatible with the rules of the ingroup, the person is moral. Abstract principles, such as found in Kohlberg's Stage 6, which is supposed to be the most "developed" level of morality, have little validity in this framework.

Lying is an acceptable behavior in collectivist cultures, especially if it saves face or benefits the ingroup. There are traditional ways of lying that are understood as "correct behavior." For example, in traditional Greece, if a person visits someone unannounced and the host is not in the mood to receive him, the host simply shouts through the door, "I am not here." The visitor can, of course, recognize the voice, but this is nevertheless an appropriate way to deal with this situation.

Individualists see lying as breaking the contract, and since contracts are very important, this is a serious offense. Trilling (1972) made the point that when people have a strong sense of who they want to be, as is characteristic of individualists, they are more likely to seek what is proper, even if it is disliked. Individualists find attitude-behavior inconsistency dissonant, whereas collectivists find it "mature" (Iwao and Triandis, 1993). Individualists may characterize the individual who acts inconsistently as a "hypocrite." Triandis (1990) reviewed studies of forced compliance among Chinese subjects. The studies showed much compliance and little attitude change, indicating that attitudes and behaviors are decoupled in such cultures.

Responsibility

In collectivist cultures the collective is responsible for the wrongdoing of one of its members; in individualist cultures, it is solely the individual who is responsible. During the Tokugawa period in Japan, if an individual behaved inappropriately and his ingroup did not punish him, the whole ingroup bore the consequences. Studies of attribution of responsibility for a wrongdoing universally have focused on the actor, role position, and social context (Hamilton and Sanders, 1983). Empirical studies done in Japan and India found that those samples gave more weight to the latter two factors, whereas the Americans gave the most weight to the first factor.

Personality

Hui and Villareal (1989) found that allocentrics were high in affiliation and idiocentrics were high in dominance, which fits well with our discussion above. Wink (1992) measured three aspects of a narcissistic personality, one of which he called *autonomy*, pronouncing it a "healthy variant" (as opposed to *willfulness* and *hypersensitivity*, which he considered unhealthy). Autonomous individuals were rated by others as more individualistic, creative, and achievement oriented.

Gudykunst, Yang, and Nishida (1987) argued that people who are high "self-monitors" try to behave in social situations the way prototypical others would behave. However, because collectivists pay much attention to who is in the social situation, they give less importance to what prototypical others would do. As a result, they are low in self-monitoring. In a study of two individualistic (United States and Australia) and three collectivist (Hong Kong, Japan, and Taiwan) cultures, they found support for this theorizing.

Tetlock, Peterson, and Berry (1993), working in an individualist culture, found that those high in cognitive integration had more idiocentric tendencies than those low in cognitive complexity. Horizontal collectivists have a tendency toward self-reduction (modesty), whereas vertical individualists have a tendency toward self-enhancement (boasting and the like), as reported by Kitayama and Markus (in press b). Collectivism is correlated with a strong sensitivity to rejection and with affiliative tendencies, and it is negatively related to the need for uniqueness and to internal control (Yamaguchi, 1994).

Professional Behavior

Collectivists are more likely to select, evaluate, and promote individuals on the basis of their loyalty and seniority than on the basis of their personal attributes; individualists are more likely to use personal attributes than group membership information. For example, the Japanese promote new employees for several years on the basis of their age and seniority in the organization, whereas U.S. corporations begin merit pay during the first months of the employee's tenure in the organization. Social loafing occurs in individualistic cultures and is less likely in a collectivist culture, when people are working with ingroup members (Earley, 1989).

Jones, Rozelle, and Chang (1990) found that it was more rewarding for the Chinese than for Americans to receive praise indirectly rather than directly. The Chinese did not want to be used as "good examples for others," although this was acceptable to Americans. Both found it quite upsetting when a supervisor criticized a group when an individual was wrong, but the Chinese tolerated this more than did the Americans. Both the Chinese and U.S. samples did not like the supervisor's giving them added work while allowing co-workers to be idle, but the U.S. sample was more upset by this practice than were the Chinese. Both did not like "average" performance ratings, but the U.S. sample was more upset about them than were the Chinese; both were unsure about the boss's giving them special treatment, such as taking them to lunch, but the U.S. sample was less upset than the Chinese sample about such actions. These findings are, in general, quite consistent with the culture-specific attributes of collectivist and individualist cultures discussed above.

        ✧   ✧   ✧

This chapter presented the culture-general and culture-specific attributes of individualist and collectivist cultures. We examined four cultural patterns: horizontal individualism, horizontal collectivism, vertical individualism, and vertical collectivism. We found these patterns to correspond to Fiske's four modes of sociality and to Rokeach's patterns of political behavior. Every individual uses all four of these patterns, in different percentages, across situations. We identified several aspects of the environment of cultures that make them tight or loose, complex or simple. Maximum individualism occurs in complex, loose cultures; maximum collectivism, in tight simple cultures.

4

Antecedents and Geographic Distribution of Individualism and Collectivism

I N CHAPTER 3, I presented the attributes of individualism and collectivism, using specific, proximal factors (e.g., cultural homogeneity) to explain the emergence of these cultural patterns. In this chapter I will consider more general, distal antecedents of the constructs and then review information about the geographic distribution of individualism and collectivism.

Advantages of Group Life

Life in groups has definite advantages for primates (Chency, Seyforth, and Smuts, 1986). It raises the probability of finding food, lessens the probability that the animal will be a victim of other animals, contributes to reproductive success, and increases the enjoyment of mutual care. In short, it is highly rewarding. However, as wide choices become available in a society, the advantages of group living become less clear. For example, wealthy and powerful males can ensure reproductive success by paying for sexual relations and by employing bodyguards for protection.

Thus a tension develops between two kinds of factors. We may call them I (individualism) and C (collectivism) factors. I-factors reflect cultural complexity, affluence, and modernity and are also a function of education, maleness, urbanism, high social class, and social and geographic mobility. C-factors require the individual to behave as the ingroup specifies and reflect cultural homogeneity, high population density, and isolation from other cultures/groups, and they are greater when there is an external threat and the members of the culture realize that survival depends on interdependence. Individualism attains its highest levels when I-factors are large and C-factors small; collectivism, when C-factors are large and I-factors are small.

Most researchers since Hofstede (1980) think of individualism and collectivism as opposites. But when we measured these tendencies empirically (see the Appendix), they emerged as uncorrelated tendencies. That is, people can be high on both, low on both, or high on one and low on the other.

Shifts from Collectivism to Individualism

As I discussed in Chapter 3, affluence, exposure to mass media, and modernization can contribute to a shift toward individualism. Yang (1988) wondered whether modernization will eventually eliminate cross-cultural differences. He identified twenty characteristics found in modern societies and noted that twelve overlap with individualism. Specifically, emphasis on personal efficacy, low integration with relatives, equalitarian attitudes, openness to innovation, sexual equality, achievement motivation, independence, self-reliance, active participation, risk taking, and a nonlocal legal orientation are found in both patterns. Yang concluded that modernization leads to changes only in those psychological attributes that are specifically functional for modern life, and in any culture there are many other cultural elements. Thus, some convergence may occur, but it will not result in the elimination of cultural differences. For example, leisure-time activities will always have culture-specific content.

The advantages of collectivism are most clear when resources are minimal but become less clear as societies become more complex and differentiated. The importance of social class and affluence as a determinant of individualism is very great. It may be the major variable that distinguishes individualists and collectivists. Thus, in societies where economic inequality is great, for example, in Latin America, where it is the highest in the world (*Economist,* November 13–19, 1993, p. 25), social-class differences result in large within-country differences on individualism and collectivism. The upper classes are very individualistic, emphasizing pleasure. That can be seen in the consumption patterns of luxury goods and vacations, carnivals, and the like. At the same time the lowest 20 percent of the population has an income of less than $500 per year (*Economist,* November 13–19, 1993, p. 25) and is collectivist. Extended family interdependence contributes to survival. At the most extreme levels of poverty, however, we see anomic individualism. In Brazil, for example, some children as young as ten are told to fend for themselves. Many of these children survive by stealing, and sometimes children are killed by vigilante groups and even indiscriminately by the police. Zimbardo (personal communication, September 1993) visited shantytowns in Brazil and reported on these conditions.

Types of livelihood also have an impact on the manifestation of these syndromes. As societies move from hunting and gathering to agriculture to being modern industrial and information societies, the advantages of group life first increase and then fade. As the advantages fade, behavior becomes more formal, trading becomes a common activity (hence market pricing), and contracts become important. Behavior becomes more a function of short-term factors (geographic mobility makes this natural) than of long-term ones.

Thus, changes in ecology (how people make a living), affluence, mobility (both social and geographic), and movement from rural to urban settings contribute to changes from collectivism to individualism. Schooler (1990b) gave much weight to the modes of production as an explanation of the emergence of individualism—if you work alone you are more likely to be an individualist.

Finally, those societies that are exposed to the mass media become more individualistic because the mass media messages are designed to create pleasure rather than to inspire people to do their duty. Hsu (1983) pointed out that in Western novels love conquers all; in Eastern novels the hero does his duty, and the heroine carries out her obligations.

Family Structure and Cultural Patterns

Family size and structure undoubtedly also contribute to these changes. If the family is large, a certain amount of regimentation and imposition of tightness, that is, collectivism, is inevitable to make life harmonious. The question is, what is the cause and what is the consequence? Is it that collectivism is associated with poverty and large families (since many sons means social security in old age), or are large families the cause of collectivism and poverty?

Although I have serious reservations about the thesis presented by Todd (1987), I will describe it in some detail. He argued that family type is the major determinant of ideology and the probability of development. Economic development, of course, is related to individualism, so his argument is relevant to our problem. Todd used percentage of literacy as his dependent variable and six kinds of family type as his independent variable. Family type can be "vertical" (strong inequalities of power between parents and children, older and younger brothers) or "nonvertical" (liberal parents, equality among brothers), and it can be "patrilinear" (kinship through the father's line is most important), "matrilinear" (kinship through the mother's side is most important), or "bilateral" (kinship through either mother's or father's side is equally important), thus resulting in $2 \times 3 = 6$ types of family structure.

In a book full of statistics and maps, Todd argued that literacy is highest in bilateral vertical families and in descending order in matrilinear vertical, bilateral nonvertical, patrilinear vertical, patrilinear nonvertical, and lowest in matrilinear nonvertical families, which is the case of polygyny.

The key behind this ranking is the position of women. The higher the position of women, the higher is the percentage of literacy and hence economic development. The age at which women marry is correlated .82 with the percentage of literacy. In the more-developed societies, many women marry after age twenty-seven; in the less-developed, they marry quite young. Later marriage means more status for women and lower birth rates.

Todd argued that the reason Japan and Germany are doing so well in their economic development, relative to Britain and the United States, is that they both have a bilateral vertical family structure, which results in ethnocentric authoritarianism, whereas Britain and the United States have bilateral nonvertical families, which results in liberal individualism. The former family pattern makes people do what is required rather than what is fun. He explicitly linked the vertical family pattern with the traditional peasant family, that is, collectivism. In sum, he claimed that the difference between Japan and Germany on the one hand and Britain and the United States on the other is that the former are relatively more collectivist than the latter.

Furthermore, he suggested that Africa is "backward" because there is so much polygyny, which although allowing women to have a certain amount of autonomy, does not allow them much influence on decisions about sexual behavior. Low development is also found in the regions where Islam, in which women have low status, is predominant.

Todd's discussion of literacy rates is interesting. He used literacy both as an indicator of development and as a predictor of future development. Theocracies have literacy rates between 0 and 5 percent; democracies between 50 and 100 percent. This translates into extreme vertical collectivism's being linked to low literacy rates, and horizontal individualism to high rates of literacy.

However, I must point out that the highest rates of literacy occur in moderately collectivist countries such as Japan (about 99 percent). Korea, Taiwan, and Singapore are close to 90 percent. The United States has rates of around 80 percent, and in some subgroups the rates are very low. In contrast, the horizontal individualist European countries have high literacy rates, like those of the Far Eastern countries.

Todd's model for development is a society with authoritarian leadership that focuses on literacy and development (e.g., Singapore). In short, vertical collectivism with emphasis on literacy is his formula for high rates of economic development. Todd's analysis results in pessimistic predictions about development in Russia and China because their patrilinear vertical family structure has only modest potential for development.

These are my reservations about Todd's thesis: First, I do not think that single-variable theories have a chance to be valid in the social sciences because social phenomena tend to be caused by multiple factors. Although I agree that the status of women is an important variable, I doubt that it is the one and only explanation of development.

Second, the fact that there are associations between family type and development does not indicate that family type causes development; it could well be the case that development causes family type. Granted, it is more plausible that family type, which comes from hundreds of years of social and cultural evolution, is the antecedent, rather than development, which is a recent phenomenon. But affluence means the freedom to choose lifestyle, including family structure, at least to some extent.

The finding that bilateral family structure is associated with high rates of development can also be argued from another angle. Pelto (1968) explicitly linked looseness with bilateral family structure in preliterate societies. In other words, an element that pushes toward individualism is linked to it. Theoretically, we can see why. There are two systems of norms—the one from the father's family and the other from the mother's family. If there are any inconsistencies between the two normative systems, the *individual* has to decide which norms to follow. Of course, if there are no inconsistencies, this does little to push toward individualism. In the case of endogamous marriages, such as those found in the Muslim world (e.g., Todd showed that large percentages of Iranian marriages involve the daughter of the father's or the mother's brother), this kind of inconsistency is minimal. Nevertheless, when inconsistencies exist, there is more individualism. Thus, the bilateral vertical family structure may be good for development because it provides a culture that is more balanced between individualism and collectivism. I will argue later that a culture that has many people whose personal goals are consistent with the goals of the relevant collectives is close to ideal.

When he made the authoritarian states his models for development, Todd missed the important point that development requires creativity, which is more likely to be found in individualistic cultures. It is one thing to have a set of inventions that only need to be manufactured and distributed, and it is quite another to have a society that produces these inventions. In short, although I see some merit in Todd's argument as part of the overall picture I have presented here, I do not think that by itself it provides adequate explanations for the presence of collectivism or individualism.

Wooddell (1989), working with an African-American sample in Detroit, found more collectivism in large than in small families. His total sample was individualistic, especially in single-parent families, where parents do not provide much control. One parent does not constitute a collective with norms that can influence a child, and thus looseness is high. Looseness is negatively related to self-control, and self-control is negatively related to criminal behavior. Thus, looseness is often related to aggression and, as I suggested in Chapter 3, to individualism.

If the family has an only child, it can develop child-rearing procedures that are totally idiosyncratic for that child, and the latter can develop its individuality to the full. In that case the important concern is not family functioning, but the child's self-actualization.

In China, population pressures have resulted in the one-child policy. This policy has the effect of increasing individualism, as the "little emperor" is spoiled by four grandparents and two parents. Jing (1994) reported on studies of such children that compared them with children with siblings. The studies concluded that the "onlies" are more egocentric, less cooperative, and have a "poor attitude toward manual labor."

Detailed descriptions of the shift from collectivism to individualism, as collectivist cultures meet modernity pressures, with vivid illustrations of the changes in child-rearing and marital patterns, were provided by Doumanis (1983) and Katakis (1984). Family structure was also the important element of Macfarlane's (1978) analysis, which I reviewed in Chapter 2: Primogeniture was adopted in England soon after the thirteenth century to preserve wealth by not splitting the land into small parcels. It forced the younger sons to seek fame and fortune in other settings and resulted in entrepreneurial activities that produced affluence, that is, individualism.

Number of Choices as a Factor in Individualism

Several other factors influence whether I-factors or C-factors are important. In most societies men have more choices than women, resulting in lower I-factors for women, and women feel more responsive to the needs of their children than men, resulting in more C-factors for women. Thus the men are likely to be more individualistic and the women more collectivist. Data reported by Ho and Chiu (1994) for China; Triandis, Chan, et al. (in press) for Japan; and Daab (1991) for Poland agree with this point. But the differences are not large.

For example, Daab (1991) did a telephone interview during which he presented ten contrasting terms describing two persons, such as "obliging or intelligent," and asked which person deserves more appreciation. The terms reflected either collectivism or individualism. He found men gave more individualistic answers ($p < .0001$) than women; those who were over fifty years of age gave more collectivist answers. Individualism was also associated with higher education, affiliation with some volunteer organization, and disapproval of religion (of course, Catholicism, in Poland, is associated with one kind of collectivism).

The Situation Can Trigger Individualism or Collectivism

The situation is the most important other factor changing the probability that collectivism or individualism will be activated. Consider the following factors that can result in the activation of one or the other pattern: First, the size of the groups one is dealing with changes from narrow, such as the nuclear family, to broader collectives, such as the extended family and the tribe, to still broader collectives such as co-religionists and members of the same political party, to still broader collectives, such as the state, and finally one is dealing with the world market and humankind. As one is relating to broader groups, one has more choices; hence I-factors are larger. Furthermore, the individual's emotional involvement with the collective is likely to diminish as the collective becomes very large. Thus, we expect individuals attached to very large collectives to be highly individualistic. Gandhi is an example. He said, "The world is my family," but he neglected his wife and children.

Second, social groups in specific situations develop different degrees of tightness concerning behaviors. At a party or bar there is more looseness; at a church, there is tightness, since key religious behaviors are prescribed (praying, kneeling), and most behaviors (e.g., making a business deal) are proscribed (Adamopoulos, Smith, et al., submitted). Thus, we can expect more individualism manifested at a party, and more collectivism in church. Generally, most religious establishments around the world are basically conservative, hence collectivist, and most centers of entertainment provide much freedom; hence they are individualist settings.

Third, bureaucracies create tightness—regulations, laws, review panels, and so on. In situations where bureaucracies are common, there is more collectivism.

The broader the ingroup one is dealing with, the more the I-factors; depending on the kind of group or behavior setting (Barker, 1968) one is in, there will be many or few C-factors. Thus, the final cultural pattern depends on the configuration of these factors. In any society we find more individualism or more collectivism, depending on the situations that are most common in that society.

The broad philosophic views of the society may also contribute to collectivism. Markus and Kitayama (1991b) reviewed literature that makes the case that in societies with a monistic philosophy "in which the person is thought to be of the same substance as the rest of nature" (p. 227) interdependence is high, and thus we will expect more collectivism. In fact, there may be some influence from mythology, as Joseph Campbell (see Segal, 1987) argued, with the West deriving more of its myths from hunting and the East from planting activities. The hunting myths lead to an individualistic perspective and the planting myths to a collectivist one.

Furthermore, since people in many societies can move to other societies, one important consideration is the match between culture and personality. If an allocentric person lives in an individualistic culture, other things being equal, she will want to move, if possible, to a collectivist culture. If an idiocentric person lives in a collectivist culture, he will want to move to an individualistic one. Most of the former kibbutzniks that I have met had left the kibbutz because they were too idiocentric. Of course, there are also situations when a person cannot move.

In East Germany the state imposed collectivism. In fact, at age fourteen there was a youth consecration ceremony (Hillhouse, 1993, pp. 48–49) in which the adolescent was asked to swear to "always unite my path to personal happiness with the struggle for the happiness of the People" (p. 49). Between 1949 and 1961 about 15 percent of the population, presumably the most idiocentric, moved to the West. In 1984 the German Democratic Republic approved 35,000 petitions to move to West Germany (p. 75). These examples show that people who do not fit a cultural pattern try to leave it.

In very collectivist cultures, such as the kibbutz and the Mennonites, Dukhobors, and Amish, when it is possible to leave the group, we can expect to find few idiocentrics. In contrast, when it is not possible to leave the culture (e.g., the USSR in 1970), we can expect the percentage of highly dissatisfied countercultural types to be high. In individualistic cultures, also, some percentage of the population are countercultural, that is, allocentrics.

Interesting parallel thinking is found in the work of Galtung (1979). He provided a macrohistory of the West, examining the past 2,500 years and anticipating the next 500. He explicitly broke the past 2,500 years into three parts: up to the fall of the Roman Empire (A.D. 476), which he called Antiquity; up to the fall of the Eastern Roman Empire (Byzantium) in 1453, which he called the Middle Ages; and up to the present day, which he called the Modern Period. He saw Antiquity as characterized by vertical individualism (and used those terms), the Middle Ages by vertical collectivism, and the Modern Period by vertical individualism.

He argued that the transition from one to the other cultural pattern was possible only because in each period there were countercultural types ready to change the society. For example, in the Middle Ages there were landed aristocrats and city burghers with individualistic tendencies, so when the old system failed, they were ready to provide a new system. He anticipated a shift toward collectivism in the next 500 years because the Modern Period is characterized by impersonal, cold, bureaucratic social structures and people are going to discover collectives that provide them with close-knit satisfying relationships. He saw the 1968 student revolutions, the revival of occultist traditions, the explorations of Eastern religious experiences, and the general trend toward the withdrawal to private life as examples of the search for meaning in the West and as the first signs of the crisis, which will eventually result in new social systems with a greater role for homogeneous, close-knit collectives. Perhaps the new "tribes" (Kotkin, 1993) I discussed in Chapter 1 are examples of emerging collectivism in modern societies.

Some Classic Cases

We might examine some classic cases of particular societies in light of the I- and C-factors. In doing so it is important to stress, once more, that there is considerable within-culture variation. Although in most collectivist cultures the authorities may be opposed to giving too many rights to the population, there will be a minority within these cultures that fervently strives for human rights. Similarly, although in most individualistic cultures people may not favor communes, or even labor unions, there will be a minority that enthusiastically joins such groups. Thus, what I present below must be seen as a trend rather than as a clear, unambiguous reality. In addition, every culture has both individualistic and collectivist attributes. It is only when a culture has more collectivist than individualistic attributes that we can call it collectivist, and vice versa.

Collectivist Cultures

Japan. In pre–World War II Japan, vertical collectivism was a powerful cultural pattern, describing the relationship of citizen and state. There was much tightness and few choices. For example, a citizen could not with impunity ignore calls to serve in the army. Although this may also have been true in individualistic cultures, the sanctions for nonparticipation increase with collectivism.

After the war the vertical collectivism of official Japan confronted the individualism of the U.S. occupational forces. The molding of the new culture shifted it from vertical toward horizontal collectivism: therefore, I suggested in Chapter 3 that Japan today was 25 percent HC and 50 percent VC.

Of course, there are within-culture variations. The older Japanese are still rather vertical, and the young generation is moving both in the horizontal direction and toward individualism. Lebra (1976), Markus and Kitayama (1991a, 1991b), Kitayama (1992), Schooler (1990a, 1990b), Hayashi (1992a, 1992b), and Iwao (1993) provided numerous examples of Japanese collectivism but also evidence of recent shifts toward individualism. For example,

Hayashi showed the importance of filial piety and repaying obligations in that country but also reported survey data where the recent Japanese responses are very similar to the U.S. responses.

Variations within the country reflect, among other factors, what jobs people do. Occupational patterns can influence cultural change, even in situations where the change is inconsistent with the prevailing cultural pattern. For example, collectivism generally puts women in situations where they are supporting the ingroup's goals and are subordinate to the men. However, in modern societies, the occupations of women may change the norms, with the result that the women are not "good collectivists." Naoi and Schooler (1990) found that those who do self-directed work are more intellectually flexible, and this is the case even among Japanese women, though in Japan it is not culturally desirable to be intellectually flexible. The intellectually flexible also have less-traditional attitudes toward the elderly, which again is not viewed as desirable in Japan. However, Japanese women are less likely than Japanese men to have self-directed work. Thus, the society takes care of a possible "problem" by minimizing the number of people who will acquire undesirable attributes.

China. China is another interesting example of collectivism. Traditional Chinese culture is vertical collectivist (Lew, in preparation), but the authorities advocate horizontal themes. Of course, cultures do not change easily, so on the whole I expect that Chinese culture is more vertical than horizontal. Perhaps 30 percent HC and 40 percent VC is a good guess.

Wang (1994) emphasized the importance of the group approach, harmony, equality, and social commitment in contemporary China. But there are nuances and a merging of certain individualist traits with specific collectivist traits. The traditions of Confucius, Taoism, and Buddhism have been wedded to new ideas in order to emphasize not only egalitarianism but also individual and team responsibility and competition. For example, teams are now rewarded according to productivity and their superiority relative to other teams. Before about 1980, only the individual's "social contribution" was considered in distributing rewards. In the past the "iron rice bowl" guaranteed a minimum income. Now, it is not enough to hold a job; one must do it well. Furthermore, people are now encouraged to do jobs they find enjoyable.

However, it is useful for us to note that certain shifts have been resisted. The success of authorities in shifting the population from narrow to broad ingroups, that is, from the family to the Communist party, has not been overwhelming. Although after 1949 the Chinese Communists forced people to denounce their parents and focus on Mao, they enjoyed only limited success. Furthermore, it created more choices, as members of the Communist party dealt with larger ingroups, and more choices resulted in disagreements among the top leadership. Major struggles for power developed that brought different kinds of leaders to the top (Deng Xiao-ping versus the Gang of Four).

Eighty percent of the Chinese population is rural and relatively poor and thus was and remains low in I-factors. Most of this vast population is collectivist, reflecting traces of the Confucian selfhood that "entails the participation of the other. ... The reason for this desirable and necessary symbiosis of selfhood and others is the Confucian conception of the self as a dynamic process of spiritual development" (Tu, 1985, p. 231).

To the extent that the Chinese are able, they engage in ceaseless learning and self-cultivation to become more loyal, filial, brotherly, and friendly to ingroup members and to be good disciples of ingroup authorities. To be filial means to worship ancestors regularly on the proper occasions, the primary duty of sons and daughters, and to repay debts to the parents and accept the spouse chosen by the family. Filial piety (Ho and Chiu, 1994) is positively correlated with age, has a low negative correlation with education, and is lower when there is exposure to the West. A person who is not responsive to those around him is considered self-centered. To be self-aware in one's roles is included in the concept of a socially desirable person. "For the son to cultivate himself, in this view, he must learn to suppress his own desires, anticipate the wishes of his father, and take his father's commands as sacred edicts" (Tu, 1985, p. 234).

Historically, collectivism in China was associated with extreme ethnocentrism. Granted, China had much to be proud of, as a civilization that went back 5,000 years and that had great cultural and artistic achievements, but China was rather high on notions of superiority over other cultures, and such ethnocentrism proved detrimental to its scientific development. The Chinese of the sixteenth century were at the same level of scientific development as the West, but they refused to pay attention to the Western scientific developments and thus got behind. Chinese collectivism is linked to considerable stereotypic thinking, uncritical fatalism, and uncreative behaviors among the vast majority of the rural Chinese population. Nevertheless, the contrast between Chinese and Americans suggests a balance in favor of the Chinese in the art of interpersonal relationships (Hsu, 1981). For example, Chinese children are more cooperative and group enhancing than American children (Domino, 1992).

The Literature on Other Collectivist Cultures. Ethnographies and other studies suggest the presence of collectivism in several traditional contemporary cultures. I might mention the Philippines (Church, 1987; Guthrie, 1961), traditional Greece (Doumanis, 1983; Katakis, 1984; Georgas, 1986, 1989; Triandis and Vassiliou, 1972), the Italians (Strodtbeck, 1958), the Latin Americans (Tallman, Marotz-Baden, and Pindas, 1983;

Holtzman, Diaz-Guerrero, and Swartz, 1975; Diaz-Guerrero, 1979), Hispanic Americans (Marin and Triandis, 1985; Triandis, Marin, Hui, et al., 1984), Indians (J. B. P. Sinha, 1982), Africans south of the Sahara (e.g., Holzberg, 1981; Fiske, 1992), Arabs (Oyserman, 1993), and Balinese (Geertz, 1963).

Of course, each type of collectivism is somewhat different. It requires future research to examine how each of these cultures is similar, how it manifests the defining attributes of Chapter 3, and different, displaying some but not others of the culture-specific attributes of Chapter 3.

Southeast Europe. Southern Italians, as described by Banfield (1958), had much in common with the pastoral society of northern Greece, the Karakatzanoi, described by J. K. Campbell (1964). Traditional Greek culture, as described by Triandis and Vassiliou (1972), had common elements with both those cultures, which suggests some generality of the cultural patterns found in Southern Europe.

Southern Italians, according to Banfield, had the narrow family as the *only* important ingroup. They were tight when dealing with this ingroup, following family norms meticulously, but loose when dealing with outsiders, improvising their behavior and doing what was apparently most advantageous in each situation.

This pattern "looks" individualistic, as so many interactions are carried out with outsiders and are individualistic. Since that kind of ingroup was not bureaucratic, the tightness was applicable only to interpersonal relationships of ingroup members toward each other and had little significance when people were dealing with outsiders, including the Italian state, politicians (who were often asked to pay in order to receive a vote), or the police. In short, behavior within the ingroup was tight; toward the outgroup loose. Banfield (1958) argued that cultures where most important associations are limited to family or tribe cannot develop a modern economy. Modern society requires broader ingroups. He said southern Italy of the 1950s was characterized by "amoral familism." People acted according to the principle: Maximize material, short-range advantage of the nuclear family, and assume that all others will do likewise. In that culture there were no extended families or voluntary organizations. The authorities consisted of individuals interested only in enriching themselves. The upper class was highly individualistic and uninterested in furthering the community. Vertical individualism when one was dealing with outgroups and vertical collectivism when one was dealing with the family seem to be the prevailing patterns.

In that kind of society, only if the interests of the family overlap with the interests of the community is there activity that helps the community. There is no sacrifice for organizations such as hospitals and schools and no trust in others. Laws are disregarded unless punishment is probable. Bribes for officials are common. Those who claim to be interested in the welfare of the community are considered frauds. Punishment is perceived as "good" because it keeps people from sinning. Those punished do not feel guilty, only unlucky. Thus, this society is collectivist with respect to a very narrow ingroup and individualistic in all other domains of activity, where obtaining the best bargain is the only aim. Banfield was criticized for drawing a picture of a society with social pathology. However, many northern Italians who voted for the Northern League seem to agree with his views and want the North to become independent of the South.

This means that these societies, and similar cultures in the former Yugoslavia, are very tight inside the family and very loose outside of it. This pattern is probably common in tribal, agricultural, and pastoral cultures. When such societies are in conflict with outgroups, some of their members consider degrading, killing, or raping members of the outgroup acceptable, as we witnessed in the former Yugoslavia.

Triandis and Vassiliou (1972) synthesized empirical studies done with Illinois and Greek college students, as well as representative samples of the populations of Athens and Thessaloniki (Salonika). A variety of ways of asking questions, obtaining ratings, making judgments, and exploring cognitive links converged in studies about the key importance of ingroups (pp. 304–307) and the major shifts in social behavior when the individual is interacting with an ingroup as opposed to an outgroup member.

Becoming a member of the ingroup requires that the person show concern and self-sacrifice for the ingroup, but once inside the ingroup, the member enjoys substantial advantages of cooperation, protection, and help. Relations with outgroups are competitive, and there is much suspicion about the motives of their members.

The empirical data showed that traditional Greeks perceived more intimacy in vertical (e.g., father-son) than in horizontal (e.g., friend-friend) relationships, whereas Illinois students showed the opposite pattern. The Greeks saw more intimacy with their extended families than did the Americans. Ingroup authorities were perceived by the Greeks as benevolent, and they did not feel comfortable about deviating from advice received from them. The traditional Greeks showed considerable apprehension about self-initiated action, which was not found among Americans. Greek adolescents wanted to achieve independence from the ingroup, yet saw breaking away from the family as painful. They were comfortable with their dependence on their parents.

The status of women was low, except for the mothers of achievers, who could bask in the glory of their children. There was much evidence of traditional Greeks' having a low self-esteem (note the similarities with other collectivist cultures, such as the Japanese; see Markus and Kitayama, 1991b), which they manifested in oversensitivity to criticism and blaming others for their mistakes. The concept *myself* rated on scales such as good-bad, strong-weak, active-passive was rated stronger by the Americans than by the Greeks. However, the concept *my relatives* showed the opposite pattern. There was evidence of close relations with the extended family; for example, *brother* was rated more "good" and "strong" by the Greeks than by the Americans.

Among the traditional Greeks, submission to ingroup authorities and defiance of outgroup authorities were the major attributes of relationships with those in power. In fact, outgroup authorities were seen as threats. In traditional Greece one must not show power before showing concern. However, it is possible to be effective when showing power *after* one has shown concern. This finding is parallel to J. B. P. Sinha's (1980) theory of leadership for India: He argued that an effective leader first shows nurturance and then becomes directive toward production goals.

Ratings of *punishment* by the Greeks showed that they considered it "good," whereas Americans considered it "bad." The perceived consequences of *punishment* included "no resentment" by the Greeks; but resentment was found in the U.S. data (Triandis, 1972). This is consistent with the notion that in tight cultures punishment is welcome and is consistent with the ideals of the society. The need for social controls (tightness) was shown in the way the Greek samples answered a number of questions, such as "I try to keep tight rein on myself at all times" (Greeks high, Americans low); "As long as so many of our teachers are afraid to administer physical punishment, our schools will continue to decline" (Greeks agree; Americans disagree). Tightness also was revealed in the Greeks' willingness to exile sex "criminals" and in agreeing that it is good to imprison those who refuse to salute the flag.

The traditional Greek key values were success of the ingroup, concern for others, and dependability. The concepts of *freedom* and *progress* were seen as collective ideas, as in the freedom and progress of Greece, rather than as individual ideas, as in "my" freedom or "my" progress. Love was seen to be the consequence of appropriate behavior. Proper behavior was much more important as a concept in traditional Greece than in the United States and was included in the concept of *philotimos,* which embodies all virtues and might be translated as "doing what the ingroup expects me to do."

Urban Villagers. There are studies suggesting considerable collectivism among urban villagers in contemporary societies. A study of Turkish urban villages by Korte (1984) provides an interesting case. There was evidence of much helpfulness within the village. Not only was much help extended toward friends, relatives, and neighbors, but also help was extended, in this case, to strangers. The traditional Islamic and rural background of the residents of these villages, which stresses the importance of generosity and responsibility toward other people, was credited for these results.

Individualist Cultures

Ancient Greece. Adamopoulos and Smith (1990) reviewed content analyses of the *Iliad* and the *Odyssey*, which showed high levels of narcissistic individualism. We must note that these books mention mostly the exploits of particular individuals and do not stress group effort as much. It may be that Homer was an individualist, which remains as a rival hypothesis to the thesis that the culture he described was individualistic.

However, it is likely that Greece was a culture that housed many individualists. The West, more generally, has been always more multicultural than the East (Dasenbrock, 1991) perhaps because the ecology has been more broken up by mountains and islands and did not have the large plains of China and India. When different cultures develop on different islands or on different sides of a mountain and the cultures meet in an urban center, people taste multiculturalism, and as we have seen, that means looseness and hence more individualism.

Germany. Although Hofstede's data indicated that Germany hosts an individualistic culture, and its affluence certainly would point in that direction, there have been historical periods in that country when collectivism was high. Authoritarianism seems to be the opposite of individualism (Gelfand, Triandis, and Chan, submitted). Yet based on behavior during the Nazi period and even now, when many neo-Nazi groups that want to exclude non-Germans from the country are making themselves heard, we suspect that collectivism is present among some segments of the population. Overall Germany is an individualistic culture, especially in recent years. In addition, I think it is rather vertical, as are France and the United States, and on that aspect it contrasts with Holland and the Scandinavian countries.

Kuechler (1993) suggested that in the 1970s a process called "individualization" took place. He explained it as follows: "In this process, ties to family, church, and community, as well as identification with social groups—for example trade unions—became less important" (p. 37). This process is responsible for the democratization of Germany, which is continuing in a rapid pace, and with it has come greater individualism. The Huelshoff, Markovits, and Reich (1993) volume also offered many examples of shifts toward individualism and made the point that women's participation in the labor force leads inevitably to lower commitment to marriage and the home environment, which "individualizes" women. One can argue that this has happened in all industrial countries except Japan and may be a further example of shifts toward individualism in most industrial democracies.

France. In an essay on French culture, Aron (1975) identified five of its attributes: down-to-earth peasants, upwardly mobile urbanites, the central
importance of Paris, monuments to the dead, and the fear of taxation. The
selection suggests a mixture of individualist (mobility, fear of taxation) and
collectivist attributes.

Aron pointed out that autocratic regimes were tolerated for centuries and
argued that France is a "patrician society," where elegance and knowing
how to live well (e.g., good food and wine) are greatly valued. But he saw a
major shift after 1945. After nine centuries during which France was *the*
major power, it had to adjust to being a power of moderate means and to
struggle with pluralism in a highly centralized state. In short, he suggested
that France was in transition between moderate collectivism and individualism. I suspect that vertical individualism is the dominant pattern.

Christin and Lefebvre (1970) reported that 85 percent of marriages occurred between people who lived in a region with the same postal code,
suggesting relatively little mobility, hence collectivism. The centralization of
decision making in Paris in the areas of education and economic planning
also suggested collectivism. Television was controlled by the state until the
1980s. In industry, management still has more status than in other industrial
countries.

An anecdote told to me by an American unionist is consistent with the last
point, that is, the vertical emphasis in French industry. As part of a friendly
visit of the U.S. labor movement to French unionism, he visited a French
plant. He was first taken to "Monsieur le Directeur," who welcomed him
and asked him to come back and comment about what he observed during
the plant tour. Then he went on the plant tour with the French unionist,
who spent most of the tour pointing to unsafe work practices. Upon comple-
tion of the tour, he was taken back to the director to say good-bye, and there
he made uninvited comments about the poor status of plant safety. His
French colleague was furious. One does not criticize the director in a face-
to-face meeting. Only a committee can face the director.

Yet, most of what Christin and Lefebvre described is highly individualist.
In the chapter entitled "A Society Against Children," they argued that there
is a major gap between the young and the old, and youth is seen as "a nui-
sance," likely to be delinquent, rather than as "interesting." The prisons are
schools for crime. Crime is a big issue, as is the case in most individualistic
cultures.

When the young were asked how they want to spend Sunday, only 18 percent said, "with my family"; 23 percent, "with friends"; and the rest, with individual activities such as watching TV, individual sports, and art shows.
Christin and Lefebvre pointed out that 62 percent of the French do not belong to any cultural, religious, or political organizations. A school group

adopted a declaration that stated: "We do not want to be told what to do; we want to decide ourselves."

The traditional family, which used to mean "extended family," has exploded, and now it is no longer important. The late 1960s divorce rate, although one-third of the U.S. rate, does not show the number of families that were separated or had other kinds of arrangements (e.g., each spouse having had a lover). There is a lot of travel, and much of the movement is designed to gain more freedom. Thus, we get a picture of people who live in one place and travel for short periods to many places. That pattern suggests "eroding collectivism" and increased individualism.

Political individualism is high in France, and the political spectrum is very heterogeneous. Although this individualism must be credited with the resistance to the Nazis and the Vichy regime during World War II, it also is associated with anomie, and there is a great deal of use of phrases with "they." The "they" are the large newspapers, the unions, and above all the government.

Sentiment against the government is expressed in anti-tax attitudes and in opposition to controls. Small business is still a very common activity in France, and there is much suspicion that the government is trying to act in ways that are not helpful to it.

France has had twelve constitutions in the past two centuries, which suggests considerable instability in sociopolitical life. Christin and Lefebvre traced French history from the first part of the sixteenth century, when the theme of personal enjoyment surfaced, as a struggle between vertical collectivism, suggesting authoritarianism (power of the king, centralization, order, socialism), and individualism (resistance to authorities, stress on the individual, criticisms of the political system, emphasis on small entrepreneurs, fighting fascism and communism in the 1914–1945 period, and emphasis on democracy after 1945). In short, the individualist elements are more numerous than the collectivist, but there is much centralization and verticality that can be traced to the "patrician culture."

United States. American individualism has been widely discussed (de Tocqueville, 1835; Bellah et al., 1985; Inkeles, 1983; and many others). Individualism includes the extreme importance of individual freedom and choice. Recently the U.S. insurance industry, aware of the importance of choice for Americans, developed a campaign against the Clinton health plan that used exactly that theme: "If the plan is adopted, you will have less choice."

American individualism has been different at various historical periods, making any description rather difficult. On the whole it is vertical, especially in business and political settings, but moving in the horizontal direction.

98 *Antecedents and Geographic Distribution*

Donohue (1990) provided an extensive discussion of "new freedoms" that have developed during the past quarter century. He traced these changes to the 1964 Civil Rights Law, which developed the concept of rights that black Americans ought to have, and which inspired other groups to seek their rights—women, gays, lawyers, and others. In popular music the concept of "good taste" disappeared as too restrictive, and songwriters were accepted no matter how outrageous their lyrics. Writers who made extreme statements, such as "marriage is a prison," found readers. The "legitimacy of illegitimacy" resulted in a 200 percent increase of out-of-wedlock births between 1960 and 1980. In short, Donohue documented major changes in the direction of looseness and hence individualism. If the United States was individualist in the nineteenth century, when de Tocqueville visited it, it has been getting even more so recently.

The extent to which a society is bureaucratic makes it tighter. In that sense, for instance, the United States is more tight than hunters and gatherers are. But hunters and gatherers do pay more attention to their ingroups (bands) than do most Americans, so we might expect them to be more loyal to their bands than Americans are to their ingroups. Again, the situation is a key factor (Ross and Nisbett, 1991). As we have seen above in discussing data from traditional Greek culture and contrasting them with American data, there is considerable evidence of American individualism across situations.

Hofstede (1980) found the United States to be the most individualistic culture. Among the factors that may have been responsible are the British influence, affluence, the open frontier, and social and geographic mobility. Most of the immigrants must have been more individualistic than their ingroups, since moving requires breaking with traditional behaviors.

The vertical aspect of American culture may derive from the fact that rather than members of the lower classes, the early settlers included many members of the upper classes, and the latter set the tone of what was acceptable behavior in North America. The writers of the U.S. constitution and the early leaders were definitely upper class. The contrast with the horizontal individualism of Australia suggests that at least initially there were not as many members of the upper class among those who organized Australian society.

Scandinavia. Scandinavia is apparently loose in some domains, such as sexuality, but quite tight in other domains, such as aggression. It seems that ingroups are more important in that part of the world than in the United States. Thus, the greater collectivism regulates behavior more tightly in family and social settings than behavior in the United States. However, in supervisor-subordinate relations the United States is tighter than Scandinavia.

Naroll (1983) checked a large number of indices of societal health and concluded that Norway had the best profile of all the countries for which he had adequate statistics. Norwegians, according to Rodnick (1955), are egalitarian, shy, inhibited, and independent, and they conform to the expectations of others. They give little praise and are oversensitive to criticism. They do not accept strangers easily and raise their children to be fairly obedient. The independence is individualistic, but the other traits are collectivist. They are a generally tight culture in which parents expect achievement but peers distrust those who achieve. I placed it in this section because its individualism was relatively high in Hofstede's data. But the number of collectivist elements is substantial, and if Naroll's viewpoint is to be taken seriously, the total information suggests that a mixture of the two kinds of elements is present and is highly desirable. Thus, I conclude that Scandinavia must be seen as a moderately individualistic region, with many horizontal collectivist elements.

A Probable Developmental Sequence

What follows is speculative, but worth thinking about. I noted that pecking orders are common among primates, who also show considerable territoriality, suggesting vertical collectivism. As humans emerged they were first mostly hunters and gatherers. Thus, a shift might have occurred from 100 percent VC to 50 percent VC and 50 percent HI. Cultural evolution moved from foragers, to agriculturists, to industry, and finally to information societies. Hunters and gatherers seemed to be 50–50 VC and HI. Since they could not accumulate food, there were few status differences and thus they were not too vertical, and since there was an advantage in exploration of new hunting grounds, they tended to be individualists. Agriculturists often found it useful to work together. There were many public works (canals, storage facilities) that could not be built by one person. Agriculture permitted food to accumulate, and there was the need to defend it. Such defense required coordinated, collective action; hence vertical collectivism was functional in that situation. Perhaps the pattern became 80 percent VC and 20 percent HI. Vertical collectivism seems to have been very common and could be found in Europe during the Middle Ages, as well as in many contemporary states.

As affluence makes more choices possible, vertical collectivism changes one of its facets, that is, it changes into either horizontal collectivism or vertical individualism. Now the profile may be 30 percent VC, 40 percent VI, 30 percent HC. When even more affluence is present and no external threats of any kind are detected, the other facet changes as well, and there is horizontal individualism, with a profile that perhaps is 30 percent VC, 60 percent HI, 5 percent VI, and 5 percent HC. In affluent, literate, self-aware cultures, there seem to be pressures in the direction of horizontal individualism. Everyone asserts a right to be equal—equal rights, votes, shares. Thus, maybe this is a 20 percent VC, 70 percent HI, 5 percent VI, 5 percent HC pattern.

We can think of the dominant cultural patterns as "default options." In any culture in a particular stage of cultural evolution, these "options" are used to define proper social behavior in ambiguous situations. For example, in a culture with a 20 percent VC, 70 percent HI, 5 percent VI, and 5 percent HC pattern, if there is any ambiguity, people use the HI pattern. However, situational factors, as discussed in previous chapters, can shift the cultural pattern from the default to another pattern. A review of and expansion on previous comments seems appropriate here.

1. Cultural homogeneity presses toward tightness, hence toward collectivism; cultural heterogeneity presses toward looseness and hence individualism. The big seven industrial countries, except Japan, are getting increasingly heterogeneous: the United States and Canada with Latin American and East Asian migrations; Britain with Indian, Pakistani, and Caribbean migrations; France with Algerian and other former colonies' migrations; Germany with migrations from Southern and Eastern Europe, especially Turkey; Italy with migrations from Africa.

2. Stability of membership in the culture presses toward collectivism; instability presses toward individualism. The big seven are all under the influence of one another and of the rest of the world, as global competition and the exchange of capital transform these societies.

3. Population density presses toward tightness, hence collectivism; an uninhabited open frontier presses toward looseness, hence individualism. There are few uninhabited regions of the world left, but there are regions of low density (e.g., Montana), generally in undesirable climates, where individualism is high. Urbanism has a mixed effect. Although it increases density, it also increases choices, and the latter factor is more important than the former. Thus, as urbanism is increasing around the world, we are likely to see more individualism.

4. External threat presses toward vertical collectivism; no threat permits horizontal individualism. In the post–cold war era, most countries are not experiencing external threat. Of course, there are exceptions, such as Bosnia and Georgia. But the great majority of countries are not experiencing threat, and that will increase individualism.

5. Resource scarcity sometimes requires that authorities regulate who is to get what. This leads to vertical collectivism. If resources are abundant, there is pressure toward horizontal individualism. This factor is likely to increase the differences between the rich countries, which are likely to become more individualistic, and the poor countries, which are likely to become more collectivist. This factor, then, may lead to support for

Huntington's (1993) thesis that the great struggles of the future will be between the collectivist and individualistic countries.

6. When there is great time pressure for a required action, the situation presses toward vertical collectivism. When there is no time pressure, horizontal individualism is likely. This is a situational variable, which changes behavior only temporarily. Only if it is a persistent phenomenon is it likely to become institutionalized and thus be incorporated in a culture.

7. When the situation calls for a particular cultural pattern to operate (e.g., external threat and vertical collectivism; or a funeral and horizontal collectivism; or someone's writing a distinguished book and vertical individualism; or someone's participating in a decision as a representative of an ethnic group and horizontal individualism), the norms of that pattern will become salient and people will act as if that pattern is the appropriate cultural pattern. Again, the same point made in number 6 is applicable.

8. Extraction of resources through cooperative action usually results in authorities' emphasizing vertical collectivism and socialization agents' approving of collectivist virtues. The presence of a clear authority in the situation presses toward vertical collectivism. If resources can be obtained through individual action, there is pressure toward individualism. This factor again is likely to increase collectivism in the relatively less affluent societies, where routine jobs are done, and to increase individualism in the affluent societies, where creativity is required. Again, this factor may support Huntington's (1993) thesis (see number 5 above).

9. If individual actions are blocked or if few options for such actions exist in a society, that situation presses toward collectivism; if no such blocks exist, individualism is more likely. The more individual social mobility is possible, as it is in many individualistic societies, the more individuals will choose to improve their status. However, those subgroups who experience discrimination and whose advancement is blocked will become more collectivist and use collective means of status improvement.

10. If reaching valuable goals is achieved through the collective, there is pressure toward collectivism; if valuable goals are better achieved through individual action, there is pressure toward individualism. This leads to the same predictions as were made for number 9 above.

11. When the individual represents a group, there is pressure toward collectivism; when individuals act for themselves, there is pressure toward individualism. Again, in collectivist societies individuals represent groups more frequently than they represent themselves, and in individualistic societies the opposite happens. Thus this factor too is likely to lead to more discrepancies between individualistic and collectivist societies, supporting Huntington's thesis.

Collectivism may result in the person's feeling good about doing what norms require (Bontempo, Lobel, and Triandis, 1990), often increases the probability of conformity to group norms, and results in the development of strong traditions. All these factors cause the collectivist pattern to become habitual. In that case, people act automatically, without thinking, in a collectivist way. Similarly, individualism rewards the individual with a sense of personal control, freedom from restraints, and enjoyment of doing what she wishes, and it can become habitual and automatic.

However, these broad prototypes must be qualified. It is important to consider the extent that central authority may influence each aspect of life, social, political, economic, religious, aesthetic, and intellectual. Mao's Communist party intruded in every one of these aspects of life. By specifying that parents had to be criticized, that the Communist party was the sole carrier of political activity, that the economy was to be centrally planned by the party, that no religions were allowed, that only "socialist realism" was good art, and that the truth could only be found in "Mao's books," the party ensured that the influence of the collective on all activities was wide and deep.

In modern Japan the penetration of collectives is less centralized. The important collectives are the corporation, the family, and the government, in that order. The corporation intrudes into family life (e.g., about 30 percent of modern Japanese, according to newspaper reports, have to spend most of their work life away from their families, returning to their family only on the weekend; there are long work hours and almost compulsory socializing with co-workers after work); political parties do exist, but membership is voluntary and most people ignore their influences; the government does intrude into economic life with its industrial policy (via the Ministry of Trade and Industry [MITI] and other institutions), and corporations do make decisions that affect economic life; collectives affect religious life in a minor way; judgments about aesthetics may be influenced by the family; collectives, with the exception of the mass media, do not have much influence on the concept of "truth."

In the United States individualism means less influence by collectives, but traces of influence can be found as families regulate aspects of social life, political parties influence political life, the Federal Reserve sets interest rates, corporations influence economic life, organized religions affect religious life, the Congress legislates that "prurient art" may not be exhibited in art galleries supported by federal dollars, and organizations that control the mass media mediate between reality and the public's understanding of what is "true."

What is striking about these U.S. examples is that the intrusion of the collectives is minor and limited, and often people can ignore the collective's directives. This aspect of voluntarism is also seen in Sweden, where the welfare state provides opportunities for individuals to be influenced by the collectives, but the influence is voluntary.

Geographic Distribution of the Constructs

Cultural anthropologists (e.g., Burton et al., 1992) have divided the world into six or seven (depending on who is writing about this) broad cultural regions. They used as bases for this classification language families, since these have been studied extensively by linguists, and family structures (e.g., monogamy, polygamy, descent through the father or mother, etc.), since they are objective and have been well studied by anthropologists.

They have identified the Circum Mediterraneum (the regions around the Mediterranean, including Europe and Africa north of the Sahara); Africa south of the Sahara; South Asia; East Asia; the Pacific; North American indigenous peoples; and South American indigenous peoples as the broad cultural areas. Particular cultures reflect influences from each area, in some proportion. For example, Mexicans were influenced by the European and North American indigenous cultural regions; Puerto Ricans by the European, African south of the Sahara, and North American indigenous cultural regions, and though both Mexicans and Puerto Ricans may be called "Hispanics," they do have somewhat different cultures.

We can expect some similarities among cultures within these regions. Thus, the area around the Mediterranean should be somewhat more individualistic, on the average, than the area of East Asia and the Pacific. However, there is no research on this topic, and whatever I say would be speculative. The research that has covered large numbers of countries is the best empirical information we have. Granted, there are limitations to this research, since countries include many cultures, and the samples have not been representative of the populations under discussion. Still, that is the best we have, so I turn to two studies of values that have covered a large number of countries.

Hofstede (1991) showed the distribution of the countries on individualism (see Figure 4.1). The data collected by S. H. Schwartz (1994) on the values of more than forty countries showed considerable collectivism in Estonia, Singapore, Slovakia, Slovenia, Turkey, Taiwan, and Malaysia and individualism in Switzerland, France, Germany, Spain, Greece, Denmark, Holland, the United States, Canada, England, New Zealand, and Australia. Similarly, the data presented by Triandis, Bontempo, Betancourt, et al. (1986) showed considerable agreement with Hofstede's measurements and indicated that California Asian and Hispanic samples are quite collectivist (see also Triandis, Marin, Hui, et al., 1984; Marin and Triandis, 1985).

Schwartz did a factor analysis of his values inventory and found two factors that accounted for 73 percent of the common variance. The first contrasted individualism and collectivism. The second contrasted harmony and hierarchy with mastery. Horizontal collectivism would appear to imply col-

104

FIGURE 4.1   The Distribution of Countries on Individualism and on Uncertainty Avoidance (uncertainty avoidance is theoretically related to "tightness")

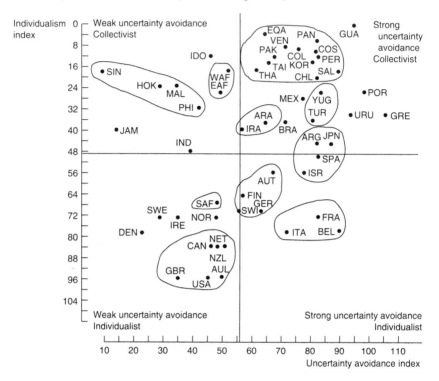

Abbreviations for the countries and regions

ARA	Arab-speaking countries (Egypt, Iraq, Kuwait, Lebanon, Libya, Saudi Arabia, United Arab Emirates)	EAF	East Africa (Ethiopia, Kenya, Tanzania, Zambia)	ISR	Israel	SAF	South Africa
				ITA	Italy	SAL	Salvador
		EQA	Equador	JAM	Jamaica	SIN	Singapore
		FIN	Finland	JPN	Japan	SPA	Spain
ARG	Argentina	FRA	France	KOR	South Korea	SWE	Sweden
AUL	Australia	GBR	Great Britain	MAL	Malaysia	SWI	Switzerland
AUT	Austria	GER	Germany F.R.	MEX	Mexico	TAI	Taiwan
BEL	Belgium	GRE	Greece	NET	Netherlands	THA	Thailand
BRA	Brazil	GUA	Guatemala	NOR	Norway	TUR	Turkey
CAN	Canada	HOK	Hong Kong	NZL	New Zealand	URU	Uruguay
CHL	Chile	IDO	Indonesia	PAK	Pakistan	USA	United States
COL	Colombia	IND	India	PAN	Panama	VEN	Venezuela
COS	Costa Rica	IRA	Iran	PER	Peru	WAF	West Africa (Ghana, Nigeria, Sierra Leone)
DEN	Denmark	IRE	Ireland (Republic of)	PHI	Philippines		
				POR	Portugal	YUG	Yugoslavia

Source: G. Hofstede, *Culture and Organizations* (London: McGraw-Hill, 1991), p. 129. Reprinted with permission.

lectivism and harmony; vertical collectivism implies collectivism and hierarchy; horizontal individualism seems to correspond to individualism and harmony; and vertical individualism to individualism and hierarchy.

Schwartz also provided measurements on the hierarchy (vertical) and egalitarian commitment values (horizontal) that we might use as clues for locating countries on our typology. Thus, based on his data, we can say that vertical collectivism is high in Singapore, among Bulgarian Turks, and in Malaysia; horizontal collectivism in Slovakia; vertical individualism in the former East Germany; and horizontal individualism in France, West Germany, and Italy. Granted, these data do not quite fit the theory of the previous chapter, but there is some correspondence. We must remember that values are but one of the elements of cultural syndromes, and there is an unknown amount of error in any measurement. Clearly, more research is needed, using multiple methods.

❀   ❀   ❀

The cultural syndromes of individualism and collectivism are the consequences of a number of different influences. I suggested in this chapter some of the most important ones, including affluence, family structure, cultural complexity, situations, and demographic factors.

5

Consequences of
Individualism and Collectivism

T HERE ARE NO STUDIES in which cultures have been randomly assigned to be individualist or collectivist and then the consequences examined. Thus whatever is said in this chapter is tentative and a matter of judgment with which the reader may disagree. I propose to approach this chapter by examining the consequences of individualism and collectivism under four headings: consequences for (1) the individual, (2) interpersonal relations, (3) intergroup relations, and (4) social institutions.

Under the last topic I could cover many institutions. I have chosen to examine the effects of individualism and collectivism on institutions for which there is literature. They include economic institutions, like the world of work; the health of the individuals in the society, including the kind of psychotherapy that is likely to be used; religion; and the politics of the society. The discussion of the last topic will bring back some of the political and philosophic issues discussed in Chapter 2.

The Individual

Family Support and Mental Health

Alienation was seen by D. Sinha (1988) to be a consequence of shifts toward individualism. He examined the rapid changes occurring in India and argued that they have direct influences on family structure by causing harm to the mental health of individuals. In cities, as traditional extended-family patterns change to nuclear ones, strong social support weakens. Although the traditional extended family puts stress on members by having them conform to authoritarian older adults, to freedom-confining norms, and to unpleasant expectations, it provides a sense of belonging that can be important, especially during life crises. The segregation of children from adults in urban settings means that peer rather than adult values are adopted by the children. There is an absence of clear models for good behavior as the roles of men and women change.

An extreme example of the implications of individualism for family members is described in the documentary film *It Was a Wonderful Life* (discussed on NPR on December 13, 1993), which described the lives of homeless women in California. Almost all of them were formerly middle class or even upper-middle class. One of them, a painter, had an honorary degree. A bad divorce, unsuccessful investments, and an inability to find a job resulted in loss of income. These women were too proud to ask for public assistance and received no help from their children, even when the children knew about their condition. As a result they slept in their cars or wherever they were able to find shelter. They avoided public shelters because of fear of being raped and robbed.

Here we have a classic consequence of an individualistic society. On the one hand, individualists have an extreme fear of dependence on the ingroup and therefore avoid getting public assistance. On the other hand, people are not close enough, especially parents and children, and in this case the children are unwilling to sacrifice to keep their mothers off the street.

The radio program did not give enough details to know why there was no help received from the children of these women. However, our theoretical discussion in previous chapters pointed to a number of possibilities: First, in individualistic cultures parents and children are less interdependent. Individualists want their children to be independent, and they push them "out of the nest." They do not make an effort to keep close, so alienation of parents and children is more common in such cultures. Whereas collectivists often try to live with their parents or in the same building as the parents, extreme individualists are likely to call their mothers only on Mother's Day. Second, people in individualistic cultures emphasize self-reliance for both themselves and others. Thus, these women would feel that it was inappropriate to ask for help, and their children may feel that it was inappropriate to offer help. Third, the ideology of individualism is that one keeps out of other people's business. "If your mother wants to sleep in her car, it is her right to do her own thing."

Well-Being

As we have seen in Chapter 3, collectivism is associated with low self-esteem. In addition, there is a smaller sense of subjective well-being, that is, happiness. Diener and his associates (Diener and Diener, 1993; Diener, Diener, and Diener, 1993; Diener, Suh, and Shao, in press) found strong correlations between individualism and a sense of subjective well-being. Japan, South Korea, and China had lower happiness and life satisfaction scores than individualistic countries, even after income was statistically controlled. Suh (1994) reported that almost 10 percent of his Chinese sample said that they had never thought about whether or not they were "happy" until he asked this question! One of the women studied by Diener in India, when asked if she was "happy," replied, "I do not know, ask my husband." In short, happiness appears to be an individualistic concept, which is understood in the context of what other people think in collectivist cultures.

East Asian countries experience low satisfaction in certain life domains, such as self-esteem, education, and health, but not in other areas, such as family and entertainment satisfaction. The low self-esteem in some cases may lead to high rates of suicide. Lester (1988) correlated Hofstede's individualism scores with suicide rates in a sample of countries. He found a correlation of $r = -.43$ ($p < .04$). Thus in collectivist cultures suicide rates were high.

Having a same-self culture, as one finds in both horizontal individualism and horizontal collectivism, may also contribute to high suicide rates, as seen in Sweden. My speculation is that people in a same-self culture are prone to embarrassment when they are not able to remain invisible. Any event that makes one different results in embarrassment. In some cases embarrassment is so high, or the individual is unable to deal with even low levels of embarrassment, that suicide is used as an escape from shame.

Individual Differences

Typical Attributions. Among individualists the causes of "poverty" seem related to individualistic factors (e.g., they are poor because they are not self-reliant) and among collectivists to collectivist factors (e.g., they are poor because the government has the wrong policies) (Zucker and Weiner, 1993). This suggests that people in the two kinds of cultures base some of their perceptions of the social environment on individualism or collectivism.

Personality Patterns. Yamaguchi (1994), theorizing that collectivists do what their ingroups want them to do, developed a collectivism scale. The scale was administered to large samples of Japanese students. Yamaguchi found that the collectivism scores correlated positively with scores obtained from standard scales measuring affiliation ($r = .29$), sensitivity to rejection ($r = .36$), public self-conceptions ($r = .29$), self-monitoring ($r = .22$), and social anxiety ($r = .14$) and negatively with the need for uniqueness ($r = -.43$). Older people scored higher on collectivism. High scores on collectivism were also related to a tendency toward "false consensus" (believing that others share one's beliefs, attitudes, and values; $r = .18$, $p < .02$). Those high in collectivism wanted people to be equal in intelligence and did not like individuals who were too competent, suggesting that University of Tokyo students' collectivism is more horizontal than vertical.

Gudykunst, Gao, Nishida, Nadamitsu, and Sakai (1992) found that those Japanese who were idiocentric were less sensitive to others, showed less attention to social comparison information, paid less attention to the status of others, and were less concerned with social propriety. They also argued that in individualistic cultures those who are high self-monitors (Snyder, 1974) pay attention to what others in general want them to do; in collectivist cultures high self-monitors simply behave more appropriately as specified by the relationships with those who are in the particular social situation. Both aspects of self-monitoring can be found in all cultures, but the emphasis on either aspect varies with culture.

Adams and Hill (1989) analyzed Japanese comic books and reported that they found repressed feelings of resentment, hostility, rage, and vengeance directed at the collective's intrusion into the individual's personal space. Blinco (1992) found that Japanese are more persistent than Americans, which has real advantages when it comes to solving difficult problems. This attribute was also found in Hong Kong (Triandis, Bontempo, Leung, and Hui, 1990) and may have been derived from the Confucian tradition.

Schmitz (1990) found that in a sample of East Germans who had moved to West Germany, the idiocentrics (as measured by items from Triandis, Bontempo, Villareal, et al., 1988) had less tendency to lie than allocentrics but were higher on neuroticism and psychoticism. The interpretation he gave was that individualism is linked to alienation; hence the relatively high levels of neuroticism and psychoticism. Idiocentrics in this study were less likely to be able to accept the norms of both East and West Germany and were either assimilated into West German culture (a tendency facilitated by their having individualistic values in an individualistic culture) or became segregated from the West German culture and linked with other East Germans in West Germany. The linking with like-minded fellow countrymen is a very common occurrence and widely found in studies of adjustment to other cultures. Thus the notable finding is that having a personality trait that matches the culture one is entering provides advantages in acculturation.

Interpersonal Relations

Relations with Members of Ingroups

In Chapter 3 we saw that collectivists have few ingroups but are closely linked to them. Collectivists tend to have few but intimate relationships, and individualists have many relationships of low intimacy. Individualists have many ingroups and enter and exit them with great frequency. Since individualists have to work at their relationships to maintain them, they tend to develop skills for effective superficial interaction with others (Wheeler, Reis, and Bond, 1989). Collectivists also have to work at their relationships, especially with non-kin, and thus the exchange of gifts is frequent. But the difference is that individualists are expected to improvise and do not have access to clear norms about social behavior, whereas collectivists simply follow the norms and do not need special skills.

Interactions

Wheeler, Reis, and Bond (1989) asked individuals in Hong Kong to keep a record of their interactions that lasted ten minutes or more, over a period of two weeks. The results are consistent with the general statements made above: Relative to the standardization norms developed in the United States for this task, the Chinese had fewer interactions (2.25) per day (U.S. = 6.00), more group interactions (29 percent) than the Americans (17 percent), longer interactions (average 61 minutes versus 53 minutes), and fewer interaction partners (Chinese 15 same sex, 10 different sex; Americans 22 and 17, respectively). The Chinese had more task and fewer recreational interactions than the Americans. The judged level of intimacy (self-disclosure) was higher for the Chinese than for the Americans, especially for men.

Conflict

Conflict occurs in both individualist and collectivist cultures, but it tends to take somewhat different forms. Both collectivist (a group fights to improve its conditions) and individualist (an individual fights to change something) conflicts occur in both types of cultures, but they have different probabilities. In collectivist cultures conflict is more likely to be intergroup, with ethnicity, language, religion, or race as the boundaries of conflicts. The conflict is between collectives, and the purpose is to improve the status or economic conditions or territory of the collective. In individualist cultures alienation seems to be the basis of the conflicts. We have seen, for instance, in the 1960s, the emergence of gangs like the one that abducted Patty Hearst, the terrorist groups in Germany, and the Red Brigade in Italy. These groups objected to the form of the societies within which they found themselves. Their aim was, not to improve the status of their group, but to change the whole society.

Social Behavior as a Function of Social Distance

Triandis, McCusker, and Hui (1990) examined the perceptions of social behavior as a function of social distance, among Chinese and American samples. The three researchers used the psychophysical method of direct estimation (Stevens, 1966), which establishes a standard against which subjects make judgments. For example, in the case of the social distance scale, the subjects were asked to "consider the person with whom you feel closest" and to assign "1" to the "distance between you and that person." They were then presented with twenty social stimuli (e.g., father, the religious group they like least) and asked to estimate the distance between themselves and each stimulus, using the same unit of measurement. Of course, if the father was the closest person in the world, he would receive 1 unit of distance. After all the judgments were made, the numbers given by each subject were divided by the geometric mean of all the judgments (the geometric mean of twenty numbers is the twentieth root of the product of these numbers). This has the effect of taking into account the fact that people use numbers differently. Some people like to use large numbers and others small numbers.

The scale values obtained from each individual in each culture were then averaged. Thus, for instance, the Chinese gave an average scale value of .34 to their father. The Americans gave a scale value of .53 to their fathers. The difference, at $p < .05$, was statistically significant, showing that the Chinese felt closer to their fathers than did the Americans. However, when all twenty stimuli were taken into account, there were relatively few differences overall (see Triandis, McCusker, and Hui, 1990, table 6, p. 1017). For instance, people of the religion liked least were given a scale value of 2.65 by the Chinese and 2.27 by the Americans, and that difference was not statistically reliable.

Next, the researchers constructed scales of social behavior. They asked the subjects to examine six qualities of social behavior: association (e.g., to help, support, like, admire, respect), dissociation (e.g., to fight with, avoid), superordination (e.g., to order to do something, criticize), subordination (e.g., to obey, ask for help), intimacy (e.g., to pet, kiss), and formality (e.g., send written invitation to, sit at a table according to rank). For each quality of social behavior, each subject constructed his/her own scale. This was accomplished by using a standard behavior, such as "to admire" for association, for which the scale value was arbitrarily set at 10. A behavior could have a larger or smaller scale value than this standard. For instance, "to ask for help" might be viewed by a person as less associative than "to admire," so the person might give a value of 8 to that behavior. The subjects judged eight behaviors for each of the six qualities of social behavior in this way, and their judgments were again divided by their geometric means to eliminate idiosyncratic ways of using numbers.

After completing scale construction, the subjects were asked to judge each of the twenty social stimuli in relation to each behavior forming the social behavior scale (e.g., "Would you kiss your father?"). The scale values of all the behaviors that were given a "yes" were averaged, and that constituted the average behavior toward that social stimulus. Each person's social behavior as a function of social distance curve was then plotted, and it had, of course, 20 points. The six average functions, for four samples, are shown in Figures 5.1 to 5.6.

The four samples shown on the curves in Figures 5.1 to 5.6 were as follows: A sample of students from the PRC who were asked to supply their own ideas of the kinds of social behavior that they would engage in with

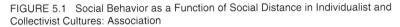

FIGURE 5.1   Social Behavior as a Function of Social Distance in Individualist and Collectivist Cultures: Association

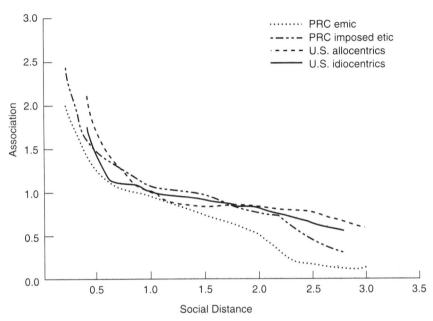

Source for Figures 5.1 through 5.6: H. C. Triandis, C. McCusker, and C. H. Hui, "Multimethod Probes of Individualism and Collectivism," *Journal of Personality and Social Psychology* 59, pp. 1006–1020. Copyright © 1990 by the American Psychological Association. Reprinted by permission of the publisher.

FIGURE 5.2   Social Behavior as a Function of Social Distance in Individualist and Collectivist Cultures: Dissociation

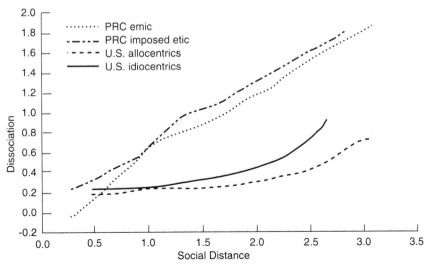

114

FIGURE 5.3   Social Behavior as a Function of Social Distance in Individualist and Collectivist Cultures: Superordination

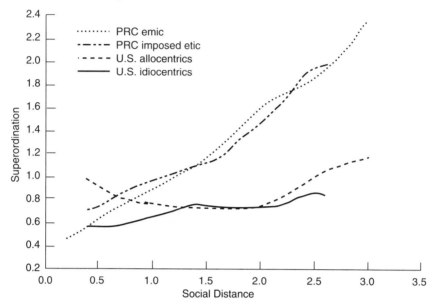

FIGURE 5.4   Social Behavior as a Function of Social Distance in Individualist and Collectivist Cultures: Subordination

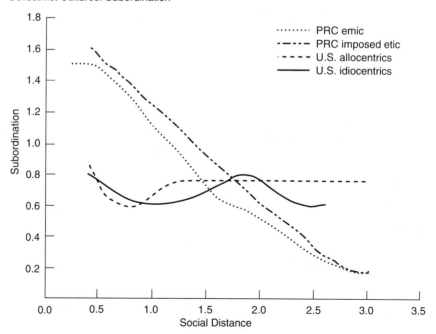

FIGURE 5.5   Social Behavior as a Function of Social Distance in Individualist and Collectivist Cultures: Intimacy

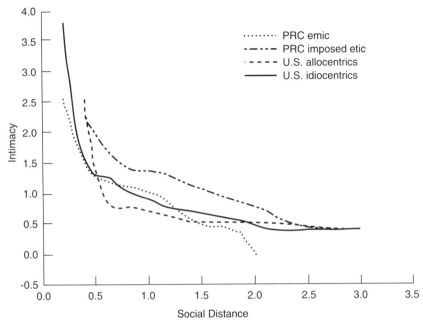

FIGURE 5.6   Social Behavior as a Function of Social Distance in Individualist and Collectivist Cultures: Formality

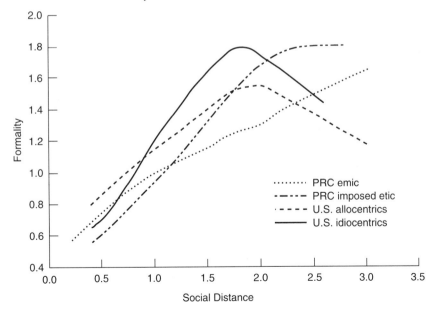

each of the social stimuli (called the PRC emic); the same people, but in this case the eight behaviors were provided by the experimenter (PRC etic). (See Appendix for a definition of *emic* and *etic*.) The U.S. allocentrics were students from the University of Illinois who had scored on the collectivist side when they answered attitude questions, such as those presented in the Appendix, and the idiocentrics, University of Illinois students who had scored on the individualist side on those questions.

We see here that the two cultural groups were fairly similar in the way they did these tasks. This is important because if they were different in every way, we would not have been sure that we had communicated the same task to them (D. T. Campbell, 1964). Thus, the fact that the curves for association and intimacy are about the same is very desirable. Next, we see that the Chinese showed more dissociation than the Americans toward their outgroups. This is consistent with the point made in Chapter 3 that collectivists make a greater distinction than individualists between ingroup and outgroup. The Chinese also showed more superordination toward outgroups, which is again consistent with that point. Finally, the Chinese showed more subordination to ingroup members and less subordination to outgroups than the Americans did. Thus social behavior across cultures was both similar and different in these studies.

Relationships of Individuals and Social Environments

Oettingen (1994) described the East Berlin school system as it existed before German unification. Differentiated performance feedback in the form of grades was given from the first grade on, in front of the entire "class collective." Teachers evaluated their students outside the classroom as well. Teaching strategies were largely group oriented and unidimensional (good at everything or bad at everything), thus enhancing the social comparisons of performance attainments. The teachers were required to adhere strictly to the curriculum, regulations, and pace of studying and were not allowed to make accommodations to the needs of individual students. A very important goal was to make every student evaluate her/himself the same way as the teacher evaluated her/him (a really vertical culture!). Moreover, every student was supposed to feel responsible for the successes and failures of his/her ingroup or class collective. This vertical collectivist system of education had much in common with the Russian school system, as described by Bronfenbrenner (1970).

By contrast, the West Berlin school system included privacy concerning grades, and teaching was multidimensional, so students could excel in one area, but not necessarily in another. There were differences in degree of regulation and teaching strategies between the two school systems. For instance, in West Berlin, there was no goal of matching the evaluation of the student and teacher. Thus, it is clear that a collectivist method of teaching was used in the East and an individualist one in the West, though both were German cultures.

The imposition of collective views, large power differences, strong uncertainty avoidance, and the masculine (Hofstede, 1980) orientation of the East Berlin system led Oettingen to expect less self-efficacy (Bandura, 1989). She reasoned that children enter school with illusory optimism about their capabilities; thus the children who were less successful would suffer losses in their perceived self-efficacy. The data supported these predictions. In addition, efficacy beliefs and course grades were correlated about .75 for those students who were very intelligent (as measured by the Raven Test) in both East and West Berlin; but for those who had a low IQ, the correlation in East Berlin was about .90 and in West Berlin about .60. Thus the collectivist method of teaching was especially detrimental for the less-able students, which was exactly contrary to what one would expect in a "proletarian state."

Development of Self-Efficacy. A study by Earley (1993) of managers, carried out in China, Israel, and the United States, found that collectivists see the self as higher in self-efficacy when they are working with the ingroup, and individualists see the self as higher in self-efficacy when they are working alone. Two variables were manipulated. The managers worked with others or alone, and when working with others the managers were told who they were. The ingroup-outgroup variable, in this study, was manipulated by telling the managers they would work with others who came from the same region and background as they did or that the people they would work with were quite different from them. The task consisted of dealing with forty in-basket items, typical of the things that managers are accustomed to do. As predicted, self-efficacy and performance were very high among collectivists working with their ingroups or individualists working alone. The other conditions resulted in lower performance.

Imposition of the Views of the Collective. The wider acceptance of the imposition of the views of authority figures among vertical collectivists was shown in studies carried out in the former USSR and Japan, on the one hand, and in the United States, on the other hand. Such studies found, for instance, that Russian and Japanese physicians are less likely to tell a patient that she has cancer than are American doctors. This paternalistic behavior is consistent with vertical collectivism. Specifically, Deeken (1992) found that 97 percent of American physicians would tell patients that they have cancer, whereas more than 50 percent of Japanese physicians would not.

Hamilton et al. (1991) reported that Japanese teachers spoke more to the group than to individuals than did ones in the United States. The Japanese spoke to the group 51 percent of the time and to individuals 47 percent of the time. The corresponding percentages for U.S. teachers were 22 percent and 72 percent respectively.

Group membership is more important for social perception in collectivist cultures. Bergeron and Zanna (1973) found that interpersonal attraction was a function of social class much more than of attitudinal similarity in samples studied in Peru, even when such attraction was assessed in situations of low intimacy. This contrasts with samples studied in the United States, where belief similarity is a more important determinant of attraction than group membership (e.g., Rokeach and Rothman, 1965), such as race or ethnicity, especially in situations of low intimacy.

Individualists apparently value ingroup heterogeneity, and collectivists value ingroup homogeneity. If our analysis of the factors that generate these cultural syndromes is accurate, this contrast may simply reflect the universal human tendency to value one's own culture, which is likely to be more heterogeneous in the case of individualists than in the case of collectivists. Preferring homogeneity also means expecting conformity from others. A meta-analysis of conformity studies employing the Asch-type paradigm looked at seventy-five studies in thirteen countries. Collectivist countries tended to have higher levels of conformity in that task (Bond and Smith, submitted).

The Importance of Face. An extensive research program examining the importance of "face" in individualist and collectivist cultures was carried out by Ting-Toomey and her associates (Ting-Toomey, 1993, 1994a, 1994b; Ting-Toomey et al., 1991). Briefly, individualists are most concerned with saving their own face (self-face concern); collectivists are *also* concerned with saving the face of ingroup members (other-face concern). Understanding face concerns leads to a better understanding of conflict styles in the two kinds of culture. Self-face maintenance is associated with a dominating conflict style, and other-face maintenance is associated with the avoiding, integrating, and compromising styles of conflict management. Communication is used to negotiate a social identity.

Whom to Consult. For advice concerning relational crises, collectivists go to informal third-party mediators, such as relatives and work supervisors. In similar situations, individualists tend to seek the advice of professional therapists and counselors.

Love and Marriage. In individualistic cultures people fall in love first and then they get married. In collectivist cultures it is more common that people get married first, and then they fall in love. Individualists tend to manage marital conflict more actively than collectivists, who often allow fate to operate, accepting and going along with the ups and downs of the relationship. Ting-Toomey (1994b) discussed how culture (individualism and collectivism) and gender construct intimate conflict in personal relationships. She noted the individualist tendency to frame conflict in the "me-you" opposition, and the collectivist tendency to frame "autonomy" and "connection" as complementary essences. She pointed out that in individualist cultures, sharing interests and activities serve as important barometers of a good relationship. In such collectivist cultures as China, shared perceptions and an exchange of intellectual intimacy are an important dimension of the romantic relationship. Romantic love is treasured where kinship ties are weak and becomes diluted when kinship ties are strong. The result is that among Chinese couples there is less passionate love and a greater emphasis on companionship than among Western couples.

Norms That Are Widely Used. Relational equity is an important element in the management of conflict in individualistic cultures; and a communal orientation model underscores intimate conflict negotiation in many collectivist cultures. The latter model refers to the importance of equality norms and rules that uphold group and relational harmony and emphasizes the importance of weighing the costs and benefits of family and personal network reactions, lifelong relational goals, a sense of indebtedness, and long-range obligatory reciprocity. It is a processes-oriented rather than an outcome-oriented model. But when dealing with outgroup members, collectivists—just like individualists—use the equity norm.

A large relational investment, Ting-Toomey argued, encourages the use of "constructive" conflict responses, such as "voice" (telling what bothers you) and "loyalty," and discourages "destructive" responses, such as "exit" (leaving the relationship) or "neglect." She speculated that collectivists more often than individualists use passive conflict responses, such as "neglect" and "loyalty." Also, she asserted that in collectivist cultures males use the "neglect" mode more and females the "active" conflict reduction methods. She also mentioned that in individualistic cultures emotions are expressed more readily in intimate conflict situations, whereas in collectivist cultures there is more evidence of the restraining of emotional expressions, which is viewed positively as reflecting "self-discipline and maturity."

Self-Evaluation. Cross and Markus (1993) tested Tesser's self-evaluation maintenance model with Chinese and American nationals. According to this model, people maintain a positive view of themselves by emphasizing their own successes or by associating with those who are successful. Tesser saw two processes: (1) reflection—basking in the reflected glory of others, and (2) comparison. People use the reflection process when the issue is not self-relevant and the comparison process when it is self-relevant. In addition, the person's performance makes a difference. People whose own performance is high use comparison and see themselves as close to the comparison other. But if a friend does better than they do, the self will be threatened. Then the perceiver will denigrate the friend's performance to prevent unfavorable comparisons.

The researchers postulated that these processes may be different in the case of collectivists, since they may not want to be superior to a friend. Hence, they may enhance the friend's performance. In the experiment, the dependent variable was the subject's rating of the friend's performance. The U.S. subjects, consistent with Tesser's theory, saw the friend's performance as more positive when the task was not self-relevant than when it was self-relevant. A stranger's performance was seen as more positive in the relevant rather than the nonrelevant condition. However, the Chinese who were high in interdependence did not differ from those low in interdependence when the partner was correct, but they were different when the partner was incorrect. They saw the partner's performance as better than did the low interdependence subjects. In short, they felt so close to their partner that they perceived the partner's incorrect performance as "pretty good." They were also slightly more positive in evaluating the partner's performance when the task was self-relevant than nonrelevant. Thus, if one is interdependent, one does not denigrate the other's performance to improve one's perception of one's own performance.

Self-Affirmation. In the same paper, Cross and Markus (1993) examined Steele's theory of self-affirmation, according to which if a person's self-esteem is threatened in one area, the person will emphasize success in another area. They reasoned that in the case of interdependent people, affirming a close other may function just as well as or better than affirming the self. There were three conditions: (1) self-affirmation (wrote an essay about own successes), (2) friend's self-affirmation (wrote an essay about their friend's successes), and (3) no affirmation (wrote an essay on a nonrelevant topic). The dependent variable was the subjects' estimate of their performance on a second administration of the test that was involved in their success story. The data showed that a friend's success functioned to affirm the self in the case of interdependent subjects.

Helping Behavior. Interpersonal relations sometimes involve different assumptions in collectivist and individualistic cultures. Specifically, in individualistic cultures it is assumed that whether a person helps or not is a matter of personal choice. But in many collectivist cultures helping is a moral obligation, thus, obligatory, not voluntary. In many collectivist cultures doing one's duty is realizing one's nature, and individual happiness is not important. Miller (1994) showed that the conditions under which one may or may not help are often different in India and the United States. In general, people must help in India under conditions where help is not required (is optional) in the United States. Greater priority is given to interpersonal responsibilities than to justice obligations in collectivist cultures.

Social Loafing. Earley (1989) showed that social loafing (doing less than one is capable of doing when one's performance is not observable) is less likely among collectivists working with ingroup members than among individualists. Similarly, Wagner (1992) showed that individualists were more likely to "free ride"—avoid responsibilities, let others do a greater share of the work, allow others to pay for them—than is common among collectivists. However, Yamagishi (1988) argued that Japanese subjects do not free ride because they are monitored very closely, and if they fail to do their share, they are likely to face severe sanctions. He showed in an experiment that when monitoring is not possible, the Japanese subjects who contribute much to the group exit the group. This is an individualistic solution to the free rider problem.

Intergroup Relations

The effect of individualism and collectivism on intergroup relations will be discussed in this section. There are consequences with respect to acculturation, communication, prejudice and discrimination, and conflict reduction.

Acculturation

It is useful to distinguish two kinds of acculturation: collective and individual. In collective acculturation the whole group changes and achieves a specific status in another culture. In individual acculturation only individuals achieve the higher status.

Lalonde and Cameron (1993) examined immigrants in Canada. They argued that within the Canadian context, black immigrants from the Caribbean and immigrants from China were more "stigmatized" than immigrants from Europe, specifically Italians and Greeks. The former cannot "pass" as regular Canadians as easily as the latter. Thus, they are more likely to adopt a collective acculturation strategy within their own cultural group. Questionnaires administered to these four groups also considered whether the immigrant was first generation ($N = 116$) or the adult child of that generation ($N = 133$). It was found that those from "stigmatized" groups perceived themselves to be at a greater disadvantage and were more supportive of a collective integration orientation than the less-stigmatized immigrants. Parents (first generation) were more likely to endorse the collective acculturation orientation and exhibited a stronger ethnic identification than their children (second generation).

More generally, similarity in the type of individualism or collectivism between a host culture and immigrants to that culture increases the probability of good adjustment (Schmitz, 1990). That means that collectivists coming to an individualistic culture have more difficulty adjusting than
individualists coming to an individualistic culture. Ulaszek (1990) examined
the perception of stress among University of Illinois foreign students and
found support for this proposition. Those from collectivist cultures had
more difficulties making friends than those from individualistic cultures.
She obtained ratings of the unpleasantness of life events from these students and found that collectivists saw some life events as even more unpleasant than did individualists.

There are a number of unstated assumptions in each cultural pattern that
can facilitate adjustment of members of one culture to another culture. The
greater the cultural distance between two societies, the more difficult is the
adjustment. Cultural distance can be measured by the following considerations: language (people can learn a language from the same language family more easily than a language from a different language family), social
structure (people can adjust more easily if the social structure is similar, e.g.,
family structure, such as monogamy, polygamy, etc.), economic structure
(people can adjust more easily if the standard of living is about the same),
religion, political system, educational level, standards of what constitutes
"truth" (e.g., derived through experience or from authorities), and aesthetic
standards (same standards help adjustment). There is literature about
American expatriates who adjust much more easily to Europe than to Africa
and immigrants who adjust more easily to a country with the same culture
than to a country with a different culture (Landis and Brislin, 1983).

Consider what happens when people with vertical or horizontal individualism move to cultures with vertical or horizontal collectivism, or vice versa.
When the two cultures have patterns represented by vertical collectivism
versus horizontal individualism, each of the attributes that distinguish the
two patterns (see Chapter 3) can be a source of conflict.

Consider the example of a supervisor from one culture and an employee
from another culture. The supervisor from a vertical collectivism culture
would expect orders to be followed without argument, much as in a military
culture. The employee from the horizontal individualism culture would
want to do what he or she wished to do to some extent and would not grant
the supervisor the right to dictate what is appropriate action. The supervisor
is likely to accuse the employee of "insubordination" and the employee to
accuse the supervisor of "authoritarianism."

Vertical collectivism versus vertical individualism would be the case
where both supervisor and employee understand "who is the boss," so the
conflict is likely to be generated on the other facet, collectivism versus individualism. In this case, for instance, the supervisor might very well expect

the employee to work extra hours for the benefit of the organization (which is very common in Japanese firms operating in the United States; see Graen and Wakabayashi, 1994), whereas the employee sees time after normal work hours to be entirely personal.

Horizontal collectivism versus horizontal individualism would lead to a situation where the supervisor expects regular contact with an employee who in turn prefers privacy and distance from the supervisor. Horizontal collectivism versus vertical individualism would include the same problem but would be further complicated by a supervisor's treating the employee as an equal. The employee subsequently feels uncomfortable and recognizes a perpetual imbalance of power.

Horizontal collectivism versus vertical collectivism would result when the supervisor expects contact and equality, whereas the employee accepts this contact but would prefer to be treated as a subordinate. And in the case of horizontal individualism versus vertical individualism, each participant is for the most part doing her own thing, anticipating orders, whereas the supervisor tries to be a cohort.

It is fairly clear from these examples that when both facets are different, as in the case of vertical collectivism and horizontal individualism or horizontal collectivism with vertical individualism, there will be more conflict. But there will always be some misunderstandings in cases where there is a difference in cultural patterns.

Although the general statement that adjustment will be best when the cultural patterns match is probably valid, there are many exceptions. One of the most interesting is the adjustment of immigrants from Southeast Asia to the United States. The family collectivism they brought with them proved to be functional for the adjustment of their children to U.S. schools. As Caplan, Whitmore, and Choy (1989) documented, within three years of arrival in the United States without knowledge of English, the children of these immigrants were performing at above-average levels in U.S. schools.

The data consisted of two rounds of survey interviews conducted in five sites: Seattle; Orange County, California; Chicago; Houston; and Boston. The 1981 round included 1,384 households, comprising 6,775 individuals. The second round, collected in 1984, used a subsample of the first sample. These refugees arrived from Vietnam and Laos. They came from average-social-status backgrounds and arrived without material possessions and little education. Eighty-five percent of them had no useful English-language proficiency when they arrived. Yet, within forty months of their arrival they surpassed many of the U.S. minorities on indices of economic achievement and their children surpassed even the average of the U.S. population in school achievement. They did not have high-level jobs, but 48 percent had incomes that were twice the income defining the poverty line.

The educational achievement of their children was remarkable. Eighty percent of the children had an overall grade average of A or B, and 48 percent averaged A in mathematics. On standardized tests, such as the California Achievement Test (CAT), 60 percent scored above the national average. Forty-nine percent were in the top quarter of mathematics CAT scores, and 45 percent were in the top quarter in spelling. (Some of the children, three years after their arrival without English, won national competitions in spelling and mathematics.)

How can these findings be explained? The cultural values of the parents, according to Caplan, Whitmore, and Choy (1989), are the bases for the explanation. Three major aspects of the culture were mentioned: household composition, values, and a longtime perspective (I will achieve through my children). Because the boat people had modest expectations (were willing to take any job) and did not have a history of experiencing discrimination in this country, they took advantage of whatever opportunities were available.

An additional factor in all probability is that in the United States, Asians find a "niche" in intellectual activities. They are not especially large and strong, as are African Americans, and did not arrive in the country early enough to occupy the best economic positions, as did the European Americans. But through education and hard work they can secure a good life, and both education and hard work are compatible with the Confucian values.

The values of these people were very clear: Ninety-eight percent agreed that education and achievement, a cohesive family life, and hard work are important. Ninety percent agreed on a number of collectivist values, such as family loyalty, morality and ethics, fulfilling obligations, restraint and discipline, perpetuating ancestral lineage, respect for elders, cooperation, and harmonious family life. Furthermore, the ratings of the importance of values obtained from parents and children correlated .83. They also rejected individualistic values such as material possessions, fun, and excitement. In fact, their values were textbook collectivist values. They were also self-reliant so as not to burden the ingroup.

They supervised the homework of their children, asking every day, "How did you do in school today?" They obtained tutors from the same ethnic group if they could not help their children and made sure that the children were model pupils. They read to their children (twice as often in their native language than in English), and those who read to their children had children who did better in schools than those who did not. They provided proverbs, for example, "When parents look away, the child becomes foolish; when they look toward the child, it becomes smart." Another similarity with other collectivists is the emphasis on persistence and effort. They said, "A knife gets sharp through honing; a man gets smart through study."

We can learn an important lesson from this study: When we study collectivist samples, we must use the group as the unit of analysis. Too often we focus only on individuals and do not examine the group dynamics behind individual performance.

Communication

East Asian collectivists use an interdependent orientation during communication, with more "we" than "I"; an emphasis more on context than on content; more emphasis on the implicit than on the explicit; more use of silence, synthesis, and ambiguity; more likely use of a climactic organization of the argument (the most powerful argument at the end); more emphasis on what was agreed than on what was said; and decisions by consensus. They use well-tried expressions and words like "maybe," "probably," "perhaps," "slightly," and phrases like "I am not sure" more than do individualists. Silence is used by East Asian collectivists as an indication of strength, power, and disagreement, whereas individualists see it is an indication of weakness, being shy, or troubled (Gudykunst and Nishida, 1994). Whether these characteristics are shared by other collectivists is not known at this time, since there are no similar communications research data from other collectivist cultures. Individualists use confrontation, pay attention to the content, use hyperbole, and adopt an anticlimactic sequence of presentation (best argument first). Research is needed to determine if this pattern is found among all types of individualists.

Prejudice and Discrimination

The relationship between individualism-collectivism and prejudice and discrimination is extremely complex. There are two contradictory tendencies that increase prejudice and discrimination. The collectivists are more likely to identify with their cultural group and thus be more ethnocentric, and the vertical individualists are more likely to put down groups that are different from their own, in an effort to be "distinguished" and to win the "competition in the market place." The horizontal individualists are probably the least likely to be prejudiced and to discriminate.

The relative strength of these tendencies depends on the vertical or horizontal character of the individualism and the collectivism. Although all collectivists identify strongly with their groups, the vertical collectivists feel more comfortable seeing themselves as different from other groups. The race riots in India (Hindu-Muslim, Kashmir, Sikhs, the persecution of the Bangladeshis in Bengal, etc.) suggest a deep-seated identification with one's own group. They also tell us that allies can turn into enemies (Hindus and Sikhs against the Muslims; Muslim and Croat Bosnians against the Bosnian Serbs) when the basic emphasis on promoting the interests of the ingroup is extreme.

Of course, whenever a cultural pattern prevails, there are countercultural individuals who adopt the opposite viewpoint, as Gandhi did with his "the world is my family." This statement suggests horizontal collectivism, but we know from his biography that he had considerable individualistic tendencies.

Similarly, vertical individualists are especially likely to want to be "distinguished," and thus we are likely to see more prejudice and discrimination among them (e.g., Americans, Britons) than among horizontal individualists (e.g., Dutch, Scandinavians), though undoubtedly other factors, such as cultural homogeneity, are also at work in this case.

Recall that in Chapter 3, I argued that every human is both an individualist and a collectivist in varying proportions. For example, American Catholics are more collectivist than American Protestants, whereas all Americans are individualists relative to the world's population. Hsu (1983) noted that the more-individualistic Protestants, presumably of the vertical type, are often more prejudiced and discriminatory (e.g., in South Africa) than the less-individualistic Catholics.

The importance of identification with one's own group was shown in Poland in studies by Otrocska, Jarymowicz, and Kwiatowska (1991). They measured the distinctiveness of "self" and "others" as well as the distinctiveness of "we" and "they." According to the analysis in Chapter 3, maximum collectivism will occur when the first distinctiveness is low and the second high. The Polish studies showed that people who had low self-other distinctiveness (i.e., the more allocentric) reported they could easily identify outgroup members (in this case Jews) based on facial features. The subjects, who were asked, "How quickly can you identify a Jew through observation?" rated their ability on a seven-point scale that ranged from "immediately" to "I can't do it." It is unclear here whether allocentrics are really able to identify outgroups more quickly than idiocentrics or they simply think they can do it. Also, even if they do identify outgroups more quickly, that does not necessarily imply resulting discrimination, though presumably if they do indeed have the ability to identify outgroups, this skill must serve a purpose and also suggests that perhaps they reject outgroups more readily.

The link between individualism and prejudice was shown in studies by Sears (1988) in which "symbolic racism" was linked to individualism. Symbolic racism is measured by attitude items that criticize current policies that they claim "unfairly favor African Americans." The data showed that those who favored individualism, hard work, thrift, punctuality, sexual repression, and delays in gratification were especially likely to express this type of attitude. However, attitudes toward equality were also important. Klugel and Smith (1988) found that those who favored equal opportunity for all were less prejudiced. These findings suggest that vertical individualists may be more prejudiced than horizontal individualists.

A relationship between one person and another can be either *interpersonal* or *intergroup* (Tajfel, 1982). In the interpersonal case the personal (individual difference) qualities of the other person are salient and the group memberships of the other person are in the background. In the intergroup case, the group memberships are salient and the personal attributes may be totally ignored. When we fire at the enemy, we are not considering individual differences.

In Chapter 3 we saw that the interpersonal pattern is more common among individualists than collectivists, and the intergroup is more common among collectivists than among individualists. The intergroup pattern is especially likely to be used when there is a history of conflict, when the groups have incompatible goals, and when there are distinguishing features between the groups (e.g., physical, behavioral, dress, language, status, religion, ideology, aesthetic standards, or other attributes that can be used to distinguish one group from another). An ethnic group that is present in large proportions in a particular social environment is especially likely to be noticed and reacted to in intergroup terms (Pettigrew, 1959).

A society with a great deal of social mobility is likely to have many individuals who are unsure about their status, and such anxiety is related to prejudice (Bettelheim and Janowitz, 1950). This condition is especially likely among vertical individualists. From these considerations it seems likely that prejudice and discrimination will be high among vertical collectivists, followed by vertical individualists, followed by horizontal collectivists, and will be low among horizontal individualists. Thus unqualified collectivism and individualism are probably unrelated to prejudice.

However, several other factors can increase or decrease prejudice and thus can change this rank order. Harsh child training has the effect of creating adults who view the world in black-and-white terms (Adorno et al., 1950), and that training is often more common among the lower classes of a society. We therefore find a social distance and prejudice pyramid (Westie and Westie, 1957), with more social distance at the bottom and less at the top of the social structure. There is also more competition for jobs between majority and minority populations at the bottom than at the top of the pyramid, which may fuel prejudice.

The extent to which government policies allow or discourage the expression of prejudice and discrimination is also an important variable. In the United States prior to 1964 it was not illegal to discriminate against groups on the basis of race, religion, nationality, and so on, and norms that were consistent with such discrimination were widely held by subgroups of society. Behaving according to norms is typical of collectivists. However, individualists were also likely at that time to follow these norms because these norms gave them various advantages (sexual, economic competition, as described by Dollard, 1937, for the American South). Inequalities of income and social position have to be justified in some way, and it is easier to justify them when a group adopts the ideology that its members are "obviously" superior in intelligence, hard work, and thrift, and that is why they are privileged.

The perceived consequences of bias against outgroups is also a factor. They can have legal (e.g., a major suit), social (e.g., acceptance by one's own group, as occurs among members of the Ku Klux Klan), and economic (e.g., boycotts) consequences. Thus although the rank order I mentioned above may be found in most societies, other factors may modify it.

Intergroup Conflict

Individualists tend to break the conflict into components, disregarding history and context. They evaluate the advantages and disadvantages of solutions and look for solutions that maximize payoffs. They like to end with a contract. They avoid discussion of vague principles and believe that everything has a price. Time is money, according to individualists. Whether the opponent likes or dislikes the contract is unimportant. The agreement must be acceptable to the majority of those who are affected. Communication emphasizes content, not context (see above).

Collectivists focus on the total picture (history, general related principles, pride, sovereignty) and many issues are nonnegotiable. Communication uses context more than content (see above). Successful negotiations require that trust first be established. Thus informal negotiations must occur before formal negotiations take place. If a contract is to be written, there should be an escape clause that ensures that disagreement will be settled by consultation rather than litigation. More time is needed for negotiations than in individualistic cultures. Collectivists usually do not show their hands in negotiations and instead wait for the other side to show its hand first. Solutions must respect nonnegotiable elements such as pride. There is evidence that during negotiations, collectivists, such as the Japanese, organize topics interdependently, whereas individualists, such as Americans, organize them more autonomously (Gudykunst, 1993, pp. 236–237).

Kirkbridge, Tang, and Westwood (1991) reported on Chinese conflict preferences. They suggested that the Chinese are especially likely to avoid conflict and to seek compromise. The Chinese are very sensitive to the status of the side with which they are negotiating and are flattered if it is more elevated than they are. Chinese negotiations tend to be formal and ritualistic. The Chinese pay much attention to the relationship and persist well beyond the patience threshold of individualists. They prefer to deal with generalities for most of the negotiation and wait until the last moment to address specifics, when concessions may be made. Thus the phases of the negotiation process are discrete, involving very different behaviors. However, whatever the phase, it is always important to give face (respect) to the other party and to emphasize holistic perspectives and harmony. The Chinese use shaming as a tactic more than individualists by pointing up inconsistencies in the arguments of their opponents.

Social Institutions

Economic Institutions

A major theory that links individualism-collectivism with work behavior was presented by Erez and Earley (1993), and Erez (1994). They called it a model of "cultural self-representation." It has four groups of variables: (1) cultural values and norms—for example, the criteria used to evaluate managerial techniques; (2) managerial and motivational techniques—especially examining their contribution to individual goal attainment, self-worth, and well-being, as evaluated in line with the cultural criteria; (3) the self as an information processor and interpreter of organizational stimuli, in line with cultural values; and (4) consequent work behavior, as exemplified by attitudes, performance quality and quantity, extra-role behavior, and commitment to or withdrawal from the job.

Erez and Earley (1993) argued that we must consider culture whenever we try to understand whether a managerial behavior will be effective. For example, a supervisor who encourages open criticism will be more acceptable in an individualistic culture, where saving face is not too important, than in a collectivist culture, where saving face is of great importance.

Other factors in the workplace have very different effects, depending on the culture. There is little need for much socialization into the job in the case of individualists and much need in the case of collectivists, who must generate a common culture that will coordinate their activities. Japanese firms typically bring a whole age group of new employees into the firm and provide extensive socialization, lasting months, often in a semimilitaristic training environment. Company songs and speeches from the top brass of the corporation are used to create maximum identification with the corporation. Zahrley and Tosi (1989) found that collective induction into the organization results in less conflict between work and family life than individual induction, which is widely practiced in individualistic cultures.

Communication is another area of difference in the two different types of cultures. It can be in writing, with a small interpersonal component in individualist cultures, but should be face-to-face in the case of collectivist cultures. Problem solving must be individual-based in the former and group-based in the latter cultures. Decision making can be based on majority vote in the former and on group consensus in the latter cultures.

Erez and Earley (1993) discussed the goals of collectives and sub-collectives and showed that the commitment of individuals to the goals of these groups is dependent on the individualism and collectivism of the culture. They recognized that collectivism has its negative aspects in organizations. One of them is that collectivists are more likely than individualists to keep important information to themselves (information is power) and not give it to members of their organizations that they see as outgroups (e.g., production people may not give crucial information to marketing people), a phenomenon documented by Triandis (1967). Collectivists compete (Espinoza and Garza, 1985) more vigorously and exploit (Pandey, 1986) outgroups even more so than do individualists. If these outgroups happen to be inside their corporation, that can be a very serious problem.

In contrast, individualists may pursue their self-interest, regardless of its implications for the collective. If getting a better job with a competitor is bad for one's former employer, that is of little concern. Individualists always look for the best "deal" they can get (Triandis, Bontempo, Villareal, et al., 1988).

The task can have an effect on individualism and collectivism and in turn may affect performance. Breer and Locke (1965) developed an eighty-three-item scale that assesses aspects of individualism and collectivism. They measured this quality after people had engaged in tasks that are disjunctive (that can be solved by one person) or conjunctive (that require everybody's contribution). They found that those who had engaged in disjunctive tasks scored higher on individualism and those who had engaged in conjunctive tasks scored higher on collectivism than corresponding control groups.

When the task requires interdependence, it is undesirable to give goals to individuals. It is better to give goals to both the group and the individuals. The reason is that goals given only to individuals make them excessively competitive and therefore less cooperative, which reduces performance (Mitchell and Silver, 1990).

Erez and Earley (1993) reviewed many empirical studies that supported their arguments. For example, the importance of different kinds of goals and feedback was supported by a study by Matsui, Kakuyama, and Onglatco (1987) that found that, in Japan, working teams with team goals rather than individual goals performed better. Team goals when used in individualistic cultures often result in social loafing and free riding. Information on both team and individual progress was helpful in increasing productivity. Thus, providing feedback on both group and individual performance was superior to providing one or another of these kinds of information only.

The importance of the task was also seen in the study by Fry, Kerr, and Lee (1986) that found that winning coaches in high interdependence sports (e.g., basketball) were more bossy than coaches who were less successful. In less interdependent sports, such as swimming and running, less coach bossiness is required.

Participation techniques used by managers are especially effective in horizontal collectivism, such as the kibbutz, and are probably least effective in vertical collectivism. Erez and Earley have done extensive research on participation and have included kibbutz samples. Three conditions were used: (1) goals are assigned, (2) goals are decided by a representative of the group, or (3) goals are decided through participation of all members of the group. Performance was quite different in U.S., Israeli urban, and Israeli kibbutz samples (Erez and Earley, 1987). Performance was more or less the same under these three conditions in the United States, a vertical individualism culture, where the assignment of goals can be accepted even though participation is desirable and has some positive effect on productivity. In Israel, a horizontal collectivist culture, performance was very different in the three conditions. In both Israeli urban and Israeli kibbutz samples it was low in the assigned goals condition and high in the participative goals condition.

Erez and Earley argued that motivational techniques that are congruent with cultural values will satisfy self-derived needs and result in high performance. Earley (1994), in both a laboratory and a field study, found that self-focused training results in self-efficacy and high performance in the United States and is less effective in China, but group-focused training leads to high self-efficacy and performance in China.

We can expect horizontal individualism or collectivism to favor an interpersonal orientation toward cooperation with fellow employees, whereas vertical individualism will not require this orientation. Erez and Earley reported a study that found that in Sweden and Japan cooperativeness was associated with the probability that the individual will be promoted; in the United States, the Netherlands, Belgium, and Germany, this correlation was not found.

During conflict resolution sessions, such as labor-management negotiations, collectivists are more influenced by their constituents than are individualists. For example, the representatives of the union are not able to deviate as much from the instructions they receive from the union's leadership or general assembly as are the representatives of management, especially if they are the owners and do not have to account to others.

The collectivist often does not distinguish self-interest and the interests of the constituents, whereas the individualist does. The individualist uses negotiation practices that highlight individual initiatives and accomplishments, which provide self-enhancement, considerably more frequently than does the collectivist.

Erez and Earley (1993) concluded their book by arguing that the West should use, not the Japanese methods of management, but methods of management that satisfy self-derived needs found in Western cultures. In short, it is not the technique per se, but the match of the technique and the culture, that makes for the success of Japan.

Consistent with the above arguments, Gudykunst (1993) reviewed communication in Japan and the United States and found it to be more informal and intimate in Japanese organizations (p. 227), especially in the downward direction, and more likely to be through vertical than horizontal information channels (p. 231) in Japan than in the United States. He found that such communication had other qualities suggesting the vertical individualism of U.S. corporations and both the horizontal collectivism (p. 231) and vertical individualism (p. 307) of Japanese corporations. Lincoln (1989) reported that frequent interaction between supervisor and subordinates is perceived positively in Japan and negatively in the United States. This is consistent with findings on child rearing, where close supervision by parents is perceived as "love" by collectivist teenagers and as "interference" by individualist teenagers.

Wang (1994), in a review of industrial and organizational psychology in the PRC, reported on practices related to the design of rewards, personnel management, testing and performance evaluation, rationalization of production procedures, and systems management that show that the Chinese are sensitive to the collectivism of their culture and have adapted their management methods to it. He argued that during the Mao period only collectivist techniques were used. In the current period both collectivist and individualist techniques are employed. For example, the Chinese now emphasize both individual and team responsibility for work accomplishment and reward not only the social contributions but also the individual contributions of employees. He reported that 84 percent of the state enterprises have set up workers' congresses that evaluate the performance of managers and supervisors. Almost 1 percent of the managers were dismissed for incompetence in 1991. The "iron rice bowl" (all were guaranteed a minimally paying job) has been replaced by more-individualistic techniques, such as an individual piece-rate bonus.

Wang also summarized his own field studies that evaluated the individual versus team reward systems in China. Under the group reward system workers tended to attribute their performance to team cooperation and collective efforts; under the individual reward system they attributed it to personal factors or the attributes of the task. He concluded that a team-oriented reward system with a clear responsibility (goal) structure is most effective in facilitating morale, cooperation, and productivity in China.

Leadership studies carried out in China have supported Misumi's (1985) theory of leadership but added one dimension to his emphasis on performance and group maintenance: moral character. The effective leader is high on all three qualities. That is, he is honest, has positive attitudes toward the enterprise, believes in team cooperation, is committed to the job and the organization, sets clear goals, and makes sure that people get to them; and he makes sure that the team has high morale by providing social support, caring about the team members' personal life, and helping team members solve their personal problems.

James and Cropanzano (in press), who developed the concept of "dispositional group loyalty" (DGL) as an aspect of collectivism, measured it in a variety of ways, including the use of collectivist items from Triandis, Bontempo, Villareal, et al. (1988). They found that the greater the DGL, the more effort individuals exerted on behalf of the group. This phenomenon is especially strong when group members are being compared with other groups. James and Cropanzano did three laboratory studies and one field study that generally supported their arguments. In the field study high DGL was associated with greater involvement in group-based organizational activities, positive attitudes toward the organization, and an inclination to perform behaviors that benefit the organization.

Among Chinese employees, Hui, Eastman, and Yee (1990) found a positive correlation between collectivism, as measured by the INDCOL scale (see the Appendix), and job satisfaction. There are several possible interpretations of this relationship. The most probable is that collectivists learn to change themselves to fit into the environment, in this case their jobs, and therefore they like their work. Other possibilities are that the individualists do not have as good interpersonal relationships on the job as do the collectivists, so they do not derive job satisfaction from good relations with fellow employees. Another possibility is that since harmony is important among collectivists, they do not want to tell a researcher that they do not like their jobs. It is likely that all these explanations are valid to some degree.

The Hui, Eastman, and Yee (1990) study is a within-culture result, which contrasts with between-cultures studies of job satisfaction in which it was generally found that collectivists have lower levels of job satisfaction than individualists (Lincoln, 1989). These lower levels are probably best explained by the importance of seeking enjoyable situations identified among individualists, the self-enhancement of individualists (since I am satisfied with myself, I must be satisfied by *my* job), and the corresponding tendency to have low self-esteem and to be worried about failures found among collectivists, which were discussed in Chapter 3.

Kashima and Callan (1994) showed how the "family" is used as the metaphor for Japanese organizations, and how this conception contrasts with the "machine" as the metaphor of organizations in the West. Redding, Norman, and Schlander (1994) examined individual attachment to organizations and showed that it is part of the explanation for the success of East Asian economies.

A final point about the influence of the culture syndromes on economic behavior was made by Han and Shavitt (1994), who found that magazine ads in the United States use more-individualistic appeals (try it, you'll like it!) and emphasize personal success, independence, and other such individualistic values, whereas comparable ads in Korea use collectivist appeals (it will satisfy your family) and emphasize harmony and family integrity themes. In an experiment, they randomly assigned individualist or collectivist subjects to advertising that used either individualistic or collectivist appeals. They found that the most persuasion, learning, and remembering occurred in the conditions where the culture of the subject matched the kind of appeal.

Health

Triandis, Bontempo, Villareal, et al. (1988) speculated that collectivism may result in lower heart attack rates. They examined data from epidemiological surveys, which showed major differences in heart attacks per 1000 inhabitants in selected samples: The lowest rate, approximately 1/1000, was found among Trappist monks. Monasteries are one of the most extreme examples of collectivism. Next, at 1.8/1000, are Japanese in Japan. A bit higher, at 3.8/1000, are Japanese in Hawaii. At the top of the list is the U.S. Caucasian population with a 9.8/1000 rate. If individualism results in almost ten times the heart attack rate of the most collectivist cultures, it is certainly worth researching the link between collectivism and heart attacks. My guess is that vertical individualism, because of the competitiveness associated with it, results in frequent hostile cognitions, associated with one of the components of type A behavior in much research, and it is this component that raises the incidence of heart attacks.

Triandis, Bontempo, Villareal, et al. (1988) also theorized that collectivists are socially more cohesive and are more likely to provide social support when unpleasant life events occur. They looked at the data from Roseto, Pennsylvania, a cohesive community that immigrated to this country as a group from the province of Foggia in Italy. The epidemiologists found a control community, Bangor, Pennsylvania, that matched Roseto in population, social class, diet, level of exercise, cholesterol levels, average weight, and so on. The Roseto heart attack rate was 5.8/1000; the Bangor rate was 9.6/1000. Social cohesion may therefore make a difference.

A third study (Marmot and Syme, 1976) intrigued Triandis, Bontempo, Villareal, et al.: It examined more than 3,000 Japanese Americans and found that the more acculturated (Americanized) the Japanese Americans were, the more likely they were to have a heart attack rate similar to that of U.S. Caucasians. Triandis, Bontempo, Villareal, et al. (1988) speculated that the emphasis on harmony and saving the other person's face in Japanese culture may reduce the vexations of everyday life.

Thus they provided a model of the determinants of disease (Figure 5.7) in which culture is responsible for different levels of social support and also for different kinds of interpretations of life events. If a member of the collective gets fired from a job, for instance, it is less devastating than if an individual who is unconnected with kin gets fired. In short, collectivist cultures pro-

FIGURE 5.7 Culture and the Determinants of Disease

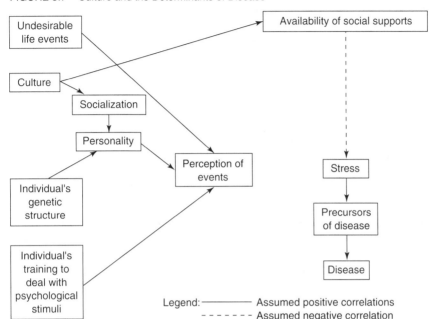

Source: H. C. Triandis, R. Bontempo, M. J. Villareal, M. Asai, and N. Lucca, "Individualism and Collectivism: Cross-Cultural Perspectives on Self-Ingroup Relationships," *Journal of Personality and Social Psychology* 54, p. 328.

vide antidotes to deal with unfortunate experiences. Triandis, Bontempo, Villareal, et al. (1988) argued that, other things being equal, collectivists will be healthier than individualists because stress in individualist cultures weakens the immune system, and that is a precursor of heart disease and other infections.

Bond (1989) examined Chinese collectivist values to ascertain whether the argument in Triandis, Bontempo, Villareal, et al. (1988) could be supported in the twenty-one countries in which he had measured these values. However, the results were rather confusing. The complicating variable is affluence. There is such a potent relationship between affluence and individualism, as well as between affluence and good medical services, that even when affluence is statistically controlled, its impact is not totally wiped out and it confuses weak relationships.

There is little doubt that social support is an important factor in good health. For example, House, Landis, and Umberson (1988) showed that the probability of death is much higher for both animals and humans who do not have social bonds. One can look at data about people who are married versus those who are unmarried and who have or do not have an extended family and see that those with social bonds have fewer accidents, fewer psychotic episodes, and more of a sense of life's meaning; they are more likely to take good care of themselves and live longer. House, Landis, and Umberson (1988) reviewed studies done among several subgroups in the United States (e.g., in California, Michigan), as well as in Finland and Sweden, which found that having relationships is a stronger predictor of death rates than is smoking.

Helgeson (1993) suggested a more complicated hypothesis concerning adjustment to a first coronary event. She dealt with "agency" (which is related to individualism) and "communion" (which is related to collectivism). Her measure of communion included agreement with items such as "I always place the needs of my family above my own," "I cannot be happy unless my family is happy," and "Even when I am exhausted I will help a friend." She argued that agency is good for the patient's adjustment and communion promotes the adjustment of the partner of the patient. Extreme agentic or communal orientation, she argued, would be bad for both patient and partner. For example, extreme agentic behavior was related to type A behavior and to longer delays before seeking help for symptoms of a heart attack. Her data generally supported her hypotheses.

Matsumoto and Fletcher (1993) reviewed studies that indicated that those individuals with the fewest social ties had the highest mortality rates; these studies supported the arguments of Triandis, Bontempo, Villareal, et al. (1988) concerning the link between collectivism and low heart attack rates. They then chose Hofstede's (1980) dimensions and obtained data on the incidence of six different types of diseases—infectious and parasitic diseases, malignant neoplasms, circulatory system diseases, heart diseases, cerebrovascular diseases, and respiratory system diseases—at five different age points in the life span. They found that power distance (i.e., the vertical dimension of our four cultural patterns) was related to the rates of infections and parasitic diseases across the five age points. The means of these diseases were high in those cultures that were high in power distance. Individualistic cultures had lower rates of these diseases than collectivist cultures. Cultures scoring high on power distance also had lower rates of malignant neoplasms and a lower incidence of heart disease.

Since power distance and collectivism are correlated, the findings for cancer and heart disease were as expected by Triandis, Bontempo, Villareal, et al. (1988). But the findings for the infectious diseases were inconsistent with these predictions. The researchers had speculated that collectivism would be associated with lower stress, and since stress suppresses the immune system, collectivists should have lower rates of infectious disease. However, in most studies of this type, factors are not equal, so it is difficult to draw firm conclusions. Nevertheless, this research area is likely to lead to some important findings in the future, as we develop detailed ways to measure individualism and collectivism in different cultures and connect these measurements with health indices.

A topic of great importance in the health area is psychotherapy. Here we find that therapists in the United States make individualistic assumptions. A survey by Fowers and Tredinnick (mimeo) examined the assumptions made by 206 practicing psychotherapists. They found that 46 percent were utilitarian individualists (if it works, let the individual do what he wishes) and 30 percent were expressive individualists (let the patient seek authenticity, spontaneity). Three-quarters of them were individualists, 10 percent were collectivists, and 14 percent were communitarian (see Chapter 2 for description of this position). Thus, U.S. psychotherapists are more likely to be effective with mainstream Americans than with minority populations, such as collectivist Asian Americans or Hispanic Americans. Marsella (1993) advised how to counsel Japanese Americans, who take their collectivism very seriously.

However, in the case of serious mental illness, the bases seem to be organic and genetic, not cultural. This is the conclusion from a study by Eaton and Weil (1955), who examined the incidence of psychopathology among the Hutterites, a highly collectivist, low-stress, stable, "utopian" community, in which there were no problems associated with cultural disintegration. Eaton and Weil found a broad spectrum of mental disorders in that community.

J. B. P. Sinha and Verma (1990), working with normal populations in India, found that allocentrics who receive social support are more likely than idiocentrics to have good mental health (psychological well-being). They used the %S measure (see the Appendix) and the allocentrism scale of Triandis, Bontempo, Betancourt, et al. (1986) and also asked whether the person preferred to do things alone or with others. In addition to the set of questions, they asked the respondent if his behavior corresponded most often to his own desires or those of others. Finally, they measured social support, well-being, and self-ratings of the extent to which respondents behaved in typically collectivist ways.

They found significant correlations of .20 between %S and collectivist attitudes, and .23 between %S and reported collectivist actions. When respondents reported receiving high social support, the %S scores correlated (in the .50 to .70 range) with (1) freedom from a sense of frustration, (2) cheerfulness, (3) optimism, (4) playfulness, and (5) psychological well-being. Allocentric attitudes correlated with well-being measures in the .49 to .60 range. Preference for being with others correlated with well-being measures in the .33 to .60 range. But when the respondents reported receiving no social support, all these correlations vanished. Thus, in a culture where receiving social support is expected, if one does not receive it, collectivism is unrelated to well-being.

Tata and Leong (1993) used measures of collectivism and other personality scales to predict the attitudes of Chinese Americans toward seeking professional psychological help. In that sample, they found that those who were individualistic (high in self-reliance) did not seek psychological help. About 15 percent of the variance in help-seeking attitude was explained by individualism.

Religion

In collectivist cultures religion takes the form of group worship. Personal salvation is often linked to what happens to relatives, and membership in religious institutions is essential for social life. In fact, it is unthinkable that one would not share the same religion with that of the collective. Thus, it seems "natural" to exterminate those who are apostates, rebels, blasphemes, and so forth. Thousands of examples, such as the Inquisition, the Salman Rushdie affair, and the persecution of religious minorities are testimonies to the way collectivism may affect religion.

However, India, though quite religious and collectivist, generally tolerates deviations from orthodoxy. The collectivism sometimes results in intercommunal fights, but given the tremendous variety of religious positions, there is tolerance. An explanation may be the difference between monotheism, which postulates only one "truth," and polytheism, which allows multiple truths. India is also interesting because the opposite of a great truth can also be true, since philosophical monism is widely held and allows every contradiction to be part of the same broad reality. Furthermore, in India individual attributes are embedded in specific situations. One can be a "vegetarian who eats meat" (i.e., be a vegetarian in most situations, but when other people eat meat, then one eats meat). Thus, even religious beliefs and practices may be seen as embedded in situations.

Perhaps even more fundamental is Joseph Campbell's point (see Chapter 2) that planters assume continuity—a dead plant is the fertilizer for the next one. Hunters tend to see discontinuities—the animal that was alive is now dead. Western religions, with their source in the mythologies of hunters, are more likely to focus on contrasts, such as God and Man, God and the Devil, good and bad, feast and famine. The Eastern religions, with their source in the mythologies of planters, see everything as being related to everything else in a continuous process of change and renewal.

In addition, many of the guiding principles of East Asian cultures are not really religious in the same sense as those of the West. Confucius provided a philosophy of life. The essence is proper action rather than faith, worship of God, or knowing "the truth." Hofstede (1991) offfered a good analysis along these lines.

Individualists see religious beliefs and salvation as personal; they do not need to worship with others. They do not require intermediaries such as the church and priests. The emphasis is on one's own relationship with the divine or with the deities. Some doctrines, such as the Calvinist notion of predestination, are excellent motivators toward becoming rich (Weber, 1930, 1958) and thus extremely compatible with individualism. Affluence allows the individuals to do as they wish, and the more that is accomplished, the better the chance that some investments will lead to more affluence and thus allow even more individualism.

This does not imply that one cannot become affluent in collectivist cultures. Economic decisions, though, must be made freely and cannot require the consent of the whole ingroup. The Japanese have found an effective way to be collectivists and make independent judgments about investments. It is also interesting to note that Gallup polls reported that the Japanese are among the least religious people on earth, with the lowest rates of regular attendance at a place of collective worship.

Politics

In collectivist cultures the political system is conceived as a way to preserve the collective, often in the form of the state, but also possibly the political party. Individual rights are secondary to collective prerogatives. Political parties can be conceived as ingroups in constant opposition to other parties that are outgroups. The more collectivist the individuals involved, the less they are willing to agree to a good proposal of the other political party. If the other party has an idea that will clearly benefit the country, it must be shot down or else it will give the outgroup too much advantage in the next elections.

One of the goals of a politician who assumes power is to enrich the ingroups to which he or she belongs. This includes one's family, friends, and party, but also all those who are introduced to the leader as good friends of his or her friends. To do any "business" in the bureaucracies of most collectivist countries requires personal contacts. One must find someone who knows someone, someone who knows the bureaucrat who will make the decision. The merits of the case are often irrelevant. What matters is that the ingroup must benefit.

In individualistic cultures the political system is designed to satisfy individual needs. The state has relatively limited control over individuals. Individual rights are protected, although an emphasis on individual liberties can lead to situations where individuals disregard the good of the country. For example, during World War II, Americans refused to conserve oil because they found it inconvenient to car pool! (Yergin, 1992).

It also means that rational laws, such as the one requiring the use of safety belts in cars, may be rejected or disobeyed in individualistic cultures if such laws are perceived as restricting freedom or one's personal rights. An interesting case was described by Demick et al. (1992), comparing Massachusetts with Hiroshima (Japan). Before the safety belt law was introduced, there was an increase in the use of belts in both sites. Although the user rates remained constant or increased after the law was passed in both Hiroshima and Massachusetts, in the latter the law was contested. The percentage that used safety belts in Massachusetts before the law was passed was 25 percent (highway driving). It went to 58 percent after the law was passed, to 63 percent a month later, and then complaints surfaced that mandatory safety belt legislation was an invasion of privacy and an infringement of human rights. Ten months later the legislation was repealed, and usage rates returned to around 25 percent. Massachusetts, along with some other New England states, still does not require seat belts.

No such changes occurred in Hiroshima, where the law was accepted. The Hiroshima percentages for highway driving were 55 percent before the law was passed, 76 percent after it was passed, 81 percent a month later, 73 percent nine months later, at which point the law required the use of belts in both the city and on the highway, and the rate went to 98 percent. Two years after the law was passed, almost all the Japanese used belts, whereas less than one-third did in Massachusetts. Kashima (personal communication, January 1994) reported that compliance in Australia is close to 100 percent. This may indicate that it is vertical individualism rather than individualism per se that leads to individuals' wanting to have the freedom not to use the belts.

As we discussed in Chapter 4, individualism is linked to modernity. Giddens (1991) argued that modernity produces specialization that causes differentiation from others, exclusion of the less competent, and marginalization of those who cannot compete or adapt to the new social environments. People need to learn new skills and occupations, which separate them from family members, which often leads to meaninglessness, and that results in high rates of divorce, the risk of living alone, children that remain unsupervised and are neglected (Pilisuk and Parks, 1985), and even narcissism. The narcissist does not attend to the important issues of the day but rather turns inward: "Bosnia is too complex for me to deal with, so I will work on my diet and exercise program." Modernity can exist to the exclusion of a historical sense and of belonging to groups.

Modernity and individualism often result in racial, religious, and ethnic tolerance, which is certainly desirable for intergroup peace. However, they also lead to diversity in marital relationships, and that seems to be detrimental to the stability of the marriage. For example, Carter and Glick (1970) examined U.S. census data to see if people who were married in 1950 were also married in 1970. They found that 90 percent of the white-white pairs were still together; 78 percent of the black-black pairs were together; 65

percent of the black man–white woman pairs survived; 47 percent of the white man–black women pairs survived. Similar results were found for differences in age, education, national origin, and religion. In short, the more diverse the marital unit, the higher the probability of divorce. Since divorce results in a 70 percent decrease in the standard of living of the women and a 30 percent increase in the standard of living of men (Donohue, 1990), and since children generally remain with their mothers, it seems that divorce plunges many children into poverty, which can hardly be desirable for a society. The extreme image is that of women and children living in poverty while men are driving expensive sports cars.

Democratic societies have a way of swinging from right to left, say from the individualism of Ronald Reagan or Brian Mulroney to the mild collectivism of Bill Clinton or Jean Cretien. Brown (1990) analyzed the situation in Britain and commented about the swing from the collectivism of the Labor party to the acquisitive individualism of the 1980s. World War II had cemented relationships because there was a common interest and common fate was salient. The Labor party emerged. But as nationalization resulted in inefficiency and in the lack of competitiveness of British products worldwide, the pendulum swung to Margaret Thatcher and nineteenth-century liberalism and laissez-faire. Unions lost much of their power, and self-employment increased. A similar pattern can be seen in the Reagan era, which was then followed by the Clinton victory.

Hillhouse (1993) argued that the shift from collectivism to individualism led to the demise of the German Democratic Republic. The Berlin Wall fell because individualism had developed among tens of thousands of citizens involved in social movements within the state, party, and church. The East German political culture changed as hundreds of voluntary associations, based on religion, music, and sexual orientation, emerged. In addition, consumerism, with its emphasis on choice among products, had an irresistible influence, as the East Germans watched West German television advertising goods they were deprived of. As the wife of the Hungarian minister of culture explained to a Western visitor, "Communism came down because we all wanted to go shopping!" (Rosabeth Cantor, in a lecture at the American Psychological Association meeting in 1992).

Hillhouse (1993) argued, in agreement with our discussion in Chapter 3, that increased pluralism and choice result in individuals with multiple identities, which are managed by the individual. She noted that attitude surveys carried out in East Germany during the period 1962–1990 show strong intergenerational value changes that correspond to a shift from collectivism to individualism. This shift resulted in democratization. Not all aspects of this shift were relevant to this political change. The shift toward consumerism was politically neutral, but the fact that the state refused to change its economic policies and provide consumer goods had important implications for the waning support citizens gave to their state. She argued then that the shift toward individualism opened the possibility of democracy, which, combined with other factors in both the USSR and West Germany, culminated in the toppling of the Berlin Wall.

This case is especially interesting because East Germany was the most successful of the Marxist-Leninist states, having relatively abundant consumer goods and the highest living standard. It was also the "only place in Eastern Europe where Marxism was taken seriously by a surprisingly large number within the population" (Hillhouse, 1993, p. 1). Yet in 1989, two-fifths of the population demonstrated against the state. Had this happened in the former USSR, there would have been 110 million demonstrators! Hillhouse pointed out that when the Politburo passed down the decision to fire on the demonstrators in Leipzig, in the fall of 1989, members of East German society, including the military, stood up and were able to prevent a slaughter. This was different from 1953 when the troops fired on striking workers. Something radical had happened between 1953 and 1989: The society had become more individualistic. One of the changes was that gross national income per capita increased by 800 percent (we have already established a link between affluence and individualism).

In her analysis, Hillhouse placed the greatest weight on the number of important ingroups present. Whereas in the 1950s, the party was the only ingroup, the 1980s saw hundreds of ingroups. In totalitarian states, such as the Nazi and Communist ones, the party makes a serious attempt to eliminate other ingroups and uses purges to expel any interior ingroups. The East German party, though, allowed numerous ingroups to flourish within itself. These groups were concerned with gardening, hobbies, hiking, environmental issues, jazz, gay and lesbian rights, and so forth. Each city had its own club that was nominally part of the Communist Youth Organization but in fact had very different norms. By 1986 there were 10,144 clubs and 5,785 interest groups within the organization. In addition, the Evangelical church had about 200 identity-based groups, concerned with issues such as the environment and feminism. Some groups included mostly handicapped persons, pacifists, or human rights activists. The pluralism that developed resulted in a situation where each ingroup provided only a fraction of the total social support or norms directing behavior. Individuation, the shift toward individualism, is a consequence of multiple ingroups. Multiple ingroups fragment social controls over an individual.

Hillhouse provided a case study of how the East Germany Politburo dealt with homosexuality. The Politburo received a report advocating that homosexuals be allowed to form their own groups within the Communist Youth Organization. The report made three arguments: (1) The party needs to keep an estimated 750,000 homosexuals from joining its rival institution, the Evangelical church, which has gay and lesbian programs. (2) If the state does not provide a place for them, they may emigrate to the West. (3) The state should provide such organizations; otherwise these people will engage in indiscriminate sexual behavior that will increase the spread of the AIDS virus. The East German Politburo approved the gay and lesbian clubs within the Communist Youth Organization.

In the former Soviet Union and its satellites, a similar set of phenomena is taking place. Powerful forces are locked into combat: the urge toward affluence and consumer goods on the one hand and the reaching for solidarity on the other. The Russian parliament, with twelve parties, provides multiple ingroups. Yet the so-called Liberal Democrats have a leader who wants to eliminate all parties.

Opinion surveys carried out in the USSR in 1985 (Umpleby, 1990) showed considerable vertical collectivism, even among elite student samples. It would be interesting to gauge radical changes in recent years. The 1985 Soviet students agreed with the statements shown below. The statements with which American students agreed in 1985 appear in parenthesis. "Human beings are unable to rule themselves, and their government should rule them" (should rule themselves); "government is necessary to provide basic stability" (best government is least government); "power must be centralized; what is not permitted is forbidden" (what is not forbidden is permitted); "the good things in life are provided by government" (by private sector); "efficiency is maximized by concentrating expertise in a single location" (by decentralization); "the customer is a supplicant" (is the boss); "the quality of goods is determined by the supplier" (by the market); "freedom permits chaos" (individual self-realization); "people should act to maximize the common good" (the pursuit of self-interest is the engine of progress); "the constitution should state what governments must do" (cannot do); "dissent is an expression of egoism" (an inalienable right); "the heroic person confronts the opponents" (compromises); "where there are four issues under dispute, a 'compromise' means that you win two and the other side wins two" (you find in-between positions on four issues).

Each political system balances between too much control by the state and too little. The equilibrium point that will be most satisfying depends on the position of the most frequently found citizen on individualism and collectivism. Democracy requires individualism. In those areas where collectivism is most strongly present, such as in Africa, there are few examples of democratic regimes. Although the Nigerian parliament architecture mimics that of the British House of Commons, it fails as an institution. Liberal democracy requires a particular cultural and psychological basis.

     ✿   ✿   ✿

In this chapter we have seen that the effects of individualism and collectivism on individuals, groups, organizations, and societies are manifested in various ways. We have yet to discover many of the ways these influences take place. In Chapter 6 we will examine some applications of the constructs, such as what can be done to train individuals from the many strains of individualist and collectivist cultures in order to avoid misunderstandings and become effective in working together.

6

Applications: Training People to Work Well Together

I HAVE ARGUED ELSEWHERE (Triandis, 1994) that all humans are ethnocentric. Ethnocentricity is an aspect of the human condition because we are raised in our own culture and see the world through categories provided by our culture. It is only when we come in contact with other cultures that we can begin realizing that we are ethnocentric. But this realization does not change our perspective entirely. All that happens is that we become slightly less ethnocentric. The more we are trained to look at the world through the eyes of other cultures, the less ethnocentric we are, but I doubt that there are any humans who are not ethnocentric.

Cross-cultural misunderstandings are very common. We tend to ignore subtle factors, for example, that the color green is "good" in many countries influenced by the Ottoman Empire and "bad" in those countries dominated by that empire. Ichheiser (1970), in his most insightful book, which anticipated Heider and many other major social psychologists, pointed out that what is taken for granted escapes our attention. Our *Kulturbrille* (cultural glasses) filter out some facts and sensitize us to other facts. Many of our conceptions are self-deceptions that serve us well. For example, if we believe that "crocodiles devour only those who have sinned," we feel relatively safe on the basis of the logic "I have not sinned, so the crocodiles will not get me," which reduces anxiety and makes life livable. This also leads to the "just world" phenomenon: "It served him right to be devoured; he must have sinned." Our perceptions of other cultures are often linked to such self-deceptions. One way to reduce our ethnocentrism is to be trained to see the world as members of other cultures see it, and that is done through cross-cultural training.

Cross-cultural training is by now a somewhat developed field of social science and continues to develop rapidly to increased sophistication. A three-volume handbook (Landis and Brislin, 1983) summarized how this training can be done, when, where, by whom, and with what effects. A book by Brislin and Yoshida (1994), which used the individualism and collectivism constructs, would be a good introduction for those who wish to have more information than is provided in the present chapter.

In this chapter I will provide a brief overview of this field and concentrate on the details of how to train the different kinds of individualists and collectivists to work together effectively. "Work together" should be interpreted broadly to include all kinds of relationships, including marital, salesman-customer, missionary–local resident, politician-citizen, teacher-student, artist-public, and so forth.

Overview

It is possible to learn about other cultures by reading books, seeing films, spending time with members of other cultures, participating in various simulations or exercises, hearing lectures, and in many other ways. More detailed discussions of the various ways to train can be found in Brislin (1993b) and Triandis (1977, 1994). Each of these ways is somewhat effective, but none is especially effective by itself. A combination of methods is highly recommended.

In general, methods that require the trainee to become involved, change behavior, and practice new behaviors are more effective than methods that only require that the trainee become aware of a cultural difference (Jackson and Associates, 1992). It is also desirable to stress the extent to which people *within* cultures are different from each other (i.e., Japan may appear homogeneous, but the Japanese are in fact heterogeneous, especially on the urban-rural dimension). Moreover, even though it is convenient to describe a culture in terms of its central tendencies, there is much variation around those central tendencies.

Some of the methods concentrate on understanding one's own culture on the assumption that then one will be able to learn about all other cultures. One technique (E. Stewart, 1966) that has been used to train Americans required them to interact with "Contrast-Americans" (actors who behave in the opposite way from the manner usually used by Americans). Videotapes of the interaction are then viewed and discussed. One of the many themes included in this training is American individualism and how it contrasts with the vertical collectivism found in many cultures U.S. military advisers are likely to work with. This has the effect of making the Americans realize that they do have a culture and what it is. Of course, the technique can be adapted to any culture.

Other methods focus on learning how to get along with people from many cultures (culture-general training). Some methods concentrate on learning how to communicate with members of very specific cultures—for example, Japanese middle managers (culture-specific training). In the culture-general training, one gets an idea of the kinds of ways in which cultures differ. In the culture-specific training, one learns how a particular culture is different from one's own culture.

Another way of classifying methods of cultural training broadly is by their cognitive, affective, or behavioral emphasis (Triandis, 1977). In the cognitive method, one is trained to *understand* cultural differences. In the affective method, the focus is on *feeling good* about members of the other culture, even though they are different. In the behavioral, the emphasis is on changing the trainee's *behavior,* so that it will not offend, and if possible will charm, the members of the other culture.

Howell (1982) identified four stages of cultural learning. In the first, the individual is unconsciously incompetent (makes a lot of errors and does not know it); in the second, the person is consciously incompetent (knows he is making a mess, but does not know what to do); in the third, the trainee has reached conscious competence (knows what to do, but has to keep vigilant so as to do it because the behavior is not yet a habit); in the fourth, the trainee is unconsciously competent (the correct behavior is under habit control). Without cross-cultural training, people are in the first of these phases. After cognitive training they are in the third stage. After additional training, including opportunities to practice the correct behavior, they reach the last phase.

The settings in which cross-cultural training takes place are many. Some corporations do their training in special training centers, sometimes called "universities" with the corporation name. Most send their employees to special training centers or bring consultants into the corporation to train them. Religious groups sometimes train those they will send to other countries as missionaries. Educational systems train their personnel in special sessions. The military does a great deal of cross-cultural training. Relative to the needs for cross-cultural training, however, very little training takes place, primarily because those who make training decisions think that it is not needed or that they cannot afford it. Some suspect that it is not effective, though the evidence is that it is (Black and Mendenhall, 1990; Deshpande and Viswesvaran, 1992).

Japanese and Korean corporations generally do more training than U.S. corporations. Some Korean corporations train their expatriates for one year, at full salary. This training includes language and culture training and extensive interactions with members of the other culture.

Corporations in collectivist countries generally train their employees much more than do corporations in individualistic countries. Two factors are responsible: First, collectivism increases the loyalty of the employees toward the corporation. It is economical to invest in employees who will stay with the firm for a long time and will not go work for its competitors. Individualists may move to the competitor if the other firm offers them more benefits or a better salary. Also, since individualists are more mobile, they are likely to leave the firm. Second, collectivist firms have a strong corporate culture that they want their employees to share. The corporate culture of firms in individualistic cultures is generally less widely shared. This difference may be traced to the preference, among collectivists, for homogeneous (like-minded) ingroups and their expectations that behavior is a consequence of norms. Training to acquire the same norms, then, is very important for collectivists. Thus, corporate policies in collectivist countries favor the creation of a common perspective and clear norms much more than in individualistic countries.

Some training takes place before the expatriate leaves; other training takes place after arrival in the host culture. Some specialists advocate giving some basic training before departure and more training after arrival in the host country.

Types of Training

Experiential Training

Experiential training is a trial-and-error method in which the trainee spends time with members of the other culture and learns how to get along with them. It has the advantage that it does not require consultants and trainers and has much face validity (appears appropriate even though it may not be). Its disadvantage is that the trainee can become discouraged, offend members of the other culture, and may even experience culture shock (Furnham and Bochner, 1986; Oberg, 1954, 1960).

Culture shock can take many forms, such as mild to severe depression and psychosomatic disorders and may even result in suicide. Bochner (1994) distinguished "push" (stressful) and "pull" (regret about leaving own culture) factors. The following are the push factors:

1. You have to watch your step, try to figure out what it all means, worry about being offensive, ripped off, or humiliated. You are uncertain that you are acting appropriately.
2. You feel helpless and unsure you will be able to cope.
3. You are confused about your role; your professional and social skills seem to you to be inadequate.
4. You discover local customs you find disgusting (for some this would include spitting on the floor or in a handkerchief, beating dogs, circumcising young girls, eating the eyes of sheep, or hanging animal heads as hunting trophies on the walls) and feel guilty that you cannot control your disgust.

The following are the pull factors:

1. You may suffer a loss of status. This is especially likely when people from developing countries come to the West. People do not realize that you are the son of a chief or that you are thought to have supernatural powers by your own people.
2. You miss your friends, your family, your cat and generally become homesick.
3. You miss places, climate, symbols, landmarks that you are used to.
4. You miss the conveniences (such as supermarkets, telephone service, help from the community) of your country.

These factors can lead to a sense of panic, a fear that one will not be able to cope with the new environment, and a feeling of worthlessness. Depression and even suicide can result. Returning home before the assignment abroad has been completed occurs in about half the cases of U.S. executives who have not received cross-cultural training. The cost can be as high as a quarter of a million dollars or more per executive for salary and moving expenses. The emotional and goodwill costs are also high. Employees can suffer from reduced self-esteem as a result of letting the company down, and the company can be humiliated in the eyes of its associates abroad.

One form of training of this type that can be recommended is placing members of the two cultures into situations that are enjoyable. For example, a good meal can result in good feelings (Razran, 1940). Programs that include traveling together, eating together, partying together, and so on have their place in cross-cultural training.

Simulations and Exercises

Trainers have developed many simulations of cross-cultural interaction (Pedersen, 1994). Descriptions can be found in Landis and Brislin (1983). Trainees play various games and do a good deal of role playing. However, there is as yet little research on the effectiveness of these methods.

Culture Assimilator Training

The culture assimilator training method, which was developed in the 1960s for the U.S. Navy (Fiedler, Mitchell, and Triandis, 1971), has been tested with experimental and control groups and has been shown to be effective (Albert, 1983). It consists of the presentation of a scenario or critical incident in which members of two cultures interact.

In this section I will use as an example the situation in which the trainees are from an individualistic culture and the training attempts to teach them how to be effective when interacting with members of a collectivist culture. In such a case, the episode would describe an interaction between a collectivist and an individualist. The learners are asked to examine the episode and make a judgment concerning the causes (attributions) of the behavior of the member from the collectivist culture. Four or five attributions are presented, and they are selected, based on research, in such a way that most of them are frequently used by individualists and only one of the attributions is usually favored by collectivists.

During the construction of assimilators, each episode and the corresponding attributions are judged by samples from the two cultures, and when there is a statistically significant tendency for a difference between the attributions chosen by members of the two different cultures, the episode and the corresponding attributions are included in the culture assimilator. In this step those episodes and attributions that are not perceived differently by members of the two cultures are discarded. Assimilators usually include about 100 episodes and their attributions, but to obtain that many episodes, those who construct assimilators usually begin with twice that number.

Once the trainee has chosen an attribution as the probable explanation of what happened in the episode, he or she receives feedback in the form of "turn to p. x to see if your guess is correct." If the trainee has chosen the wrong attribution, the feedback simply says, "Try again." If the correct attribution was selected, the feedback is half a page or so and provides several clues about the other culture and the way members of that culture look upon their social environment. Thus, it is possible to teach the trainees to make the kinds of attributions about social behavior that members of the other culture make about their own behavior. This broadens the trainee's perspective.

To avoid creating stereotypes, some assimilators (e.g., Albert's on Hispanic culture) also include the percentage of the subjects in the pretest groups who selected a particular attribution. For example, in the case of a particular wrong attribution, it may say, "Only 7 percent of our Hispanic sample chose this explanation." In the case of a correct attribution, it may say, "When we pretested this attribution, we found that 85 percent of our Hispanic sample thought that it was the best choice." Such statements have the advantage that they show that Hispanics may at times pick an attribution that the trainee selected, but that they are not likely to do so, and it is better for the trainee to keep checking the attributions until the correct one is identified. Empirical evidence reviewed by Albert (1983) indicated that people who have been trained with this method feel more comfortable in the other culture and are less likely to experience culture shock.

The training can be culture-general (e.g., Brislin et al., 1986) or culture-specific (assimilators have been developed for specific cultures listed in Albert, 1983, Appendix). The impact of the culture-general assimilator has been found to be substantial. It was helpful in improving the adjustment of students from collectivist cultures to New Zealand, an individualistic culture (Cushner, 1989).

Fox (1993) developed a twenty-five-episode assimilator for members of individualist and collectivist cultures to learn about each other, especially taking gender issues into account. The advantages of this method of training are that (1) once the assimilator has been constructed, it can be used with thousands of trainees; (2) it is effective, and its validity is assured by the way it is constructed; (3) the trainees can make mistakes without offending members of the other culture and in private, thus without being embarrassed; (4) the trainees have a sense of progress, as they are able to pick the correct attribution while progressing through the assimilator; (5) some people (especially those who like puzzles) find this method of learning engaging.

The disadvantages are (1) the cost of production, which can be substantial, since it requires extensive interviews with bicultural people who can supply episodes and attributions, tests of samples from the two cultures to find out if the cultures differ in the kinds of attributions they make, editing of the episodes, and printing of the assimilator, and (2) some trainees find working with a book too much like "schoolwork," and prefer methods of training that include interpersonal contact.

If funds are available, putting the assimilator information on an interactive software makes it a bit more like interaction with actual members of the other culture. In this case, actors can be videotaped while they portray the events in the episode. This has the advantage that "mistakes" such as using the "wrong" tone of voice, gestures, body posture, eye movements, and distance between the bodies can be included in the assimilator. The attributions can then be presented on the computer screen, and the trainee can select the correct one by using the computer keyboard. The feedback can be made more graphic by having the actors give it in the form of criticism or approval.

Unfortunately, at the present time, interactive computer technologies are expensive. The costs of employing the actors, plus the equipment, means that an investment of a quarter of a million dollars may be needed. However, if a large number of people are to be trained, that may not be an impossible obstacle.

Behavior Modification

In this procedure a trainer is present to criticize the trainee whenever a behavior is inappropriate and to praise the trainee for correct behaviors. Thus, the trainee's behavior is shaped to become appropriate for interaction in the other culture. The method has the advantage that it is very effective. However, it is expensive, since a trainer is required to work with the trainee.

Combinations of Methods

We do not yet have research on the optimal combination of methods. One guess is that frustrating the trainees by placing them in experiential learning settings, where they make a lot of mistakes, may increase their motivation, at which point they will be especially receptive to the assimilator. After they have learned what behaviors are correct, the behavior modification approach may be used to "stamp in" the correct behaviors.

Evaluation of the Effectiveness of Training

In my opinion, training should be evaluated and modified as a result of the evaluation. There are two kinds of evaluation procedures: formative and summative. Formative evaluation is done while the training is developing, and the information is used to modify the training. Summative evaluation is done at the end of the training, often by an independent observer, since the trainer may be biased in favor of the training.

The ideal evaluation is one that randomly assigns trainees to training and no-training (or later training) conditions and measures the effects of training as the difference between the two conditions. Detailed discussions about evaluation can be found in Triandis (1977).

Measuring before and after the training must be done carefully. If the training is given after the trainee has learned to avoid making mistakes in the new culture, it will look as if it is more effective than it really is. A related complication is that there is often a U-curve relationship between time spent in the other culture and how one feels in a new environment (Furnham and Bochner, 1986). Usually, people feel rather good when they first arrive at a new culture because they are received by colleagues and may live in a hotel where the environment is more or less the one they already know. It is after they have to cope with the new culture that they may experience culture shock. Thus they go from feeling good to feeling bad. When they learn how to cope with the new culture, they go back to feeling good. In fact, the sequence may well be good, bad, very bad, bad, good, very good. If the U-curve is present, the measurements of performance will be contaminated: Measuring training during the down part of the curve suggests that training harms performance; measuring it on the up side of the curve makes the training look more effective than it really was.

What should be measured in order to evaluate the training? One of the best measures was developed by Bhawuk and Brislin (1992). It consists of forty-six items (reliability $r = .84$), similar in format to the episodes of culture assimilators. Each item examines behaviors relevant for collectivists operating in an individualistic culture. The test measures whether a collectivist knows how to behave in individualistic cultures and whether an indi-vidualist knows how to behave when interacting with a person from a collec-tivist culture. For example, disagreeing with others in the United States is scored as "good" and doing so in Japan is scored as "bad." The test also mea-sures the open-mindedness of a person concerning cultural differences and the person's flexibility concerning behaving in unfamiliar ways that call upon norms of other cultures.

The test was given to visitors to the East-West Center, in Hawaii, where there are numerous visitors from Asia. Those who received high scores were rated by members of the staff of the East-West Center as more effec-tive in adjusting to American culture than those who received low scores. The high scorers enjoyed working on complex tasks requiring intercultural interaction, enjoyed eating different kinds of foods, and often had spent three or more years in another culture. A factor analysis of the items showed that people use the collectivism and individualism constructs when interact-ing with members of their own and other cultures. Thus, it is possible to use the constructs to teach people to interact more effectively with members of other cultures.

Multimethod measurement of the adjustment of expatriates is highly rec-ommended. In fact more than one method should be used to understand (1) how the person feels about being in the new culture, (2) how the person's spouse and significant others feel about the expatriate being in that culture, (3) how the person's colleagues from both cultures feel about the person's interpersonal skills, (4) how the person's objective performance is evaluated in the head office and in the local office abroad, and (5) how successfully the expatriate has developed friendships and other relationships that are consis-tent with the job.

It is important also to keep in mind that judges providing criterion mea-sures have their own biases. For example, people in the head office often do not understand the conditions in the field, and even if they have visited the field, they see matters from the point of view of tourists rather than from that of people who live in the culture.

The culture of the corporation can interact with the measurements. Some U.S. corporations use the philosophy that their subsidiaries abroad should be exact copies of the home office. For example, the accounting firm of Ar-thur Andersen argued that its clients are buying "American expertise" when they use them as consultants, and thus the firm had to maintain American culture all over, from Argentina to Zambia. This strategy has the advantage that communications within the corporation are very good because people think alike and use the same assumptions. In contrast, it may not be optimal for firms that have to sell in the local market. The difference between the American culture of the office in Buenos Aires and the people they want to sell to can impede the effectiveness of the sales. If the culture of the corporation is the culture the expatriate knows well, that makes adjustment easier, and the measurements should show that.

Other corporations such as ITT take the position that each subsidiary should develop its own culture that is appropriate in the specific setting in which it operates. ITT went as far as to let its German subsidiaries side with Germany and its British subsidiaries side with Britain during World War II. This strategy is bound to endear the company to the local population but will create problems of communication between head office and subsidiaries. Corresponding to this difference is the need to train everyone to absorb the company culture or provide a lot of manuals and other communications that tell the local people how to operate, but to allow the local people to use their own interpretations of how the company rules are to be implemented. In that case an ITT employee from New York would have difficulties adjusting to the local culture, and the measurements should show that.

One can argue that when the company culture and the local culture are compatible, there will be fewer difficulties for the local company. For example, it is reported in the press that Japanese companies operating in the United States are involved in an unusually large number of lawsuits brought about by female employees. Both male and female employees, even though they are selected as among the more collectivist Americans, are individualists and find some of the demands for sacrifice for the company impossible to comply with (Graen and Wakabayashi, 1994).

If there is a difference between the two cultures, how should the culture of the company be related to the culture of the nation? Here the tight-loose dimension is especially significant. If the national culture is tight, it may be desirable to keep the company culture a bit loose, in order to soften the harshness of everyday life. Conversely, if the national culture is loose, it may be optimal to provide a somewhat tight culture to compensate for that. Thus, the rule seems to be: Try to be as similar as possible, but to the extent that you are different, be different by *complementing* the national culture.

Training Collectivists to Interact with Individualists and Vice Versa

In the modern world, one of the most frequent types of cross-cultural interaction is between people from collectivist and people from individualistic cultures. Not only is the East-West relationship very important, but also many of the people who move from traditional cultures to modern information societies are collectivists. Thus, training each group to interact more effectively with the other is going to be an increasingly important activity.

I will review aspects of this training by organizing it around the four defining attributes of collectivism. Then, I will mention some additional topics that should be covered.

Self-Definition

Since collectivists define themselves as members of groups and individualists define themselves as autonomous entities, individualists are likely to ignore information about the group memberships of collectivists, and that might result in incorrect judgments. For example, an individualist might ask a collectivist to work with a colleague of the "wrong" status. It is desirable for individualists to be trained to look for and learn about the attitudes and norms of the authorities of the collectivist's ingroups, since collectivists are likely to get guidance from ingroups more than is typical in individualist cultures.

Conversely, the collectivists may add information about groups in perceiving the actions of individualists, information that has no applicability to these individuals. For example, the collectivist might not have scheduled an important meeting, thinking that the individualist would visit his mother on Mother's Day, when in fact the individualist only called his mother on the phone that day.

Goals

Collectivists need to learn that individualists give priority to their personal goals when these goals are in conflict with group goals. Conversely, individualists must learn that the personal goals of collectivists often overlap with the goals of their collectives, and when they do not, collectivists are quite likely to subordinate their personal goals to those of the collective.

Norms

Since collectivists use mostly norms to explain behavior and individualists use mostly internal attributes, misunderstandings can occur. For example, the collectivist's norm may be that people must attend certain events, such as funerals of all colleagues, whereas the individualist's belief is that one attends only the funerals of colleagues one liked. Conversely, the individualist may have a negative attitude about people who smoke, whereas the collectivist sees nothing wrong with smoking, as long as the norm allows it.

One of the obvious differences in classrooms is that vertical collectivists rarely ask questions, but individualists often do. Individualist teachers often feel upset that the vertical collectivist students participate so rarely. However, the correct attributions they should make is that vertical collectivists have been trained to get instruction from their ingroups and not to make contributions to their ingroup unless they are asked. In contrast, individualists are socialized to make their individual contributions known (Brislin, 1994, p. 240).

East Asian collectivists use apologies as a social lubricant. Apologies are usually reciprocated, so that both parties "take the blame." It is important to remember that when a collectivist apologizes, it is only a social form, not to be taken literally. For example, he may say, "Here is the inadequate food prepared by my wife; unfortunately she is not a good cook." In fact, she may be a terrific cook. In one case a collectivist entertaining an individualist in a fashionable London hotel was overheard by the management of the hotel apologizing for the quality of the food; he was taken to court for slandering the hotel!

Remember that for collectivists reality does not have to match the interpersonal relationship. It is the relationship that matters to the collectivist, and the fact that he is making an outrageously incorrect statement about the food does not matter, because it is the right statement for creating a good relationship through a humble self-presentation. In response to the statement about the inadequacy of the food, the other person may apologize for the food he served on a previous occasion or say something else that will please the collectivist and thus cement the relationship. For example, the individualist might apologize for not giving enough choices to a collectivist. The ideal host in collectivist cultures knows the tastes of the guest and provides the food; the ideal host in individualistic cultures provides a wide selection for the guest to choose from (Shinobu Kitayama, personal communication, 1993).

Brislin (1994) pointed out that individualists get training in many activities that are expected in their society but not expected in collectivist societies with as much frequency. These include public speaking, calling attention to themselves, and making their own personal opinions known to others. Collectivists, in contrast, have excellent skills in promoting harmony with others and in not calling attention to themselves.

In sum, in predicting social behavior, the collectivist will rely too much on group norms, and the individualist too little on such information. Collectivists need to be trained to expect less compliance with norms among individualists than is typical in their own culture; and individualists have to be trained to expect more compliance with norms than they are used to seeing.

Individualists will do well to learn as much as possible about the ingroups of collectivists, since their behavior is much more dependent on ingroup norms, symbols, attitudes, and values than is usually the case in individualistic cultures. Especially important is to train individualists not to use themselves as the yardstick of how people will behave in social situations; collectivists are much more sensitive to these situations, and self-information is likely to understate the influence of groups and the setting on a collectivist's behavior.

Emphasis on Relationships

Individualists need to learn that collectivists not only are willing to continue relationships that are more costly than profitable but also will do so in more situations than is true for individualists. Exchange relationships tend to be different in the two kinds of cultures: Collectivists tend to exchange more in the areas that Foa and Foa (1974) described as "particularistic"—love, status, and services. Individualists are more likely to exchange in areas that Foa and Foa called "universalistic." That is, individualists tend to exchange money, goods, and information, which are resources that can be given to anyone, whereas collectivists tend to exchange resources that can only be given to a particular person. Clearly, people give status to a specific person. Also, collectivist exchanges take considerable time. People do not give love as quickly and easily as they give money in a store or the stock exchange.

This is a very important point because individualists tend to offer money for services for which the collectivists expect the individualist to give another service. For example, a baby-sitter is usually paid in individualist cultures, whereas in collectivist cultures the repayment is in the form of baby-sitting for the other person's child at another time or giving a language lesson or a letter of recommendation.

Individualists visiting collectivist cultures will do well to have one or two friends with them, since a lot of activities occur in groups. For example, they may not be served in a restaurant that is set up to serve only banquets. Conversely, collectivists should learn that being alone is not only acceptable but is even preferred by some individualists. The concept of privacy is something collectivists must understand, so that they will leave individualists alone when they receive signals that the individualist wants to be left alone.

Attributions

Collectivists need to learn that individualists are likely to stress internal causes of behavior; individualists need to understand that collectivists, relative to them, are more likely to stress external causes of behavior. Specifically, collectivists focus on relationships; individualists focus on personality.

Success is often attributed by collectivists to the help of others, and by individualists to their own abilities. One can easily imagine a misunderstanding of a successful meeting: "We succeeded because we had a good team" versus "we succeeded because our negotiator was very able" could easily result in ruffled feathers.

Collectivists tend to explain failure by lack of effort, and individualists by task difficulty or bad luck. An individualist employee who tells a collectivist supervisor that the task was too difficult is likely to be perceived as finding excuses for his laziness. Had he indicated that he had not tried hard enough, the supervisor would have found the explanation quite "realistic."

Changing Self or Situation

Collectivists should learn that individualists try to change social situations into which they do not fit. If collectivists expect that kind of behavior, they will find individualists less arrogant and aggressive than if they do not expect such behavior. Conversely, individualists should know that collectivists try to change themselves to fit into social situations. If individualists know that, they will find collectivists less passive and "spineless."

In the context of interactions between East Asian collectivists and Western individualists, I suggest that collectivists should also learn the following about individualists:

1. They have an unusually good opinion of themselves and have a need to express their high self-esteem. Their apparent arrogance is a reflection of the culture.
2. They are much more enthusiastic and use an expressive style in social interaction that East Asian collectivists use very rarely. Individualists may say, for instance, about a gift, "I love it!" or about an event, "Great! Terrific!" East Asian collectivists are much more tentative in such situations. Such differences can be misinterpreted, for example, "I love this gift" may be heard as "she loves me." Conversely, the low-key response of a collectivist may be seen as "she does not like the gift" or "she is a bore."
3. They stress pleasure and fun. Happiness is a very important value for them.
4. They decide quickly, but the implementation of the decision is often inadequate because too few people were involved in making it.
5. They place great value on consistency, especially on consistency between attitudes and behavior. When there is inconsistency, individualists are likely to label the other person a "hypocrite."
6. They do not make a sharp distinction between private and public behavior.
7. They are more likely to do something because it is fun than because they have an obligation to do it.
8. They expect a clear statement about their relationships, such as "if I give you this, you will give me that."
9. They expect the relationship to last a relatively short time.

Individualists should learn the following about collectivists:

1. They like modesty. Individualists, who have a tendency toward self-enhancement that is not found among collectivists, should hide their high self-esteem and learn to present more modest selves. They will thus appear less arrogant in the eyes of collectivists.
2. They do not consider happiness so important and consider doing their duty much more important.

3. They sometimes have difficulties making decisions. Individualists should respect collectivists' tendency to make decisions slowly, after much consultation, and preferably when there is consensus about the best course of action. This tendency is not as "inefficient" as it appears. After all, every decision can be seen in a broader context as involving the time that is required to reach it and the time needed to implement it. Taking time to decide by involving all those affected by the decision may result in quick implementation.

4. They are less concerned about cognitive consistency than is the case with individualists.

5. They pay much attention to the difference between private and public behavior.

6. They often think that it is rewarding to do their duty.

7. They expect relationships to last a long time. Often they cultivate relationships for some time before expecting the relationship to provide benefits.

8. They are quite vague about how relationships will evolve. Thus, individualists are well advised to be patient, take time to build relationships, and establish long-term relationships.

Privacy and Personal Space

Individualists value privacy; collectivists do not value it much and often find being alone frightening. Related to these points are differences in the way personal space is used. Collectivists do not respect the personal space of others as much as do individualists. For example, in a restaurant in a collectivist culture, one person occupying a table for four may find three people sitting at the table without asking for permission. The same action in an individualistic culture would be extremely rude.

Collectivists need training on how a person gets in and out of new groups, makes social conversation, compliments, in short, how one lubricates superficial relationships. Individualists need to recognize that they tend to be more superficial in their social behaviors, and that collectivists expect them to reveal much more about themselves, including financial details. Such "intrusive" questions are the means through which social behavior is lubricated in collectivist cultures. The lesser barrier between person and others is seen in collectivist cultures in the ease with which a passerby will criticize a parent who is raising a child "incorrectly" (Bronfenbrenner, 1970) or will join in ongoing conversations in public places.

In addition, individualists need to learn more about the proper exchange of presents and gifts, which are also important ways to lubricate relationships in collectivist cultures. Individualists need to practice the habit of attending to the needs of others, especially at banquets and other formal occasions, when they are supposed to keep their neighbor's glass full.

Advice to Individualists and Collectivists

Triandis, Brislin, and Hui (1988) specified what training should be given to collectivists and individualists so that they can be more successful in interpersonal relations. Individualists need to learn that there is a high probability of change in collectivists' behavior—and even in what appears to be personality—as they move from one group to another. Especially significant is the behavior of collectivists interacting with ingroups versus outgroups. When interacting with outgroups, the collectivist is likely to be seen by individualists as a "different person."

Individualists have to learn to look for clues on whether they are perceived by collectivists as ingroup or outgroup members. The assumption that because you are both working for the same company or even because you are related (kin) you will be ingroup is often unjustified. Working for the same company or being a relative predisposes the collectivist to make you an ingroup member, but it is *not* sufficient. Some actions are also necessary. For example, some indication of self-sacrifice for the benefit of the ingroup might result in your becoming an ingroup member.

Collectivists need to be trained to use compliments more, because compliments lubricate social relationships. Collectivists often do not compliment others much because they are used to interacting with members of their kin group, whose relationship they can take for granted.

It is important for individualists to learn that in some cultures, such as India, people rarely say, "Thank you." This is because, according to the Indian beliefs, giving help is a blessing to the giver, and thus there is no point thanking the giver: By receiving the benefit one has helped the giver to be a good person. Westerners who expect to be thanked are likely to become annoyed if they are not thanked in appropriate ways, but if they are trained to interpret correctly the "no thanking" behavior, they will feel much less annoyed.

Ting-Toomey (1994a) provided suggestions to individualists on how to reduce conflict in intercultural situations with collectivists. She suggested taking into account the way people use the face concept, controlling their sense of egocentric superiority, becoming proactive in dealing with low-grade conflict before the conflict escalates, learning to "give face" and not push the opponent against a wall, and being sensitive to the importance of quiet, mindful observation (individualists should learn to avoid asking too many "why" questions). They should practice attentive listening skills and use more qualifiers, disclaimers, and tentative statements. Finally, they should let go of the conflict situation, if the other party is not able to deal with it directly.

Harmony in social relations is often expected in collectivist cultures (especially in East Asia), whereas individualists are trained to be frank and to "tell it as it is." This can produce major problems when criticism is given in ways that the collectivist culture considers inappropriate, especially when criticism is given directly, without placing it in context. In collectivist cultures it is often desirable to convey criticism indirectly by using a close friend of the employee, so the employee will not lose face by being criticized directly by the supervisor (P. B. Smith and Bond, 1994). Presumably, also, the close friend can "hold the hand" of the employee while the bad news is being communicated.

Collectivists need to be trained to expect individualists to be less attached to their ingroups. If the relative of an individualist fails in school or is fired from a job, the collectivist will expect this event to be extremely traumatic; however, the individualist may not see it that way. This misunderstanding can be even more significant if it is the relative of the collectivist who has had a problem. The collectivist will expect the individualist to understand that a major trauma has occurred, but the individualist is likely to minimize the significance of the event. A collectivist subordinate may expect special consideration, for example, an offer to take a week off after such traumatic events, whereas an individualist supervisor may not pay attention to the events, giving an impression of "total insensitivity" to the subordinate. The distance from ingroup members characteristic of individualists may be misinterpreted by collectivists as a "personality defect" when in fact it is normal behavior.

Collectivists are likely to find vertical individualists "too competitive." They need to be warned that competition is important in vertical individualism. They also need to be trained to understand the individualist tendency to define status as a function of specific accomplishments; individualists might need to be trained to pay more attention to group memberships as definers of status.

Collectivists must avoid dependence on persuasive arguments based on cooperation and the avoidance of confrontation, because these conditions are not valued as much by individualists as by collectivists. Similarly, they should expect relationships from the point of view of individualists to be based on costs and benefits. Conversely, individualists need to learn to sacrifice themselves in order to maintain good relationships with collectivists.

Collectivists need to see that social relationships with individualists can be pleasant but will rarely become intimate. If there is no time and place attached to an invitation, it is only a polite form, not a "real" invitation. Most collectivists do not know that: Because invitations are very important in their cultures, when they are given, they are really meant.

Because the timing of business transactions occurs much sooner and with fewer preliminaries in individualistic cultures, the collectivist has to learn not to take too long before starting the business of the meeting, lest the individualist interprets it as "wasting my time." Conversely, the individualist has to be trained to slow down and engage in more preliminary interactions before jumping into the business discussion.

Cohen (1991) urged individualists to establish warm interpersonal relationships before they negotiate with collectivists. He suggested they consider how messages are interpreted in historical-cultural context; pay attention to symbols, indirect formulations, and nonverbal gestures; be aware of status and face; start high and do not compromise too soon; do not show too much flexibility; use a tit-for-tat strategy; be patient; and pay a lot of attention to the outward form and less to the substance of the agreement.

Communication must be handled differently in different cultures. It can be in writing, with a small interpersonal component, in individualist cultures but should be face-to-face in the case of collectivist cultures. Problem solving must be individual-based in the former and group-based in the latter cultures. Decision making can be based on majority vote in the former and group consensus in the latter cultures.

Collectivists need to pay more attention to contracts, signatures, and the written word than is commonly done in their cultures. Foreign student advisers in the United States sometimes have to extricate collectivist students from contractual relationships they did not intend. The student, for instance, may see five apartments and write to all landlords telling them that he is interested in the apartment, thinking that the landlords will simply hold the apartment until the student can consult his friends and decide which one to take. In the meantime the five landlords think that they have a deal. When they discover that they do not have a deal, they complain to the university authorities. Conversely, individualists need to be trained to focus on oral agreements, which sometimes have more validity in collectivist cultures than in individualist cultures.

Social relationships are likely to be superficial and short-term and thus disappointing to collectivists, unless some training is given to prepare them. Training for individualists could focus on the building of long-term relationships with little immediate benefit.

Collectivists need to pick up the point that individualists remain unimpressed by the prestige of their place of birth, their lineage, older age, male sex, or family name. They need to be trained to talk about their accomplishments. At least, they need to have a friend do so. Although they should not boast, if they say nothing, the individualist will think of them as "nobodies." Conversely, individualists need to understand that heritage and association really do matter in collectivist cultures. And if they do not want to be seen as self-centered, they need to moderate the presentation of their own accomplishments.

Collectivists should acquire some insight about the way they see ingroups and outgroups. Collectivists see them as very different, but individualists do not see them as quite so different. For instance, a collectivist might see a "regular customer" as somebody that deserves a much larger sales discount than a customer who comes in for the first time. The individualist is not likely to see such a difference. In fact, the individualist would insist that pricing a product according to who the customer is rather than according to how much it costs to acquire it from a wholesaler is unfair, if not immoral. Conversely, the individualist needs to learn that collectivists exaggerate the difference between ingroups and outgroups and must learn to expect much difference in the behavior of collectivists during social interaction with different groups. Individualist bureaucrats value dealing with people in an evenhanded way. Collectivists often do not value evenhandedness. They take the view that if they are not going to give special benefits to their ingroup, who will?

What collectivist cultures define as a "normal fee" individualist cultures may see as a "bribe." The appointment of a relative is seen by collectivists as natural, given the need for a manager to have a person of trust work for him; individualists see it as "nepotism."

Collectivists expect more help from their ingroup than is usually given in individualist cultures. For example, if they visit the individualist's city, they expect to be met at the airport and that the individualist will spend time with them until they settle in. This can involve taking them to see their landlord, for grocery shopping, and generally helping them with their chores. Refusal to do these chores will be seen as most ungracious, if not insulting. Individualists who receive such assistance may take it as a slight on their self-reliance. Individualists who know about these expectations will appear to be more successful hosts than individualists who ignore the demands of these social situations.

Because collectivist ingroups make more demands on their members than the members have time or energy for, people in such cultures develop special strategies to avoid being in situations where they have to respond to these demands. For example, if the collectivist will arrive at the airport and expect to be met, the member of the ingroup may arrange to be out of town. Of course, it is essential to tell the traveler that this will happen and to give advice about getting a cab or other transportation that will substitute for being there. Since collectivists are expected to bring gifts for every member of the ingroup whenever they visit, they often decide not to visit at all. That is an extreme form of avoiding the demands of ingroups.

A good skill for individualists to learn is to make requests of collectivists that will allow them to back out without saying no. The Japanese use long intervals of silence between partly made invitations to allow for nonverbal communication of acceptance or nonacceptance that will allow both parties to save face.

Training Those from Horizontal and Vertical Cultures to Work Well Together

A major consideration in learning to work well together is understanding what kinds of relationships are most important. Horizontals emphasize horizontal relationships, such as spouse-spouse, friend-friend, employee–fellow employee; verticals emphasize parent-child, boss-subordinate, and teacher-student relationships. This means that people will seek different kinds of relationships and when possible "convert" a relationship to the kind that they are most comfortable with. Thus, a professor from a horizontal culture may convert a professor-student relationship to a friend-friend relationship, which may well confuse a student from a vertical culture. Conversely, a friend from a vertical culture might convert a friend-friend relationship to a counselor-client relationship and provide all sorts of unrequested and unexpected advice.

In general, people from vertical cultures going to horizontal cultures will do well to avoid extremely superordinate (bossy) or subordinate (submissive) behaviors. Conversely, people from horizontal cultures going to vertical cultures may have to practice more extreme behaviors on the superordination-subordination axis that fit the roles they are in in the vertical culture.

People in horizontal cultures are distrustful of authorities, whereas people in vertical cultures have been trained to accept authorities. This can have important implications because nonacceptance of authorities can be interpreted as insubordination or arrogance and may be seen as a character defect by people in the vertical cultures; the acceptance of authorities can be seen as servility and spinelessness by members of horizontal cultures.

Members of vertical cultures do not realize that administrators in horizontal cultures have very limited power because there is a complex system of checks and balances limiting it. Some training along these lines will reduce surprises and misunderstandings. A person from a horizontal culture trying to get a person from a vertical culture to do something is well advised to consider what the supervisors of that person are likely to say or do. Another useful component of persuasion is to argue that the changed behavior will benefit the person's ingroup.

In general verticals are comfortable with competitive situations and horizontals are quite uncomfortable. That means that horizontals are likely to minimize competition and verticals are likely to inject competition into social situations. It will help a vertical to learn to emphasize harmony and cooperation, to be careful in saving the other person's face, and to avoid confrontation.

❖   ❖   ❖

This chapter provided a perspective for making both individualists and collectivists able to interact effectively with members of cultures that differ from them. The final chapter will provide an evaluation of the two cultural syndromes.

7

Evaluation of Individualism and Collectivism

IN THE PREVIOUS CHAPTERS we discussed the use of the terms *individualism* and *collectivism* in the literature and the content, measurement, antecedents, consequences, and practical utility of the concepts they represent. In this chapter we will examine the advantages and disadvantages of the two cultural patterns. Clearly, this is not a scientific chapter but one of matching my values with what I presented in the previous chapters. If your values are different, you may well arrive at different conclusions. Nevertheless, by stating how I evaluate the cultural patterns, I give you a chance to think about your own way of evaluating them.

I am going to be frank about my own values so that you can take my biases into account when you read this chapter. I am, across situations, a horizontal individualist 37 percent of the time, a vertical individualist 23 percent of the time (i.e., 60 percent individualist), a horizontal collectivist 27 percent of the time, and a vertical collectivist 13 percent of the time (according to the way I responded to the scenarios discussed in the Appendix). Thus, my biases should be clear. I am an individualist, but my 40 percent collectivism allows me to be sympathetic to that point of view. I am definitely a horizontal person (64 percent); that is, I dislike powerful authorities.

You may well ask: Why bother with an evaluation of individualism and collectivism? I think it is useful to do that, because (1) the way we vote can make the country more or less individualist or collectivist, (2) we can chose to live in places that are more or less individualist or collectivist, and (3) to understand the conflicts of the future, we need to decide if we are going to help the individualist or collectivist side in these conflicts.

Relationship to Politics

In the modern world we constantly try to change things. For example, when we vote we try to move a society toward a vertical individualistic side, of the

Reagan-Thatcher-Mulroney variety, or toward a horizontal collectivist side, such as the Labor party. Both the extreme right (fascism) and extreme left (communism) of the political spectrum are extremely collectivist (the individual must subordinate self to the state).

Remember the discussion in Chapter 3: Horizontal individualism goes with social democracy, or the liberal side of the Democratic party in the United States; vertical individualism goes with free market thinking, or the right wing of the Republic party in the United States; horizontal collectivism corresponds to kibbutz-type political entities; vertical collectivism to communalist movements. In short, extreme versions of collectivism go with totalitarianism. Democracy, pluralism, multiculturalism, and the like are compatible with individualism.

Regional Differences

When we decide where to live, we might well be interested in whether the place is more or less individualistic. For example, Canada is less individualistic than the United States (Lipset, 1990). Lipset brought together massive data from surveys to show that Canadians are more likely to go for "law and order" than for "unrestricted freedom," whereas Americans show the opposite patterns. Thus, even when two societies are very individualistic, one might be less individualistic than the other.

In my observation, Hawaii and New York City are less individualistic than Arizona or Idaho. For example, Hawaii offers to those who live on the island of Oahu, the majority of its population, virtually free transportation for those over sixty-five and medical insurance for the whole population residing on the islands. New York State has a much higher income tax than most states; New York City has an additional tax but provides a superb library system. A free library is an example of Fiske's communal sharing. Voting patterns match these points exactly. Hawaii and New York City vote for Democratic candidates almost all the time.

Studies by Francisco Morales in Spain showed meaningful regional differences in responses to items such as the ones in Triandis, Bontempo, Villareal, et al. (1988). In short, each province of Spain has a different profile on individualism and collectivism. Studies in Italy showed the South to be more collectivist than the North. Studies in Greece (Georgas, 1989) showed that the countryside, especially the mountains and islands, is collectivist and the cities are individualist. Observations by Tanaka in Japan showed a similar pattern, with the countryside more collectivist than the cities. Similar findings were reported by Daab (1991). Triandis and Singelis (submitted) suggested that we can use the scenarios of the Appendix to train people to pay attention to age, social class, and other demographics in order to "place" members of both individualistic and collectivist cultures more accurately on these dimensions. Thus, they will not use national origin as the sole basis for predicting a person's collectivism.

In short, minor differences by region, state, and country do exist, and people do have choices concerning where to live, how to vote, what religion to join (e.g., Catholicism is more collectivist than most Protestant denominations). If choices do exist, we may want to evaluate the constructs, so we can decide how to make these choices.

The Conflicts of the Future

In addition, as we discussed in Chapter 1, Huntington (1993) argued that the conflicts of the future will be along cultural lines, that there will be a confrontation between collectivists, who value group rights more than individual rights and argue that "overemphasis" on human rights interferes with central planning; and individualists, who insist on human rights all over the world. If Huntington's prediction is supported by future events, we should decide whether we want to be sympathetic to one or the other side of the argument.

The implication in Huntington's thesis is that open conflict will take place between the two camps. He quoted me (Triandis, 1990) as showing the cohesion of the two sides. However, in my view, these particular two sides are not cohesive enough to lead to war. I see the West and the "rest" as too large, amorphous, heterogeneous. However, the idea of future conflicts along cultural lines has merit.

Specifically, Moynihan (1993) pointed out that the principle of self-determination that can be found in the UN charter remains undefined. What is the unit that will seek self-determination? What is the idea of "sovereignty" in the modern world? Moynihan asked if language is the attribute that will define the state. But there are 6,170 languages, and some (English, for example) clearly require more than one state, so one would need a UN with, perhaps, 7,000 states instead of one with 186. Most other categories, such as race and religion, do not provide satisfactory criteria. When we consider several criteria simultaneously, we might end up with 10,000 states. That would be *pandaemonium,* Moynihan's title for his book. This raises the question of what is the kind of group that is likely to be involved in future conflicts.

In my opinion such groups will have to have at least three attributes:

1. They should have common goals, including a "clear" enemy. Without a clear enemy the energy required for conflict cannot be garnered.

2. They should be sufficiently small for people to be able to identify with them. Just as most people cannot identify with "mankind," so is identification with enormous entities difficult. Even the "state" is in some ways too large an entity, as the Soviets discovered in their failed experiment to create

"Communist humans," whose personal goals would be identical to the goals of the Communist party.

3. The group needs a homogeneous common culture. That means shared ways of talking, thinking, and feeling. Common unstated assumptions are essential aspects of such a culture. Common culture results in the possibility of each human's predicting what other humans will do. Such prediction leads to trust and a sense of "control." Control is an extremely important aspect of well-being (Langer, 1983) and is thus highly reinforcing, and people will fight to get it. Furthermore, similarities in subjective cultures permit humans to validate their own. Since many aspects of subjective culture are not "objective" and require subjective judgments, such as what is a "good life," "what should be the most important principles in one's life," the major way to validate them is to find other humans who make the same judgments. Homogeneity, then, has great value in bolstering the sense of certainty that one's ideas are valid.

However, to get homogeneous shared culture, language is not enough. It is necessary to have similar economic status, occupations, the same concept of "truth" (e.g., it is not possible to get along with people who think that truth comes from authorities when one thinks that it comes from observations), and the same social structure. Similarities in religion and in the sense of aesthetics are also desirable but may not be essential for the creation of a stable ingroup in all cultures.

This argument, then, makes Kotkin's (1993) "tribes" (see discussion in Chapter 1) much more plausible entities for future conflicts than individualist and collectivist states. The tribes will be in conflict along cultural and economic lines, but the binding element will be similar occupations, lifestyles, and ideology. The women's movement, if it develops a clear focus, gays and lesbians, racial groups of similar ideology, the green lobbies, and refugees are most likely entities for future conflicts. Much of this conflict will be economic, but some will involve burning the house of the "enemy," as we see among contemporary German Nazis reacting to Turkish *Gastarbeiter.*

In short, yes, the conflicts will be cultural but, in my opinion, not along the collectivism-individualism divide. However, the behavior of these "tribes" will have much in common with the behavior of collectivists, so what we discussed in this book may well have wide applicability in understanding the conflicts of the future.

A General Thesis

The general thesis of this chapter, in agreement with B. Schwartz (1986), is that collectivism has definite advantages for those social relationships that include small groups, such as family and co-workers, where people are deal-

ing with face-to-face situations and with people they are going to be inter-
acting with for a long time. We might call these "interpersonal situations."
In most of these relationships, achievement is not the central purpose.
Rather, people are either enjoying themselves or are consuming goods.

In contrast, individualism has major advantages for situations where the
individual is dealing with large collectives, such as the state, or for situations
where achievement within the world economy is a central concern. We may
call these "large collective situations." In short, from the point of view of individuals, in interpersonal situations, there should be collectivism; in large
collective situations, individualism.

Let us consider some preliminary support for this position. Naroll (1983)
reviewed much empirical evidence suggesting that if gross national product
per capita is kept constant, very positive social indicators, such as longevity,
low suicide and divorce rates, low rates of homicide and drug and alcohol
abuse, and high rates of mental health are found in those societies where
the primary group (family or equivalent) provides strong social ties. In such
societies, the primary group also functions as a normative reference group
(i.e., people do what the ingroup norms specify), provides emotional
warmth and prompt punishment of deviance, is homogeneous, uses active
gossip to control behavior, has frequent rites, memorable myths, a plausible
ideology, and badges of membership (i.e., is collectivist and rather tight).

Nevertheless, one must admit that sometimes in interpersonal situations,
collectivism is a burden on individuals. Individuals sometimes feel they
have too many obligations; ingroup members make too many demands;
ingroup authorities have too much power; individuals may want to carry out
a project and the ingroup opposes it; investing in a new enterprise may be
impossible because the ingroup absorbs the surplus and thus there is no
capital to invest. In short, all is not ideal in interpersonal situations in collectivist cultures.

In those situations where individuals are dealing with large ingroups or
the production and distribution of goods, individualism is to be preferred.
Human rights, a public setting that allows individuals self-actualization, and
freedom of movement and thought will be found in individualistic cultures
more than in collectivist ones. This will result in better science (e.g., more
Nobel prizes in science), multiculturalism, creativity, and high achievement
in both the arts and economic enterprises.

But again disadvantages can be identified rather easily. Low voting rates
in some individualistic countries indicate alienation from politics. The opposition to taxation is a classic individualist response that undermines the
health of the collective. Individualists too often prefer to spend their money
on a larger yacht rather than on improving the country's elementary education. The great products of the past civilizations, like the Great Wall of
China, the Acropolis, and the medieval cathedrals, were financed through

taxation. Support for the infrastructure in communications, education, research, public health, and so forth requires public money. The arts are flourishing in cities of modest size in Northern and Western Europe because public moneys support them. Versions of central planning in Japan, Korea, Singapore have cornered markets of products invented in the West, so the same products are no longer produced in the West. Thus, even in this domain one cannot claim that individualism is always to be preferred.

It seems likely that some form of balance between individualism and collectivism is optimal. The great sages of the past, such as Confucius and Socrates, emphasized balance. Many of the knee-jerk proponents of the free market have forgotten this. Balance requires cognitive complexity. Any extreme position is simple, couched in terms that the crowd can support and the voters can understand. The lack of balance is "corrected" in democracies by switching from one side of the argument to the other, that is, by changing parties in power. That is the strength of democracies. But it may be more profitable to develop middle courses that can be steady and provide predictability for social and economic planners (e.g., the strategic planners of corporations). In any case, these considerations suggest that neither individualism nor collectivism is desirable unless one is balanced by the other.

Furthermore, although collectivism is desirable in interpersonal situations, too much of it can be undesirable; and although individualism is desirable in large collective situations, too much of it is also undesirable.

Advantages and Disadvantages of Collectivism

Advantages

The advantages of collectivism may be seen in the areas of social indicators of the type mentioned above. It is not difficult to see that delinquency and crime rates are relatively low in rural compared to urban settings, and in stable compared to fast-changing societies. But a more fundamental issue is the kind of morality that is more frequently found in these cultures.

Studies of morality reviewed by Eckensberger (1994) indicated that universally children go through certain stages of moral development. In Stage 1 the child focuses on punishment and obedience is considered essential. This is a universal "primitive" view of morality, seen even in the U.S. Congress when it tries to control crime with more police and prisons. In Stage 2 one follows rules only if it is to one's advantage to do so; what is right is an equal exchange, a good deal. That view is already individualistic, but it is a primitive individualism. In Stage 3 one does what one is expected to do by the ingroup and by one's role. This is a primitive collectivist position. In

Stage 4 one does one's duty, and laws must be upheld unless they are in conflict with other fixed social duties. This is a more sophisticated collectivist position. In Stage 5 the emphasis is on social contract and individual rights. This position argues that people hold a variety of opinions and that most values and rules are relative to the group one belongs to and should usually be upheld because there is a social contract. However, there are also nonrelative values, such as life and liberty, that must be upheld regardless of the opinion of the majority of the ingroup. This is a more advanced individualistic view, one that does contain, however, some collectivist elements. Finally, in Stage 6, humans may reach the most individualistic view. In this stage the focus is on universal ethical principles. Particular laws and rules are valid only if they are consistent with such principles. Principles such as justice, the equality of human rights, and respect for the dignity of human beings as individual persons are not negotiable. This is clearly an individualistic view.

Reviews of cross-cultural studies of these stages showed that in general children develop their ideas about morality by following these stages. The findings indicated that Stages 1, 5, and 6 are rare and that Stages 2, 3, and 4 are found in most cultures. The highest stage reached by a child seems to reflect the socioeconomic level of the parents (wealth of parents implies higher stages), the religion (e.g., fundamentalist positions are associated with lower levels of economic development), and the rural-urban background of the sample (the more urban reach higher stages). The more educated samples also reach higher stages.

In short, many of the factors that shift people from collectivism to individualism are also associated with the attainment of the higher stages. However, the correlation between collectivism-individualism and the level of the stage reached by a child is quite imperfect: The measurements of the levels of moral development found the highest scores in Israel (in the kibbutz) and among the upper classes in Germany, the United States, Taiwan, and India.

Members of the lower classes generally obtain lower scores, and the lowest scores have been obtained in less-developed countries. The key point for our discussion is that Stages 5 and 6 have few elements that collectivists would find appropriate. There is no mention of the common good, of social harmony, family security, self-control, or the Indian values of nonviolence and the sacredness of all life or the Chinese values of collective happiness, filial piety, and collective utility. In short, this work, done by Western psychologists, is "rigged" so that individualistic cultures will get high scores! Ma (1988) remedied that problem by providing a Chinese perspective on moral development.

It seems to me that the issue of the crime that is associated with individualism is going to be one of the key questions of the moral and political debate concerning the advantages and disadvantages of individualism and collectivism. There is no doubt that as social controls, especially self-controls, are lowered, crime increases. The 1980s, marked by extreme individualism and competitiveness in the industrialized countries, saw the tripling of the crime rate in all of them except Japan. A National Public Radio (1993) report on the Thatcher era in Britain made an explicit connection between her policies and the tripling of the crime rate. We can note major increases in crime and corruption in Russia, Poland, and other former Communist countries, as well as after the economic liberalization in the PRC (Hao, 1993).

The Committee on Law and Justice, Commission on the Behavioral and Social Sciences (1994), examined violence in urban America and concluded that this part of the world has a "violent culture" that promotes violent behavior, especially among young people. The committee emphasized the need to change that culture. It proposed that all civic and religious organizations charge all elements of the community with the mission of violence prevention; discourage actions that aggravate ethnic tensions or promote violent stereotypes; enlist celebrities in voluntary antiviolence campaigns; and encourage the media to publicize early successes in responding to violence. In short, it advocated a pro-social, less violent culture.

Policies in the individualist industrial countries emphasize short-term goals (getting elected) over long-term goals (a good economy, low social conflict, and little anomie in ten years). Even in collectivist countries the leadership is likely to consist of individualists, and thus from a long-term perspective, policies are not that different from those of individualist countries. Therefore, we see in many countries the neglect of the infrastructure (roads, educational systems) and huge national debts.

We also see anti-tax sentiment in all countries, but its motivation in individualist countries is different from its motivation in collectivist countries. In individualist countries it is "myself and my nuclear family" against everyone else; in the collectivist it is my ingroup versus the outgroups.

The global economy is making vertical individualism more respectable than it was. Dog-eat-dog competition is now seen as inevitable, and the neglect of those who cannot compete (e.g., jobless, sick, mentally disturbed) is seen as the price that must be paid for the success of those who can compete.

In many industrial countries, taxes were used to redistribute income, that is, move toward horizontal individualism. However, global competition presses toward vertical individualism: Inequalities are tolerated, and there is relatively little concern for those who have no jobs. Naturally, if there is no safety net to provide for the jobless, they will turn to crime. What else can they do? Without a national full-employment policy, crime is inevitable. But such a policy requires taxation, and that means that the upper class will have fewer yachts and less fun. They are the ones who vote more reliably than the poor, so they control many political decisions. As long as crime is restricted mostly to the inner city, there will be little political will to do something fundamental about it.

One study mentioned by Naroll (1983) was especially revealing. It was based on U.S. data, and the dependent variable was the probability that a young man would be classified as a delinquent. It found that when such a young man frequents five households, for example, among neighbors, relatives, parental friends, and school chums (where he is sufficiently intimate to open the refrigerator and get a drink without asking for permission), the probability that he will become delinquent is essentially zero. As the number of such households goes down, the probability of delinquency goes up. There could not be a better demonstration of the significance of ties to the community for delinquency.

Homicides, drug abuse, and divorce and suicide rates are also low where people are tied to others with bonds of emotional attachment. Trimble (1994) reported that among the Amish, Mennonites, and other tight, religious communities in the United States and Canada, there are hardly any cases of drug use. Bacon (1973) found that cultures that allow children to be dependent have less drug abuse, especially abuse of alcohol. Thus, collectivist cultures have an advantage in this area.

Many collectivist parents set high standards of achievement for their children and provide warm support as their children attempt to reach those standards. Thus we see in the United States many of the top prizes in spelling and science going to young people of collectivist backgrounds. However, some of these parents push their children too hard and create resentment. Some children revolt against their parents. Parents also try sometimes to push in directions in which the child is not talented, creating further problems.

Disadvantages

Collectivism has disadvantages at both the private and the public levels. At the private level, we find less willingness to cut the bonds with the family when that is required for study abroad or for occupational achievement. There is evidence of high levels of homesickness when a collectivist is away from the family (Cardem, 1993).

The worst aspect of *some* collectivist child rearing is that it undermines the self-esteem of the child. It makes for adults that are compliant but not innovative. The lower levels of happiness and well-being reported by collectivists, after the data are statistically controlled for GNP/cap (e.g., Diener and Diener, 1993; Gallup, 1976), probably reflect, in part, dissatisfaction with the burdens of doing one's duty and the suppression of strivings toward self-actualization.

At the public level of the relationship of individuals to the state, extreme collectivism has the most disadvantages. For example, both the Nazis and the Communists established regimes that strongly subordinated individual to state goals. Extremist political groups, such as the Ku Klux Klan (KKK), are also highly collectivist. Both Norman Lincoln Rockwell of the American Nazi party and Malcolm X (at one time) wanted to split the United States into distinct white and black states (homogeneity goes with tightness, which is correlated with collectivism), and they once collaborated in a rally in Madison Square Garden in New York City (Hughes, 1993) promoting the idea of separate black and white states within the United States.

We have observed ethnic cleansing in extreme conflict situations where collectives fight. In the former Yugoslavia, in the 1992–1994 period, those who were individualistic were silenced by authoritarian regimes. The peasants, who are strongly collectivist, have been in control. Their leaders use nationalism to stay in power.

As mentioned in Chapter 3, collectivists are extremely supportive of ingroups and in situations of conflict treat outgroups very harshly. That is not to say that individualists are incapable of atrocities of the My Lai variety, which occurred during the Vietnam-U.S. war in 1968. But incidents such as the rape of Nanjing, China, in 1937 by the soldiers of a militaristic Japan, the extermination of 6 million Jews by the Nazis, the liquidation of masses of opponents by Stalin, are more frequently associated with extreme collectivist than with individualist societies. We must remember again that in every society there are both individualists and collectivists. When the Nazis came to power, they managed to expel from Germany many individualists who had the means to live abroad and they subordinated the rest. There is also, among vertical collectivists, a de-emphasis on science, since dictators do not want competing sources of "truth" (e.g., Hitler did not mind losing Jewish scientists, such as Albert Einstein). Religious authorities have been consistently antiresearch throughout history, and in fact in Greek Orthodoxy there is the dogma: "Believe and do not research." Collectivists often emphasize a collectivist ideology that can be political (e.g., Hitler), religious (e.g., the Spanish Inquisition), and even artistic (e.g., Stalin's and Mao's "socialist realism").

Dealing with outgroups brutally means that in some cases wife beating will be a greater problem in collectivist than in individualist cultures. In many collectivist cultures (e.g., traditional China, India, Africa) the ingroup does not include spouses from the outside in the early stages of the marriage. The wife lives in the household of her in-laws and is expected to be a kind of obedient servant. In many of these cultures, only when she gives birth to a male is she widely accepted as a member of the ingroup. Even if she lives in a nuclear family, her husband is supposed to be the master. Thus, according to a National Public Radio report on October 3, 1993, about 50 percent of the wives surveyed in Zimbabwe claim they are beaten regularly. The local saying is, "We beat our wives because we love them" (i.e., to improve them). The assumption is that the husband's will is the "law" of the household. A wife that does not obey (e.g., refuses to have sex) is beaten. If she goes home to her family, she may be beaten by her brothers, who do not want to have to return the bride price they obtained when she married. Some of those interviewed stated that wife beating is a "valuable aspect of African culture that the white man wants to destroy." One of the incidents mentioned was the beating received by a wife when she nagged her husband for not taking responsibility for his son born out of wedlock!

Even more extreme cases can be found, such as the wife killing that takes place in large cities in India and elsewhere. According to a report I read in the local press in New Delhi in 1983, there were about 200 criminal investigations per year of cases in which a woman was killed, usually in a kitchen accident in which her mother-in-law was involved. The suspected motive was to make it possible for the husband to remarry and get another dowry.

Collectivists also are much more tied to the past than are individualists, a phenomenon that may make economic progress more difficult. Political parties in collectivist cultures are perceived as ingroups and outgroups: This results in the ingroup's fighting a good proposal of the outgroup party so that the latter will not gain in popularity by actions that are good for the country (Triandis, 1972).

In many collectivist cultures, for example, the Karakatzanoi of northern Greece (see J. K. Campbell, 1964), the continual feuds as one or another kinship group attempts to restore its honor result in perpetual armed hostilities. Of course, the gang wars of American cities are similarly collectivist. Fighting along ethnic, religious, and tribal lines is found in the struggles of Basques and Spaniards; Armenians and Turks; in Northern Ireland; Azerbaijan; Georgia; Uganda; Burundi; Rwanda; Turkistan; Tibet; and in the Kurdish search for a national state; the Hindu-Muslim and Sikh-Hindu struggles on the Indian subcontinent, East Timor, and Indonesia; and in the Palestinian, South African, Sudanese, Somali, and Bosnian situations. The racial riots of the large American cities are still another example.

In collectivist cultures people have so many obligations toward their ingroups that they do not have the interest or energy to do volunteer work. That is a real disadvantage, especially when activities are required that do not fall into the categories "required by the norms of the ingroup" or "advantages exceed disadvantages." For example, serving on the board of civic associations is not required by ingroup norms and usually is more time-consuming and costly than advantageous in terms of personal contacts or other advantages. One has to do it because one is ideologically committed to a good cause.

Finally, collectivists hoard information even more than individualists do and do not share it with outgroups. Since their ingroups are often narrow, they deprive colleagues from the same organization of important information. For example, they may not give valuable information to colleagues working in the same corporation (Triandis, 1967). This turned out to be a major problem in the USSR (Kaiser, 1984), where one part of the bureaucracy did not know what the other parts were doing. Cooperation in collectivist cultures occurs only within the ingroup; extreme competition is used with outgroups. Leonid Brezhnev was exasperated by the Soviet bureaucracy's inability to cooperate; each small face-to-face group fought all other groups (Kaiser, 1984).

In sum, when collectivism operates in personal situations, it is generally a very desirable social pattern, but with a major qualification: *as long as ingroup members are involved.* It becomes undesirable when large collectives are involved, especially when outgroup members are targets of the actions of ingroup members.

Advantages and Disadvantages of Individualism

Advantages

The major advantages of individualism can be seen in the relationship of individuals to large collectives and in production and distribution activities. With respect to large collectives, individualism means that human rights can be observed; multiculturalism is possible in the society; there is democracy; if a person commits a crime, that person, not his whole ingroup, is punished; the culture favors progress and technological innovation; and it emphasizes creativity, freedom, mastery, and achievement.

A high GNP/cap is strongly associated with individualism (Hofstede, 1980). Whether that will be the case in the future requires further research. Some economists have argued that the best economic development occurs in collectivist settings, such as Hong Kong and Singapore. However, I suspect that other variables, such as small size and the ability to take advantage of inventions made in other countries, may be more important determinants of the phenomenal economic growth of those states.

It is likely that the relationship of affluence and individualism is circular, each fostering the other. Those who are affluent can do their own thing, including investing in projects that their ingroup finds too risky. Some of these projects succeed, and the entrepreneur becomes more affluent. Affluence means more choices that the individual rather than the group makes, hence more individualism.

Economic development, according to Pareek (1968), is a function of high "need for achievement" (which is often linked to individualism and competition), multiplied by high "need for extension" (use of large ingroups, not just the narrow family concerns, which is a special form of collectivism we might call "large ingroups collectivism"), minus the "need for affiliation." In other words, need for both achievement and extension are required: If one of these two is very low, the other cannot be effective; in addition, if people spend most of their time enjoying social relationships, they will not develop the economy.

This conceptualization was supported by a study reported by Gorney and Long (1980), who as far as I could determine had not read Pareek. They had the ethnographies of fifty-eight cultures rated by ten cultural experts on the dimensions of competition (related to need for achievement) within the culture, interpersonal intensity (related to need for affiliation), amount of aggression, and "synergy" (related to need for extension). They found that social development (high economic success of the ethnic group) was present in cultures high in competition and synergy and low in interpersonal intensity.

Individualists have a sense of high self-efficacy. Because their self-esteem is high, they are more likely to try risky activities, so achievement is often associated with individualism. We see in the biographies of famous people from collectivist cultures (e.g., Japan) that they were idiocentric members of those societies. For example, Davey (1960) provided a biography of a Japanese Christian missionary by the name of Kagawa. A brilliant son of a rich father, he did not fit in with the boys of his age group, who scorned him and ridiculed him. He shifted from Buddhism to Christianity on the basis of a personal decision, a sure sign of idiocentrism. He was the only Japanese who signed, in 1927, together with Gandhi and Einstein, a declaration that stated that forced conscription into military forces was immoral. He was a pacifist in militaristic Japan. He condemned the war with China (1937) and the United States (1941–1945) and proclaimed loyalty to Christ rather than the emperor. After Japan's defeat, the emperor proclaimed to his people that he was not divine and asked Kagawa to instruct him about Christianity. The biography included hundreds of incidents reflecting personal decisions inconsistent with the Japanese social order.

Finally, individualists insist on equal treatment under the law. This is especially significant in political situations. Many vertical collectivists, for instance, were extremely surprised that President Richard Nixon had to resign. After all, he was the boss, so why could he not check the books of his opponents?

Disadvantages

Individualism is linked to loneliness and poor social support (Triandis, Leung, et al., 1985) and high probabilities of family conflict and divorce (Brodbar and Jay, 1986). It tends to "leave people vulnerable to feelings of alienation and narcissistic self-absorption and tempts them to pursue narrow self-interest" (Spence, 1985, p. 1293).

Culture has a broad influence on individuals. It tends to push individuals in a particular direction, but individual differences also "spill" some people further in the direction of movement, past the culture mean. Thus, although an individualistic culture usually pushes toward democratic cognitions, behaviors, and institutions, it also pushes some people toward narcissism. Narcissism undoubtedly increases the divorce rate and number of one-parent families. Narcissism is more common when resources are abundant (e.g., entertainment stars) or extraordinarily limited (e.g., Brazilian shantytowns, described by Scheper-Hughes, 1985). Thus, it is not surprising that we see many one-parent families in the economically deprived segments of our cities. Individualism may well exaggerate these trends. For example, Britain is the most individualistic country in Europe (Hofstede, 1980) and also has the highest rate of one-parent families (17 percent, see *Economist,* November 13–19, 1993). Clearly, these statements cannot be viewed as definitive, but they certainly suggest important hypotheses for further research.

The extreme competitiveness found among vertical individualists can result in both anxiety (am I doing well enough?) and frustration (I am not doing well enough). It fosters discrimination (I am better that these groups) and was responsible for some of the arms race (Hsu, 1983; if "they" have 10,000 nuclear warheads, "we" must have 20,000). Klugel and Smith (1986) found that white Americans who were more individualistic were more likely to perceive the policies of the U.S. government as "favoring the blacks" than were those who were less individualistic.

Extreme competitiveness can interfere with creativity when competitiveness becomes an all-absorbing concern. For example, Helmreich, Beane, Lucker, and Spence (1978) found that extreme competitiveness was negatively related to scientific achievement. Instead of doing their job, high competitors spent their time keeping score on how well they were doing. K. Smith, Johnson, and Johnson (1982) found that cooperatively structured instruction leads to greater achievement and retention levels in all kinds of students. Norem-Hebeisen and Johnson (1981) found that cooperative students have a stronger feeling of personal worth, whereas competitive and individualistic students are more vulnerable to failure. Cooperatively arranged classrooms lead to more assistance, encouragement of achievement, friendship, and high self-esteem levels among students (R. T. Johnson and Johnson, 1981, 1982).

Violence in the streets, delinquency, and crime as well as loneliness, insecurity, and family tensions have been linked to individualism (Hsu, 1983; Macfarlane, 1978; D. Sinha, 1988). In fact, Macfarlane asserted that "loneliness, insecurity, and family tensions which are associated with the English structure outweigh the economic benefits" (p. 202).

Sinha saw the mental health of Indians under threat because of rapid social change, which weakens the family and results in social violence, riots, terrorism, suicide, delinquency, crime, and other forms of social disorganization. Westcott (1988) argued that excessive freedom results in loneliness, alienation, and relentless competition. Donohue (1990) associated excessive freedom with childhood crime, early pregnancies, drug abuse, suicide, homicide, homelessness, separation, divorce, and AIDS. Unbounded freedom, he claimed, results in no moral hierarchy. He focused on the looseness of 1990s American culture, where "no fault" laws result in irresponsibility, where there is too much civil liability, too many arguments about the rights of this or that group or person. He traced these developments to the 1964 Civil Rights Law, which, according to him, resulted in other groups' seeking their rights. Looseness means that there are no limits provided by the concept of "good taste" in song lyrics and art. He cited popular writing that includes extreme arguments, such as favoring the elimination of the institution of marriage. Although clearly a conservative critic of American culture, Donohue did a good job of describing the disadvantages of unconstrained individualism.

We can remind ourselves that the child-rearing pattern that pushes children toward early independence, although good for achievement, is bad for drug abuse (Bacon, 1973). In short, "there is no free lunch."

Hughes (1993) also claimed that the "self is now the sacred cow of American culture" (p. 7). The individual is no longer responsible for his or her own actions, since other people have created the conditions that resulted in individual behavior. The unconstrained self is always right. "The culture of complaint," as Hughes called it, blames all those who have power and allows people to claim only rights and to have no duties or responsibilities.

Because I believe in balance, that is, in checks and balances, I personally believe that some of these criticisms are sound. The extreme freedom that is advocated by some individualists does not seem to have any constraints. Although I am a member of the American Civil Liberties Union, I do not agree with all its positions.

Humans are simply not constituted to operate without controls from the physical or social environment. We note among some individualists a lack of understanding that too much of a good thing is a bad thing. We see them playing their music at higher and higher decibel levels, destroying their hearing. We see them striving for more and more money, not realizing that this shifts their level of adaptation (Helson, 1964), so the ordinary pleasures of life, like enjoying the beauty of a landscape or the moon, disappear. The frantic competition leads to high levels of anxiety and more people in therapy than ever before (Donohue, 1990).

At the same time, I recognize that some collectives are oppressive and can demolish all striving toward individuality. In fact, observers of child rearing in collectivist cultures (Guthrie, 1961) have noted that in certain cultures parents often try to break the will of the child, emphasizing total obedience.

When we look at the ethnographic extremes on the dimension of aggression, we see some interesting data. Robarchek and Robarchek (1992) provided a very informative contrast between the extremely individualistic Waorani of Ecuador and the very collectivist Semai of the Malaysian forests. The Waorani are independent, autonomous, and "in control"; the Semai are helpless, overwhelmed by obligations, and not in control of their life. In most respects the ecology of these two tribes is the same—a tropical forest. Social organization is similar. The only apparent difference is the population density, which is sixty-eight times greater among the Semai. As I argued in Chapter 3, density seems to be linked to tightness and hence to collectivism.

The aggression levels of these two tribes are diametrically opposite. The Waorani had a male homicide rate of 60 percent (that is, six out of every ten males were killed by someone). The Semai were extremely peaceful. Robarchek and Robarchek (1992) reported that some of the women of the Waorani fled from the tribe to escape the violence of the men. After some time they returned with two female American missionaries, who proceeded to work on the self-image of the Waorani males. Changing the view of the self resulted in a dramatic decrease in violence.

In some U.S. inner cities the level of violence is similar to that among the Waorani. Should Americans think of themselves as more linked to others, as a means of reducing violence? A research project along these lines would be well worth the effort. In short, is a shift from extreme individualism to more balance with collectivism desirable from the point of view of the level of aggression in American society?

The unbounded search for material success, so typical of American individualism, also seems to fail to provide happiness. Brickman, Coates, and Janoff-Bulman (1978) studied twenty-two lottery winners and twenty-two control subjects. The lottery winners were *not* happier than the controls. The researchers also checked to see if there was a difference in the happiness levels of buyers of lottery tickets and controls and found none. For example, the happiness levels of the winners, with happiness judged "in the past," "now," and expected in the "future," were 3.8, 4.0, and 4.2, for the lottery winners and 3.3, 3.8, and 4.1 for the controls, and the differences were not statistically significant.

The reason for these findings is that happiness is relative to our expectations. Our expectations are shaped by past events and have a neutral point (the level of adaptation, Helson, 1964), which is the geometric mean of the values of salient events. Winning a lottery has the effect of raising the level of adaptation. The result is that after one wins, most mundane, pleasant events in life (such as looking at a beautiful landscape) significantly lose some of their power to delight. Life becomes more drab, and to counteract that, the winner acts irrationally (e.g., buys a mansion that he cannot afford). A few months after winning the lottery, many of the winners were in worse shape than they had ever been!

High rates of heart attacks (see Chapter 5), irresponsibility in the public domain indicated by low voting rates (e.g., 50.1 percent in 1988 in the United States, which has one of the lowest rates of any industrial democracy, Hughes, 1993), and poor adjustment (Kasser and Ryan, 1993) have been noted by some writers as being linked to individualism. Kasser and Ryan (1993) found that values and expectancies for wealth and money are negatively associated with adjustment and well-being when they are more central to an individual than other self-relevant values and expectancies. Their measures of the centrality of money-related values and expectancies among college students were negatively related to their measures of well-being and mental health. Extending their sample to noncollege subjects replicated the findings, with evidence of lower global adjustment and social productivity and more behavioral disorders among the most materialistic. Similarly, Emmons (1991) found that distress levels were associated with higher strivings for power, which reflect desires to control, impress, and compete with others, a complex of motives that is found more often among individualists than collectivists.

Finally, individualism has a serious disadvantage in the area of international economic competition stemming from the fact that as jobs become more complex and more demanding, they require more training. However, for corporations to provide such training, they must be reasonably sure that their employees will stay with them for some time. Individualist employees are mobile, and that often makes training risky for the employer. Corporations certainly do not wish to train the future employees of their competitors! In short, for firms in individualistic countries, individualism is making competition in the global marketplace more difficult than it has to be.

A Synthesis

Studies carried out by survey organizations (e.g., Gallup, 1976) in different parts of the world indicated that when people are asked about their wishes and hopes for the future, they voice similar goals:

1. Improve personal character
2. Keep healthy and enjoy life
3. Have more money
4. Do better at work
5. See my family thrive
6. See improvements in the general economic conditions
7. See improvements in the general political conditions
8. Improve the social situation

   9. Serve others
   10. See a better world
   11. Keep things as they are

   I judge the first to be more collectivist (it is a classic Confucian value) than individualist, because there is a definite "tightness" in the idea. The second serves both the ingroup and the person. As S. H. Schwartz (1990) observed, there are many values that serve both. Perhaps a good society promotes these values even more vigorously than other values. The third looks more individualistic than collectivist, though obviously the ingroup would benefit from more money. The remaining goals seem to me to be collectivist, only indirectly helping the individual. Of course, in a worldwide perspective, individualists are a minority, perhaps not exceeding 30 percent of the population. Thus, it is not surprising that most goals are collectivist. There is also the problem of social desirability: It may be more socially desirable to endorse collective goals in such a survey. But perhaps there is a lesson in this: To pursue goals that are broader than ourselves and benefit us indirectly is more desirable than to pursue strictly individualistic goals such as pleasure, a variable, exciting life, and the like.
   A useful theoretical integration of the argument about the relative advantages and disadvantages of individualism and collectivism can be attained by examining the arguments of Foa and Foa (1974). The Foas argued that there are six kinds of exchanges that humans engage in. Three are "particularistic" in the sense that it makes a large difference *who* the particular person is with whom one exchanges. They are *love, status,* and *services.* The other three are "universalistic" in the sense that one might exchange them with anyone. They are *money, information,* and *goods.* People do not care who buys their stock in the stock exchange or their product in the store or who gets information from their books. But people do care who gets their love and their services and to whom they give status.
   As a society moves toward modernity, which means, as we have seen, more individualism, time gets to be a premium. Employees get paid by the hour, and productivity is measured in units of goods or services produced or provided per hour. The particularistic exchanges require more time than the universalistic. One can give $1 million by writing a check in less than a minute, but one can not make love in that length of time.
   We note that in traditional societies people take a lot of time exchanging particularistic resources. The Trobrianders in the South Pacific (Malinowski, 1922, 1960) take long trips to give bracelets (which are worthless to Westerners) to people with whom they want to maintain good relationships. This so-called Kula Ring is sustained simply to create solidarity. Malinowski compared it with the display of the crown jewels: It does not produce something of commercial value, but it gives satisfaction.

In collectivist cultures greetings take a long time and include giving status with proper honorifics and expressions of concern for the other person (the Chinese greeting, Have you eaten?) and the other person's kin (How is your family?). As time becomes more valuable, many of these exchanges are first shortened and then dropped and are substituted by exchanges that do not require so much time. Thus, the parent who might take an hour interacting with a child instead gives him or her some money to go to the ice cream parlor. Modernity, affluence, and individualism are linked and make particularistic exchanges less frequent and universalistic exchanges more frequent.

Triandis (1990) argued that collectivists are good at exchanging particularistic resources and poor—relative to the individualists—at exchanging universalistic resources (e.g., husband-wife joint estate management planning); conversely, individualists are good at exchanging universalistic resources and relatively poor at exchanging particularistic resources (e.g., giving status).

We noted above that the problems of the collectivists are in exchanges of universalistic resources, that is, in actions that involve large publics or the government. We also saw that the problems of the individualists are in exchanging particularistic resources. They are not so good in intimate, face-to-face relationships.

Thus, if we can train our children to compensate for our cultural background, train individualists in intimate, self-disclosure, and face-saving interactions and train collectivists on how to deal with the government and (especially if they are government bureaucrats) on how to deal with the public, that will result in improved societies. One consistent observation I made in many of my travels in the two kinds of societies is that in collectivist cultures authorities tend to relate to the public in an authoritarian, unhelpful, abrasive way, whereas in individualistic cultures by and large the authorities are respectful of their citizens and helpful.

We need also to distinguish between narcissistic individualism, where only the individual's goals determine behavior, and communitarian individualism, where the individual's goals are integrated with the goals of the community. To the extent that individuals pursue goals that are desirable not only for themselves but also for their societies, the societies will function well. Since there are many such goals (see the list above) and they are valued universally, there is a definite direction for the evolution and change of societies toward the kinds of societies that we would like to live in.

Advice to the Young

Suppose a young couple, one a collectivist and one an individualist, asked me where they should live. What advice would I give them? Clearly, it would depend on their values. Individualists on the whole would feel most comfortable in individualistic cultures, and collectivists in collectivist ones. But here we have a couple that is split on background. What advice can I give?

One important consideration is the competence of these young people. Individualistic societies, with their emphasis on achievement, competence, competition, science, and modernity, are affluent and well designed for people who are successful. If that is important for them, they would be better adjusted in such cultures. If it is important for them to be happy, creative, and free and to feel that they are high in self-efficacy, they should chose an individualistic culture. Also, individualistic cultures tolerate differences better, and since they are different as a couple, that would suggest that they should choose an individualistic culture. Furthermore, if they are concerned about democracy, human rights, good relations with authorities, and equal treatment under the law, the choice is individualism.

However, this option has many disadvantages, and they must choose it only if they feel able to accept them. They will be faced with much crime and drug abuse and with homicide rates much higher than in collectivist cultures. If they are successful, they might be able to protect themselves from these problems by living in the "right" neighborhoods, hiring bodyguards, and so on. The competitiveness, the insecurity that one will or perhaps will not do well, often lead to anxiety and high rates of heart attacks. One may also be lonely and not receive sufficient social support. Interpersonal relationships are likely to be curt and less intimate than they would be in a collectivist culture.

Thus, maybe they should consider a collectivist culture. Such a choice would result in more-pleasant interpersonal relationships, as long as they are dealing with ingroup members. There will be law and order and relatively little crime and drug abuse, and they would be able to emphasize group achievement.

However, they would have to pay a price for these advantages. They may be overall less happy, less affluent, more under the control of others; people will demand more conformity; and they will feel more tied to the past. They may also have trouble in relations with the authorities and may find themselves having to support the harsh treatment of outgroups. When the culture is both collectivist and very tight, there may be more suicide because that combination is especially linked to low self-esteem. I mentioned earlier the study by Lester (1988) that found a correlation of .43 between collectivism and suicide rates.

Obviously, the young people, having heard the advantages and disadvantages, would have to decide for themselves. But you and I, as we think about these issues, would do well to explore what we can do to change our societies toward a greater balance between these two tendencies. We need societies that do well both in the citizen-authorities and the person-to-person fronts, that provide both freedom and security, that have something not only for their most competent members but also for the majority of their members.

In addition, my advice for the couple would be to self-monitor their behavior and make sure that they use more particularistic behaviors than is normal in individualistic cultures. I would say to them: Provide more compliments, status, and more services to others than is expected of you. Furthermore, try to emphasize values that are shared by the vast majority of your society. Finally, when dealing with interpersonal relationships try to be collectivists. That is, seek stability, loyalty, the long term; define yourselves as members of ingroups, try to line up your personal goals with the goals of ingroups; pay attention to the norms of ingroups and be willing to sacrifice personal gain for the sake of keeping the ingroup happy; try to tolerate old relationships that are no longer profitable (i.e., where the gains no longer exceed the costs) for the sake of the stability that I advocate.

At the same time, when dealing with large-scale collectives, be individualistic. You need to think of what is best for you and how you can achieve, succeed, and compete.

In the final analysis, then, my best guess is that good mental health depends on including both individualistic and collectivist tendencies in one's repertoire of behavior and using the individualistic in some situations and the collectivist in other situations. Mental health also requires that personal goals be compatible with the goals of our collectives. Thus, when we strive for success, we should not be the only ones who succeed; our collectives should also succeed.

Appendix: Measurement of Individualism and Collectivism

Level of Measurement

The measurement of these constructs can be done at two levels: the cultural and the individual. The two levels are often highly correlated, as in the work of S. H. Schwartz (1994), where the correlations of the two levels were in the .80+ range. However, it is not wise to assume that kind of correlation. It must be checked empirically for each set of data.

It may be easier to understand what is meant by "levels" if we take a concrete example. Suppose we have a 20-item attitude questionnaire that we think measures different aspects of individualism and collectivism. Suppose we obtain responses to this questionnaire from 10 cultures that are widely scattered around the world. Assume further that we were able to get 100 people in each culture to answer this questionnaire.

Now consider how the data may be analyzed. One option is to add the responses of the 100 people in each culture, that is, ignore individual differences and simply say we have 200 numbers (10 cultures times 20 items) that index what we are interested in measuring. In the literature (e.g., Hofstede, 1980), this is called an ecological-level analysis, though Leung and Bond (1989) preferred the term "cross-cultural." In any case, that is a cultural level of analysis.

Another option is to analyze the data separately in each culture. For example, a factor analysis could determine similarities in the way people respond to the items. In each culture we could have a different factor analysis and thus end up with 10 different analyses. Leung and Bond (1989) called this the "intracultural level," and it is an individual-level analysis.

Leung and Bond (1989) also discussed the "pancultural" way of analyzing such data. The pancultural factor analysis would be based on the correlations of the 20 items across the world, that is, the 20 by 20 matrix based on 1,000 observations per variable would be factor analyzed. This kind of analysis gives the universal factors that underlie this data set.

Cross-cultural psychologists use the terms *etic* for universal and *emic* for culture specific (see Triandis, 1994, for a description of why this is useful, where the terms come from, and how to measure etic factors with emic items). Leung and Bond (1989) developed a statistical procedure that extracts "strong etics" and "weak etics" and identifies emics; it also eliminates response sets.

Response sets have been a problem in cross-cultural work (Triandis, 1972), because people do not use scales the same way. In some cultures (e.g., around the

Mediterranean, especially among the Arabs) if one is truthful one must make strong, clear statements, and thus the use of the extreme ends of scales is very common. One does not just say, "I like this food"; one must say, "This is among the best food I have ever had." In other parts of the world, such as in East Asia, people place great value on modesty and on controlled emotional expression. One does not say, "I strongly agree"; one is more likely to say, "Perhaps I agree." This results in the frequent use of the middle positions of scales (Hui and Triandis, 1989) when answering questionnaires.

These tendencies, although annoying to cross-cultural psychologists, are not impossible to deal with. One can standardize the data within each culture, removing the mean of the data set obtained in each culture and dividing by the standard deviation of the data set. Thus, each culture has a mean of zero and response sets are neutralized. This technique, of course, assumes that the questions asked are sufficiently heterogeneous that there is no reason to expect a culture to average more or less than zero.

Leung and Bond (1989) did something analogous. They standardized the data first within subject and second across items. A factor analysis based on these doubly standardized scores can extract factors that are independent of culture. A "strong etic" is obtained when these factors are in agreement with the factors extracted from the cross-cultural (or ecological) factor analysis. Factors that are extracted from the doubly standardized scores, but not found in the cross-cultural analysis, are "weak etics." Factors that are extracted by the cross-cultural (or ecological) method, but not from the Leung and Bond method, are cultural factors that do not describe individuals. Factors extracted only in the intracultural analyses are emic factors that can describe individuals in their particular culture, but should not be used to compare cultures.

Another statistical procedure that has been used to study the individualism and collectivism constructs is discriminant function analysis (e.g., Triandis, Bontempo, Betancourt, et al., 1986). Here functions that look like factor patterns, that is, consist of loadings of items, are extracted. These functions are designed to provide the most discrimination possible among the data sets from each culture. This analysis has many similarities with pancultural analysis, though because it is not based on doubly standardized scores, may have the weakness of including distortions traceable to the way the subjects use scales.

In general, we need etic measures to compare cultures and emic measures to fully understand them. Depending on the purpose of our research, we should use both. If we need to compare, we should work on the etic measures; if we need to test a theory within culture, we should use the emic measures.

It is possible to focus on different elements of subjective culture, such as beliefs, attitudes, and values, in assessing the levels of collectivism and individualism. Since I hold that individualism and collectivism are cultural syndromes, I use all elements of subjective culture and look for consistencies among them. However, other researchers have used only one type of element of subjective culture, and for certain purposes this is an advantage, since the more-focused measures are more reliable (have high Cronbach alphas). Focusing on a particular ingroup rather than covering all the important ingroups of a cultural group also has the benefit of allowing the measures to be more reliable (high Cronbach alphas). However, my interest has been in developing the most general measures possible, and I have been willing to pay the price of low reliabilities in order to do that. For different purposes, researchers will want to use different strategies. There is no such thing as "the best method." All methods have limitations. The use of multimethod approaches that converge is the only strategy that can be recommended.

Historical Overview of Measurement

Hofstede (1980) provided scores based on an ecological factor analysis. His data extracted one of four factors, which he called individualism versus collectivism. However, as we have said, a factor that exists at the cultural level may not be found at the individual level of analysis.

Hui (1984) was the first to measure the construct at the individual level. He used 63 items and a 6-point strongly agree–disagree format, which he called the INDCOL scale. He analyzed the data by considering different collectives (spouse, parents, kin, neighbor, friend, co-worker). Hui (1988) showed that the collectivism scores of this instrument were valid because they correlated in meaningful ways with "social interest" (Crandall, 1980), a construct that has much in common with collectivism, and numerous scenario-generated scores. He found that collectivism was correlated with social desirability among his Chinese, but not among his American, subjects. Presumably, in an individualistic culture, collectivism is not socially desirable.

Hui (1988) considered models that predict behavior from attitudes, norms, and other such variables (Fishbein and Ajzen, 1975; Triandis, 1972, 1977, 1980) and reasoned that collectivists would show a greater correspondence between an obligation to do something and the intention to do it, whereas individualists would show more correspondence between liking to do it and intending to do it. He used the following scenario: "A classmate whom you have only recently met, suggested that the two of you should go out for lunch and chat. So, you and your classmate went to a restaurant. You had agreed to each pay for your own meal. The cost for each of you was about $6. Before leaving the restaurant, your classmate put a tip of $1.50 on the table." The subjects were asked for their felt obligation to pay the classmate for the tip (from 0 to $1.50) and in addition to indicate how much they intended to give to their classmate. A similar scenario was also used where the words "classmate" were changed to "good friend." Among collectivists (determined by INDCOL) the obligation and intention to pay the classmate and good friend were correlated .71 and .87 respectively. Among individualists the corresponding correlations were −.50 and .69. This data suggested some predictive validity for INDCOL. In addition, Hui (1988) found that collectivists favored sharing others' burdens more than individualists. The appendix of Hui (1988) includes the wording of the INDCOL items.

Other Studies of Attitudes

Bellah et al. (1985) reported the content of interviews with 200 Americans about their lives. Content analyses suggested the following themes: self-reliance; independence; separation from family, religion, and community; hedonism; utilitarianism;

emphasis on exchanges, contracts; helping the community only if the self gets something for it; competition; wanting to be distinguished; emphasis on competence, equity, and fairness; trust in others; involvement in community life; rejection of arbitrary authority; and the self as the only source of reality.

The best items from Hui (1984) were used by Triandis, Leung, et al. (1985), who broadened the measurement by including a number of scenarios and asking the subjects to indicate how much they were influenced by different kinds of people in different situations. This study established both the convergent and discriminant validity of attitude items as measures of individualism and collectivism. Allocentrics were more cooperative (the D. W. Johnson and Norem-Hebeison, 1979, measure) and less lonely (the Schmidt and Sermat, 1983, measure).

Triandis, Bontempo, Betancourt, et al. (1986) used items suggested by colleagues from nine diverse cultures, in addition to attitude items that had proven successful in the Hui (1984) and Triandis, Leung, et al. (1985) studies and ideas from Bellah et al. (1985). These items were administered to samples from Illinois, California (Hispanics, Anglos, Asian-Americans), Hong Kong, Chile, Costa Rica, Indonesia, India, Greece, the Netherlands, and France. An attempt was made to obtain 100 men and 100 women in each culture, but that did not succeed in every place. A pancultural factor analysis was done (see above for description of this type of analysis), and in addition a discriminant function analysis was performed. The pancultural factor analysis clustered items indicating four factors (selected items are listed below).

Self-Reliance with Hedonism
What happens to me is my own doing.
If the group is slowing me down, it is better to leave it and work alone.
The most important thing in my life is to make myself happy.

Separation from Ingroups
Children should not feel honored even if the father was highly praised and given an award by a government official for his contributions and services to the community.

Family Integrity
Aging parents should live at home with their children.
Children should live at home with their parents until they get married.

Interdependence and Sociability
I like to live close to my good friends.

The discriminant function analysis showed that "Family Integrity" provided the most separation among the samples, accounting for 57% of the common variance. It correlated .73 with Hofstede's (1980) collectivism scores.

The top scorers on "Family Integrity" were California Asians, Indians, Hong Kongers, Costa Ricans, and Indonesians. The bottom scorers were from the Netherlands, France, Greece, and Illinois.

Triandis, Bontempo, Villareal, et al. (1988) examined the structure of idiocentrism and allocentrism in the United States, using 158 items. In addition to the 63 INDCOL items, they used 95 U.S. emic items. In this study three factors emerged:

Self-Reliance with Competition
  If the group is slowing me down, it is better to leave it and work alone.
  Winning is everything.

Concern for Ingroup
  I like to live close to my good friends.
  I would help within my means if a relative told me s(he) is in financial diffi-
    culty; and reversed: It is foolish to try to preserve resources for future gen-
    erations.

Distance from Ingroups
  I am not to blame if one of my family members fails.
  My happiness is unrelated to the well-being of my co-workers.

A second study, with 145 items, with subjects from Illinois, Japan, and Puerto Rico, again showed that individualism and collectivism are multidimensional and replicated the findings by Triandis, Leung, et al. (1985) that allocentrics report receiving more and a better quality of social support and idiocentrics report that they are lonely. These results were found in both Puerto Rico and Illinois.

Several additional questionnaires allowed a second-order factor analysis (a factor analysis of the factors obtained from each questionnaire), which showed that "Subordination of Ingroup Goals to Personal Goals" was the underlying factor for collectivism. This is "Vertical Collectivism."

Finally, these studies suggested that the meaning of self-reliance is different in collectivist and individualistic cultures. In collectivist cultures it means not being a burden on the ingroup, which echoes vertical collectivism. In individualistic cultures it means not being dependent on the ingroup, which echoes horizontal individualism.

Lortie-Lussier and Fellers (1991) used some of the items from this study with English Canadians, French Canadians, and Italian Canadians and found that the English Canadians were the most individualistic, the Italian Canadians were most peer oriented, and the French Canadians the most family oriented.

Multimethod Measurement

There is a need for multimethod measurement because each method has its own biases and limitations. In addition, if individualism and collectivism are cultural syndromes (see Chapter 3), there should be tendencies to find correlations among self-descriptions, attitudes, values, and other such elements of subjective culture. Triandis, McCusker, and Hui (1990) used five methods: (1) The meaning of the self in collectivist and individualist cultures; (2) the perceived homogeneity of ingroups and outgroups in these kinds of cultures; (3) responses to attitude items; (4) responses to value items; and (5) perceptions of social behavior as a function of social distance in these two kinds of cultures. I will now discuss these methods in more detail.

1. The meaning of the self in collectivist and individualist cultures used an adaptation of the Kuhn and McPartland (1954) method, which required subjects to complete 20 sentences that begin with "I am … " Content analyses of the responses examined whether a social category was suggested by each answer. Social (S) responses were considered to be completions, such as "a son" (family), "a Roman Catholic" (religion), "a resident of Pearl City" (common residence), and so on. The percent out of 20 responses that were scored S provided the %S score. The means of this score in collectivist samples ranged between 20% and 52%. Several individuals had scores of 100% in a sample obtained in the People's Republic of China (PRC). However, this may simply exaggerate the score because in Chinese "I am" must be followed by a category, not a personal quality. The means for individualist samples ranged from 11 to 19%, with the mode of the 519 Illinois subjects equal to zero!

This measure is sensitive to the cognitions that the respondent has had just before responding to it. Trafimow, Triandis, and Goto (1991) randomly assigned students from the introductory psychology subject pool at the University of Illinois to two conditions: "For the next two minutes, you will not need to write anything. Please think of what makes you different from your family and friends. What do you expect yourself to do?" or the same initial instruction and "Think of what you have in common with your family and friends." A two-minute interpolated task was followed with the request that they complete the 20 statements described above (beginning with "I am").

Eighteen respondents had Chinese names; 24 had English names. The "what makes you different" instruction generated 30% S-responses from the students with Chinese names and 7% S-responses from the students with English names; the "what you have in common" instruction generated 52% S-responses from the students with Chinese names and 23% S-responses from the students with English names. Both the student's name and the instructions had highly statistically significant effects. The fact that the Chinese students, who in some cases were members of the third or fourth generation in the United States and were responding in English, provided significantly more collectivist responses than the students with English names tells something about the importance of culture.

It is interesting to compare the average levels of the %S-responses obtained in this experiment with the levels of samples responding without any sort of priming. When the students with Chinese names were given the collectivist prime, their %S scores averaged the same as the respondents from the PRC. The students with English names, in the same condition, reached the level of the Chinese-background respondents from Hawaii. On the other hand, the individualistic prime pushed the students with Chinese names to the level of the Chinese students from Hawaii and the students with English names to the lowest average ever recorded for the %S scores.

A second experiment was done with students with English names only. Twenty-four students were randomly assigned to the condition that included a collectivist prime, which consisted of a paragraph about the king of Sumeria who sent a member of his family to help another king, or an individualistic prime, a paragraph about the king of Sumeria who sent his most talented general to help the other king. Again the %S was measured. This time the collectivist prime gave 20% and the individualist 9% S-responses. Thus, the data obtained from students with English names in this second experiment were comparable with the data obtained from the students with English names in the first experiment.

Trafimow, Triandis, and Goto (1991) argued that people have a cognitive schema (a set of interrelated ideas) that includes individualistic ideas and a different schema that includes collectivist ideas. By priming one or the other of these schemata, we can obtain a different score in the %S. This makes this measure highly sensitive to the conditions of administration, which can be desirable, if we wish to measure the effect of particular situations on the respondent, and undesirable, if we are looking for stability. The presence of a cognitive schema is parallel to the findings by Alan Fiske (1993) I discussed in Chapter 3. He found that people from diverse cultures had schemata for each of his four types of sociality.

The major conclusion that I have derived after ten years of use of this measure is that it is very good for cross-cultural comparisons and very poor for intracultural work. It just does not have sufficient range for intracultural work.

In addition, I found that this measure is very good when I lecture on collectivism to Chinese audiences. I can ask an audience to take 10 minutes to write on a sheet of paper 20 statements that begin with "I am." After that, I tell them how to score their statements. That takes about 5 minutes. Then, I ask them to raise their hand if their score was between 0% and 9%, 10% and 19%, and so on, till I get to between 90% and 100%. There are no hands until we get to 30% and quite a few hands when we are in the 90 to 100% range. In contrast, with people from Western backgrounds, there are hardly any hands after we reach 30%. In short, the distributions are essentially nonoverlapping. It is also interesting that the reporting mistakes made in this demonstration exercise, if any, occur at the 30 to 39% range. In other words, some Chinese and some Westerners in the 30% area may not raise their hand when their score is 30%, suggesting that the Chinese are embarrassed to have "so few" and the Westerners are embarrassed to have "so many" S-responses.

2. The second method used by Triandis, McCusker, and Hui (1990) used judgments of the homogeneity or heterogeneity of ingroups and outgroups. Collectivists tend to see their ingroups as very homogeneous; individualists see them as heterogeneous. I think that collectivists value homogeneity, and that has some relationship to their preference for harmony within the ingroup. At the same time, individualists value some heterogeneity because they value people who are "distinct" and "unique." In any case, the data did show these differences.

3. Responses to attitude items, such as the ones used by Hui, Triandis, and others described above, usually were on a 6- or 9-point scale from strongly agree to strongly disagree. Collectivists agreed with items such as "aged parents should live at home with their children," which were rejected by individualists.

4. Responses to value items, such as the 56 values developed by S. H. Schwartz and Bilsky (1987), where a subject indicates whether a value (e.g., *equality,* equal opportunity for all) is "a guiding principle in my life" on a scale from 0 = not important to 7 = of supreme importance, and where a −1 may be given to a stimulus that

is not a value. Collectivists gave greater importance to values such as "honoring parents and elders," and individualists gave greater importance to values such as "an exciting life."

5. Measuring perceptions of social behavior as a function of social distance is based on the theory that collectivists will behave more differently toward ingroup and outgroup members than will individualists. Subjects were required to make psychophysical judgments by the Stevens (1966) method of direct estimation. This study was described in Chapter 5 in considerable detail, and the curves that were characteristic of collectivists and individualists were reproduced in that chapter (see Figures 5.1 to 5.6).

Starting from these curves, one can estimate whether a person is a collectivist or an individualist by the extent to which his curves are like the curves of the collectivists or of the individualists in the study. Similarly, from each method, a score for each individual was obtained, and the scores obtained from all the methods were intercorrelated.

The interrelations among the results of the five methods were small, but positive. Thus, we are dealing with a cultural syndrome, and rather diverse methods of measurement showed convergence.

Hui and Yee (submitted) obtained a shorter version of the INDCOL scale, and with a second-order factor analysis obtained an ingroup solidarity factor (share things, help, closeness to parents, share honors) from 852 subjects. This appears to be a measure of horizontal collectivism. They found a small, but significant, association with age (i.e., the older subjects were more collectivist); males were lower on this factor than females; the factor correlated with job satisfaction ($r = .19$, $p <$ .001) and felt social obligation ($r = .09$, $p < .05$). Those high on ingroup solidarity did not want autonomy in their jobs and did not want to be consulted by their boss. But they did want to work for a prestigious company more than those who were low on this factor.

Triandis, McCusker, Betancourt, et al. (1993) submitted the data used in Triandis, Bontempo, Betancourt, et al. (1986) to a Leung and Bond (1989) analysis and compared the results with intracultural and cross-cultural analyses.

The Leung and Bond factors had six themes. The first three were clearly individualistic:

1. Separation from Ingroups: One can't feel honored just because an ingroup member is honored.
2. Independence: self-reliance, struggle to be alone; thinking one can do without friendly co-workers.
3. Personal Competence: Judge people on their own merit, not the company they keep.

The fourth was bipolar. It emphasized:

4. *Task:* If the group is slowing me down, it is better to leave it and do the job alone, versus *social* emphasis: I enjoy meeting my neighbors everyday.

The remaining two factors were collectivist:

5. Dependence on Others: Children should live at home until they get married, versus self-sufficiency: What happens to me is my own doing.
6. Sociability: I plan to live with my parents; I enjoy meeting my neighbors.

The "Separation from Ingroups" factor was a strong etic because it appeared not only in the Leung and Bond analysis but also in the pancultural one. It may reflect an independent versus an interdependent self (Markus and Kitayama, 1991b). The samples that were high on independence were France, Illinois, Poland, and Venezuela; the countries that were high on interdependence were Hong Kong, Indonesia, India, Chile, Japan, and the PRC.

The "Independence" factor seems to be a strong etic also. It contrasted Illinois and Japan with Venezuela and the PRC.

The "Personal Competence" factor was also a strong etic, contrasting those high, which included Japan, France, Chile, and the PRC, with those low, which included Poland, Venezuela, and Hong Kong.

"Family Integrity" was a weak etic; those high were in India and Indonesia and those low were in Chile and France.

There were also several emic factors, some of which were very interesting. For example, the Indonesians had a factor suggesting "Insecurity When One Is Far from the Ingroup."

Even more interesting was the observation that in the intracultural analyses, factors that appeared in collectivist cultures such as "Serving the Ingroup," "Cooperation," "Harmony Within the Ingroup," and "Attention to the Needs of Family and Friends" were entirely missing in individualistic cultures.

Similarly, factors that appeared in the intracultural factor analysis of the data from individualistic cultures were entirely missing from the analysis of the data from collectivist cultures. These included "Distance from Parents" and "Competition." "Self-Reliance" was correlated with "Compassion" in Illinois and with "Insecurity" in Indonesia.

In conclusion, this study suggested that "Separation from Ingroups," "Independence," and "Personal Competence" are factors found at both the cultural and the individual levels of analyses. "Family Integrity" is a cultural-level factor (remember, this factor correlated .71 with Hofstede's scores, according to Triandis, Bontempo, Betancourt, et al., 1986); it does an excellent job of discriminating across cultures, but not across individuals within culture because it has very little range within culture.

"Dependence on Others" and "Sociability" are good measures of allocentrism. "Separation from Ingroups," "Independence," "Personal Competence," and "Task Orientation" are good measures of idiocentrism.

In sum, this study has sorted out what is important in cultural-level analyses (Family Integrity), and what should be used to locate people who are allocentric (Dependence, Sociability) or idiocentric (Separation from Ingroups, Independence, Personal Competence, and Task Orientation).

Triandis, Chan, et al. (in press) developed additional scales and also used items from Triandis, Leung, et al. (1985); Hui (1988); Triandis, Bontempo, Villareal, et al. (1988); and Triandis, McCusker, and Hui (1990) to see whether the various measurements of individualism and collectivism converged, and if one of them was more "central" in the sense that it correlated with all the other measures.

They used:

1. the %S
2. a set of Thurstone-scaled "Family Integrity" items
3. the subject's perceptions of whether their culture was collectivist or individualist
4. the subject's judgment of whether they are "the kind of person who behaves" in an individualistic or collectivist manner
5. a scale developed by Yamaguchi (1994) that measures the extent subjects saw themselves as doing what is consistent with their own goals or with the goals of their friends
6. the Yamaguchi items but substituting "friend" with "parent"
7. a measure developed by J. B. P. Sinha of whether the subjects feel that their own desires, opinions, and interests are more or less important than the desires, opinions, and interests of others.

Triandis, Chan, et al. (in press) used the logic of item analysis. They had 12 standardized scores (7 collectivist, 5 individualist) and asked which of these measures correlates the most with the total, that is, the sum of all the other methods less the one being tested.

This analysis showed that the "I am the kind of person who acts this way" scale was the most central. It correlated .41 with the total of all other scales ($p < .001$). However, several other scales had almost equally central positions, and since the correlations were not statistically significantly different from each other, it was concluded that all the methods are usable.

Noting that the %S is an excellent measure across cultures, but not within culture, because it has too little range within culture, the authors suggested that depending on the purpose of the study, it may be desirable to use the %S and one or two of the other methods. Certainly, the "I am the kind of person ... " scale has much merit.

The second study in Triandis, Chan, et al. (in press) examined the responses of Japanese subjects to (1) the attitude, (2) the value items, and (3) the Thurstone-scaled "Family Integrity" scale. Both the attitude and the value items were useful, but the Thurstone-scaled "Family Integrity" scale was recommended especially because it correlated well with both attitudes and values.

The low alphas suggested the addition of items that are essentially synonyms of the ones that were used in the previous study. Items added by Singelis, Triandis, et al. (in press) produced considerable improvements in the alphas.

The Work of Other Scholars

The measurement of individualism and collectivism was reported by several other scholars. Because of limitations of space, I will not describe it in detail, but the reader is directed to the references.

Wagner and Moch (1986) used items such as "People in a work group should be willing to make sacrifices for the sake of the work group." This kind of item suggests vertical collectivism.

Yamaguchi (1994) used items such as "I don't sacrifice self-interest for my group" and "I think it is desirable for members of my group to have the same opinion."

Oyserman (1993) developed different items for different studies and was able to obtain meaningful patterns of results with outside variables.

Weissman et al. (1993) developed the California Cultural Assessment Inventory (CCAI). Subjects were asked to rate the importance of 25 values in relation to family, close friends, colleagues, and strangers. Subjects rated these values on a 0 = Not at All Important to 6 = Very Important scale and also on how much they actually engage in those types of behaviors in relation to the same four groups on 0 = Never Do It to 6 = Do It All the Time. They reported good reliabilities, factor structures, et cetera.

Bhawuk and Brislin (1992) developed 16 items that measure individualism and collectivism, which together with items measuring flexibility and open-mindedness had excellent alphas ($r = .84$). This was achieved by focusing very narrowly on the issue of direct versus indirect communication and a few other related concepts. For example, they had collectivist items such as "I prefer to give opinions that will help people save face rather than give a statement of the truth" and "I have respect for the authority figures with whom I interact." They had individualistic items such as "I say no directly when I have to" and "I prefer to be direct and forthright when dealing with people."

During a conference held at the East-West Center in 1989 several participants suggested ways to get a class of students interested in the collectivism topic. C. Harry Hui told of an exercise consisting of a list of 25 social stimuli (e.g., grandfather's brother and different types of acquaintances) and the students are asked to enter a check mark next to those who are "indispensable to your happiness." He reported that British respondents placed few check marks and Chinese respondents used many. In addition, this list can be used to estimate the distance in kilometers between "you and those listed above who are still alive," the frequency of telephone calls to these people, assuming no financial limitations (suggested by Cigdem Kagitcibasi), and the chance that one might say to them, "I love you."

A participant from a collectivist culture suggested: "Think of the three most recent parties you have attended. What percentage of the people, on the average, did you know prior to the party?" The assumption is that collectivists will enter a higher percentage than individualists. Another one suggested: "What percent of the people at the average party did you talk to?" Again it was supposed that collectivists would provide higher entries.

These suggestions were published in the *Cross-Cultural Psychology Bulletin,* and one of the readers, V. S. R. Vijaykumar, of the Department of Psychology at the University of Madras, India, subsequently reported that he had used these items. He worked with Tamils and Telegus living in Madras. He found that the number of people who were checked as being indispensable, the frequency of telephone calls, and the intention to say "I love you" were intercorrelated. But the distance in kilometers item was unrelated to the other measures. The author concluded that the three intercorrelated items do capture collectivism. The people who are indispensable for happiness and the intention to say "I love you" items were strongly correlated in all samples (Tamils .96; Telegus, .85, other cultures .93). The Telegus were more collectivist than the Tamils.

Bierbrauer, Meyer, and Wolfradt (1994) distinguished between a normative and an evaluative component of social behavior and devised a scale that measures these components. It discriminated Germans from collectivist populations.

Chan (1994) used the %S, attitude, and value measures in Hong Kong and Illinois. He trichotomized each distribution, calling the lowest third 1, middle third 2, and highest (most collectivist) third 3, then summed the 3 indexes. He called this sum the COLINDEX score. Those with scores of 7, 8, and 9 were called collectivists, and those with scores of 3, 4, and 5 were called individualists. The distributions of these scores were as expected: In Hong Kong there were more collectivists and in Illinois more individualists. The scores also predicted the behavior of subjects in an experiment during which they negotiated with a computer program while they were thinking that they were negotiating with a stranger or a friend. As expected, the collectivists behaved much more differently than the individualists when they negotiated with a friend compared to with a stranger, and this difference was related to the COLINDEX score.

Singelis (1992, 1994) developed scales that measured interdependent and independent self-construals. They had alphas in the .69 to .74 range. Interdependent self-construal was correlated with the tendency to communicate contextually rather than directly.

Gudykunst, Matsumoto, et al. (1994) developed measures of self-construal with alphas around .80+. They used items from many of the scales mentioned above and developed additional items. Examples of their items follow: For interdependent self-construal: "I maintain harmony in the groups of which I am a member"; "I consult with co-workers on work-related matters"; "It is important to me to maintain harmony within the group." For independent self-construal: "My personal identity is very important to me" and "It is important for me to be able to act as a free and independent person."

Ways of Measuring the Constructs

Goals

Tanaka (1978) surveyed samples from the Pacific Rim and found more individualism among Australians and New Zealanders than among East or South Asians. For example, "to do what I think worth doing" was considered an important goal by 50% and 64% of the Australians and New Zealanders respectively, and by only 32% of the Japanese, 12% of the Indians, and 8% of the Pakistanis. Consistent with my contention that the Indians are vertical collectivists and the Australians horizontal individualists, "to acquire high status" was an important goal of 35% of the Indians and of only 1% of the Australians. Thus, goals may provide good methods for measuring the four kinds of cultural patterns I discussed in Chapter 3.

Values

Hofstede's (1980) study focused on values, as did those of Hofstede and Bond (1984) and the Chinese Cultural Connection (1987), which started with a set of values generated in Chinese culture and applied it to diverse cultures.

The S. H. Schwartz and Bilsky (1987) method has been used in more than 40 countries. Schwartz (1994) obtained data from 200 teachers and 200 "others" (usually students, sometimes a representative sample) in each country. This project was reviewed in Chapter 3.

Content Analyses of Autobiographies

Content analyses of autobiographies (Morsbach, 1980) have suggested the presence of more individualistic themes in the West than in Japan. Shannon (1986), in a content analysis of U.S. young children's books, found a very strong tendency for the self to be the focus of activities and very little evidence of harmony with others.

Other Content Analyses

An ingenious method that gets at the individual-collective dimension was used by Semin and Rubini (1990). It consisted of a content analysis of insults carried out in Catania, in the collectivist Italian South, and Trieste, in the individualist Italian North. Semin and Rubini used insults directed at the person (you are a pig, stupid, cretin, ugly, uncivil, sucker) or at the person's collective (f— your mother and 36 other relatives!).

There were more collective insults in Catania than in Trieste, but no significant differences were found on individual insults. There was no difference in the number of insults exchanged per unit of time; however, the North made more use of intellectual insults (e.g., stupid).

Observations

Kernis et al. (1988) observed whether people walked alone or with others. Triandis (1990) also made systematic observations of people walking as well as riding cars alone or together in an American and in a collectivist Greek town. Triandis (1990) found that the alone/together ratio was larger than 1.00 during the day and dropped to less than 1.00 during the leisure periods. Thus, it appears to reflect "sociability."

The alone/together index for walking did not show cultural differences; the one for riding in cars did. It was 3.94 in Urbana, Illinois, versus 3.42 in Kozani, Greece. Observations carried out by Triandis (1990) in China suggested that more social interactions occurred in groups of 3 or more in that country than in the United States. This is consistent with the observations by Brandt (1974), who noted that Korean skiers ski in larger groups than American skiers.

Distribution of Amount of Attention Received

Derber (1979) discussed the pursuit of attention in American life. He argued that attention is a unique resource that Americans seek. Clearly, attention has special value in a vertical individualist culture. Thus, the extent people get attention may be a useful measure of vertical individualism.

Derber reported field studies in different settings in which trained observers coded who gets attention, the inequality in the distribution of attention, and the disposition of individuals to get attention. He examined factors that cause extreme inequality of attention.

In addition, Derber and his assistants tape-recorded 320 after-dinner conversations and coded the interactions. They found that attention getting was a function of status. Some people monopolized the conversation. Quoting a line from Oscar Wilde, "I hate people who talk about themselves, as you do, when one wants to talk about oneself, as I do," Derber suggested that the measurement of attention getting and seeking is quite revealing of social dynamics. Especially interesting is the person who has a way of shifting attention from the other to the self. He noted that the wealthy in most cultures buy attention with flashy cars or high fashion and by talking about "my therapist." Note that therapists are paid to pay attention!

Derber's findings indicated that those with more education and other status-linked attributes get more attention. Men got more attention than women. Those who were insecure sought more attention.

Laboratory Behaviors

Knight (1981) used chips that represented different outcomes when resources were divided. Children in collectivist cultures tended to divide such chips more equally than children in individualistic cultures. However, even in vertical individualist cultures, children divided resources in a way that indicated that they wanted to have more than another child, but not much more than the other child.

Current Recommendations for the Best Methods of Measurement

Both Singelis, Triandis, et al. (in press) and Triandis and Singelis (submitted) were based on the judgments of undergraduates from the University of Illinois in Champaign, Illinois ($n = 96$), and the University of Hawaii at Manoa ($n = 171$). The Singelis, Triandis, et al. (in press) study asked these undergraduates to respond to items that included ideas from the horizontal and vertical individualism and collectivism constructs. Both samples included men and women.

Triandis and Singelis (submitted) used a questionnaire that started by describing the constructs of individualism and collectivism. The subjects were then guided through a set of steps that allowed them to estimate their own tendencies toward individualism and collectivism. These measures were called the "Subjective Individualism and Collectivism" (SINDCOL) scores. Convergence between responses to the ordinary scales that used attitude items, such as those described above, and SINDCOL indicated that SINDCOL has convergent validity. Instrument 2 below presents the actual instrument we recommend for use by those who wish to measure subjective individualism and collectivism.

To eliminate the influence of the social desirability of the terms *individualism* and *collectivism,* half of the subjects were randomly assigned to a condition in which they read a page that indicated that each construct had many highly undesirable aspects (e.g., individualists are more likely than collectivists to die of heart attacks; collectivists are more likely that individualists to die of cancer), and the other half did not see that page. Results indicated no difference in the scores. Informal interviews with the subjects suggested that most of them did not read the page. As one subject put it: "I know what these constructs mean. I did not need to read about them."

After making 12 individualism and 12 collectivism ratings, the subjects were invited to sum the points so as to find out whether they were individualists or collectivists. In our analyses we used the total individualism and collectivism scores and regressed the 12 predictors of that score to see which of these ideas "worked." We also correlated the total scores from SINDCOL with the factors obtained from attitude items measuring collectivism and individualism. Finally, we obtained the usual demographics, such as sex, age, social class, ethnic background, and religion.

The items in Singelis, Triandis, et al. (in press) were presented as "a new personality test." Unless otherwise noted, items were answered on 9-point scales, where 1 = Never or Definitely No and 9 = Always or Definitely Yes. After each item there was a space for the subjects to write a number between 1 and 9 that corresponded to their sense of how frequent was the event or how much agreement they felt with the statement. Instrument 1 (below) reproduces the instructions; they are recommended for future use as well. The Triandis, Chan, et al. (in press) study used several methods that are described below.

Method 1. Consisted of 13 statements, developed by J. B. P. Sinha, to reflect Indian collectivism or Western individualism. Triandis, Chan, et al. (in press) had found that the sums of these items correlated very well with all the other methods used in their first study to measure these constructs. The judgment, and two examples, were "Please indicate if you are the kind of person who is likely to":

1. ask your old parents to live with you _____ (collectivism); 2. spend money (e.g., send flowers) rather than take the time to visit a sick friend _____ (individualism).

Method 2. A pool of 94 items was developed from previous measures of individualism and collectivism (e.g., Triandis, Chan, et al., in press) and additional items written for this study. Seventy of these items were identified a priori as measuring two kinds of individualism (horizontal and vertical) and two kinds of collectivism (horizontal and vertical). The horizontal types refer to emphasis on equality and the perception of people having more or less the same self, as is typically found in homogeneous cultures. The vertical types refer to acceptance of inequality. Vertical individualists are competitive and try to be on top of the social structure. Vertical collectivists are willing to sacrifice themselves for the benefit of the collective. For example, "one should live one's life independently of others" was identified as a horizontal individualism item and "I would do what would please my family, even if I detested that activity" as a vertical collectivist item.

Method 3. Measures of an interdependent and independent self-construal were obtained through the Self-Construal Scale (SCS), constructed by Singelis (1992). Subjects responded to items on a 7-point scale: 1 = Strongly Disagree to 7 = Strongly Agree. Previous Cronbach alpha reliabilities for the two dimensions were in the .69 to .74 range. Validity has been established through interethnic comparisons and associations with collectivist communication behaviors (see Singelis, 1994, submitted; Singelis and Sharkey, in press). "Being able to take care of myself is a primary concern for me" (individualistic) and "even when I disagree with my group, I keep my opinions to myself to avoid an argument" (collectivist) are examples of items.

Items from the Sinha scales (Method 1 above) were summed to give scale scores. The 6 individualist and 7 collectivist items from this scale had alpha reliabilities of .42 and .53 respectively. The Self-Construal Scale (SCS) items (Method 3) were also summed to give scale scores with alphas of .70 for the 12 independent items and .71 for the 12 interdependent items.

Each a priori group of items for the vertical and horizontal dimensions of individualism and collectivism (Method 2) was separately subjected to a principal components factor analysis that extracted a single unrotated factor. Items with low communalities (loading less than .35) were dropped. Items not previously classified were then correlated with scales derived from the previous step. Items correlating more than .30 with a scale were added to that scale, provided they did fit the theoretic description of the dimension. Finally, the scales were reduced to 8 items each by dropping items with the lowest item-total correlations. These procedures yielded 32 items divided evenly among the 4 dimensions (VI, HI, VC, HC). The alpha reliabilities for the scales were horizontal individualism .67, vertical individualism .74, horizontal collectivism .74, and vertical collectivism .68.

The horizontal and vertical items were combined in order to give overall measures (16 items each) of individualism and collectivism. The alphas for the two scales were .66 and .78 respectively. In addition, 8 item measures of individualism and collectivism were developed by eliminating items from the combined measures. The 4 horizontal and 4 vertical items with the highest item-total correlations were retained for individualism and for collectivism. Alpha correlations for the 8-item combined scales were .59 and .70 respectively.

The SINDCOL (see Instrument 2 below) items (Triandis and Singelis, submitted) were divided into their individualism and collectivism components, and items with low (below .25) item-total correlations were dropped from their respective scales. This yielded a subjective individualism scale containing 9 items (numbers 3, 4, 7, 12, 13, 19, 21, 22, and 23) with an alpha of .71 and a subjective collectivism scale containing 11 items (numbers 1, 2, 5, 6, 9, 11, 15, 17, 18, 20, and 24) with an alpha of .69.

To determine the convergence of the various methods of assessing individualism and collectivism, the 12 scales described above were intercorrelated. Whereas the horizontal and vertical collectivism scales were strongly correlated ($r = .39, p < .001$), the horizontal and vertical individualism scales were not ($r = -.00, p = NS$). The two horizontal dimensions ($r = .20, p < .01$) and the two vertical dimensions ($r = .14, p < .05$) were slightly, but significantly, positively related.

Subjective individualism was related to horizontal individualism (H-I) ($r = .39, p < .001$), vertical individualism (V-I) ($r = -.02, p = NS$), horizontal collectivism (H-

C) ($r = -.17, p < .01$), and vertical collectivism (V-C) ($r = -.23, p < .001$). Subjective collectivism was correlated with H-I ($r = -.28, p < .001$), V-I ($r = .07, p =$ NS), H-C ($r = .24, p < .001$), and V-C ($r = .49, p < .001$). In multiple regressions the 4 vertical and horizontal scales accounted for 23% of the variance in subjective individualism and 31% of the variance in subjective collectivism.

Singelis, Triandis, et al. (in press) reported considerable convergence among the various methods of measurement of the horizontal and vertical, individualism and collectivism, constructs. In addition, subjects whose cultural background was from East Asia were significantly higher ($p < .001$) in collectivism than subjects whose background was European. Such convergence suggests the validity of all the scales.

We are still testing different methods in our attempt to find the *shortest* scale that has acceptable reliability and validity. At the moment of this writing, my recommendations are as follows: First, consider whether you are measuring at the cultural or at the individual levels. Our experience is that at the cultural level the %S score, described by Triandis, McCusker, and Hui (1990), is quite useful. In addition, you might use the items of Instrument 1 below, and some of the values used in Triandis, McCusker, and Hui (1990). Instrument 1 can give you 12 scores (see below for a full explanation). Thus, you will have 12 + 2 (the %S and the values) = 14 distributions. Trichotomize each of these distributions and call the lowest third 1, middle third 2, and highest third 3. Then sum to obtain the total collectivism score, which can be as low as 14 and as high as 42.

At the individual level, use Instruments 1 and 2. For scoring responses to the items of Instrument 1, add the responses to the 8 items that are shown as measuring Horizontal Individualism (HI), Horizontal Collectivism (HC), Vertical Individualism (VI), and Vertical Collectivism (VC) to obtain 4 scores measuring these qualities. Of course, reverse-score the items that are marked as reversed. Instrument 1 also includes some scenarios that provide an additional method for the measurement of horizontal-vertical, individualism-collectivism. The scenarios that follow can be scored by taking into account the percent of the time that the HI, HC, VI, and VC responses were given rank 1 and, separately, the percent of the time they were given rank 2. The subjective individualism measures of Instrument 2 are self-scoring. Unfortunately, we have not yet developed the best set of scenarios. We should have a set that represents the most common situations found in most cultures. That requires a major research project. We see the current set as a first approximation of the ideal.

It is recommended that you correlate the 4 HI, HC, VI, and VC scores, the 4 percentages given rank 1, and the 4 percentages that are given rank 2, and the subjective individualism and collectivism scores. These 14 scores should correlate to form a multimethod, multitrait matrix. In other words, for example, the correlations among the measures of HI should be higher than the correlations between HI on the one hand and HC or VI or VC on the other.

If your research requires that you derive two groups, individualists and collectivists, we recommend that you trichotomize each of the 14 distributions and give to each variable a 1 (minimum collectivism), 2, or 3 (maximum collectivism) score, so all your subjects will have a minimum theoretical score of 14 and a maximum theoretical score of 14 times 3 = 42. Then you will have a continuous variable measure of individualism-collectivism. You could consider those scoring 14 to 23 as one of your groups and those scoring 33 to 42 as your other group. For tests of theories that assume individualism-collectivism to be opposites, this approach can have some utility. An even better way, but slightly more time consuming, is to standardize each variable and add the standard scores to obtain the total collectivism score.

Instrument 1

This questionnaire is anonymous, and there are no right or wrong answers.

We want to know if you strongly agree or disagree with some statements. If you strongly agree, enter a 9 in the blank space; if you strongly disagree, enter a 1 in that space; if you are unsure, enter a 5 next to the statement.

If you think the question does not apply to you, use a 5 and draw a circle around the 5.

In short, use this key:

Strongly										Strongly
Disagree	1	2	3	4	5	6	7	8	9	Agree

1. I prefer to be direct and forthright when I talk with people_____HI

2. My happiness depends very much on the happiness of those around me _____HC

3. I would do what would please my family, even if I detested that activity _____VC

4. Winning is everything_____VI

5. One should live one's life independently of others_____HI

6. What happens to me is my own doing_____HI

7. I usually sacrifice my self-interest for the benefit of my group_____VC

8. It annoys me when other people perform better than I do_____VI

9. It is important for me to maintain harmony within my group_____HC

10. It is important to me that I do my job better than others_____VI

11. I like sharing little things with my neighbors_____HC

12. I enjoy working in situations involving competition with others_____VI

13. We should keep our aging parents with us at home_____VC

14. The well-being of my co-workers is important to me _____ HC

15. I enjoy being unique and different from others in many ways _____ HI

16. If a relative were in financial difficulty, I would help within my means _____ HC

17. Children should feel honored if their parents receive a distinguished award _____ VC

18. I often do "my own thing" _____ HI

19. Competition is the law of nature _____ VI

20. If a co-worker gets a prize I would feel proud _____ HC

21. I am a unique individual _____ HI

22. To me, pleasure is spending time with others _____ HC

23. When another person does better than I do, I get tense and aroused _____ VI

24. I would sacrifice an activity that I enjoy very much if my family did not approve of it _____ VC

25. I like my privacy _____ HI

26. Without competition it is not possible to have a good society _____ VI

27. Children should be taught to place duty before pleasure _____ VC

28. I feel good when I cooperate with others _____ HC

29. I hate to disagree with others in my group _____ VC

30. Some people emphasize winning; I am not one of them _____ VI (*reverse-scored*)

31. Before taking a major trip, I consult with most members of my family and many friends _____ VC

32. When I succeed, it is usually because of my abilities _____ HI

We now have a set of scenarios. Each scenario is followed by four options. Please place yourself mentally in that situation and rank these options by placing a 1 next

to the option you consider the best or the most "right" or "appropriate." Place a 2 next to the next best option; and a 4 next to the least good option.

33. You and your friends decided spontaneously to go out to dinner at a restaurant. What do you think is the best way to handle the bill?
Please rank the four options
A. Split it equally, without regard to who ordered what_____ HC
B. Each person decides how much to contribute to the total, and if that does not cover the bill, each person is assessed inversely proportionally to what s/he has contributed_____ HI
C. The group leader pays the bill or decides how to split it_____ VC
D. Compute each person's charge, according to what that person ordered_____ VI

34. Suppose people are participating in a sports day. There is not enough time for every player to play every other player. What do you think is the best way to organize the events of the day? (Assume that the ranking of the skills of the players is well known.)
A. The winners of past contests play one another. At the end two players are left to compete for the prize_____ VC
B. Divide the players according to skill, and then play in the appropriate category _____ HC
C. Have people play one another based on a lottery system. At the end of the day everyone gets a ribbon for participating_____ HI
D. Have people play according to a lottery system. Each game results in a player getting some points. The winner is the person who accumulated the most points. Points earned against high-skill opponents count more than points scored against less-skilled opponents_____ VI

35. A community has been devastated by a natural event. The government is planning to distribute funds in that community. What principles should be used?
A. Those who lost more should receive a greater share_____ HC
B. Everyone should get the same amount_____ HI
C. Those who are more useful to the community (physicians, teachers, et al.) should receive more than those who are less useful (e.g., the unemployed) _____ VI
D. Those who are nationally famous should receive more that the others _____ VC

36. A big event is taking place in your community, and you have received four requests from people to stay with you overnight while they are in town. You only have space for one guest. Which one will you invite?
A. a relative_____ HC
B. a high-status member of your profession_____ VC
C. the one person who is most fun to have around_____ HC
D. someone well connected in political circles_____ IC

37. You have received four invitations for social events for the same night, and the events are sufficiently far from each other that you can accept only one invitation. Which invitation will you accept?
A. The invitation from a high-status member of one of your groups (e.g., sports, philosophical, religious)_____VC
B. From the one person who is known to be good company_____HC
C. From a relative_____HC
D. From a person who is well connected nationally_____HI

38. You are buying a piece of art for your office. Which one factor is most important in deciding whether to buy it?
A. It is a good investment_____VI
B. Your co-workers will like it_____HC
C. You just like it_____HI
D. Your supervisor will approve of it_____VC

39. You are deciding whom to vote for, for an important political job. Which is the most important consideration in deciding how to vote? The candidate is, other things being equal,
A. a high-status member of your community_____VC
B. powerful (influences national policy)_____VI
C. a relative_____HC
D. someone who appeals to you personally_____HI

40. You are buying a used car. What is the most important consideration when buying it?
A. The seller is a trusted relative_____HC
B. The price makes it "an excellent buy"_____VI
C. An expert mechanic, who is one of your longtime friends, recommended it _____VC
D. It is beautiful; it rides like a dream_____HI

41. A controversy has developed in your workplace, and you need to take a position. Which is your most likely course of action?
A. You assemble all the facts and make up your mind_____HI
B. You discuss it with your boss and support his position_____VC
C. You discuss it with your friends and take their views into account_____HC
D. You consider which position will most likely benefit you in the future_____VI

42. Which factor is most important when hiring an employee? The applicant
A. is easy to get along with_____HI
B. has worked for a competitor before_____VI
C. is a relative_____HC
D. is a respected member of the community_____VC

43. You are in a conflict situation with another person. Which procedure would you find best to resolve the conflict?

A. Use a mediator_____HI
B. Present all the evidence to a judge and have him/her decide_____VI
C. Negotiate with your opponent until you find a satisfactory solution_____HC
D. Have a respected member of the community who is acceptable to both parties tell each of you what is right and proper to do_____VC

44. Suppose you had to use one word to describe yourself. Which one would you use?
A. unique_____HI
B. competitive_____VI
C. cooperative_____HC
D. dutiful_____VC

45. You are considering joining a club. Which one factor is most important in deciding which club to join?
A. The one where people have the most fun_____HI
B. The one that is most prestigious_____VI
C. Some of your family members are already members of that club_____HC
D. The one suggested by your parents_____VC

46. You are buying some new clothing. Which is the most important factor that you will consider in choosing the style? The style that is
A. most suitable for your unique personality_____HI
B. most impressive in social situations_____VI
C. worn by your friends_____HC
D. recommended by your parents_____VC

47. You are starting a new business, and you are looking for a partner. Which is the most important factor in choosing a partner?
A. Someone with the same business interests_____HI
B. Someone who has been successful in previous business ventures_____VI
C. A close friend_____HC
D. A senior, successful, experienced member of the community_____VC

48. You are operating a company in the tropics, and air conditioners have become available for the first time. Who should get the first one?
A. The company president_____VC
B. The person whose work area is the hottest_____HC
C. The person who makes the greatest contribution to the enterprise_____VI
D. The person who wins a drawing for the air conditioner_____HI

49. You are dividing a bonus among different kinds of workers. What principle should be used?
A. To each according to contribution_____VI
B. To each equally_____HI

C. To each according to need_____HC
D. To each according to status within the corporation_____VC

50. You have been asked to suggest how the divorce rate might be reduced. You recommend that people should marry
A. for love_____HC
B. those who are similar to them in many ways_____HI
C. persons of high status, so if they are divorced they would lose status_____VI
D. according to arrangements made by their parents_____VC

51. The meaning of life can best be understood by
A. paying attention to the views of parents_____VC
B. through discussions with friends_____HC
C. through individual meditation_____HI
D. through individual exposure to the views of wise people_____VI

52. Happiness is attained by
A. gaining a lot of status in the community_____VC
B. linking with a lot of friendly people_____HC
C. keeping one's privacy_____HI
D. winning in competitions_____VI

53. You are planning to take a major trip that is likely to inconvenience a lot of people during your absence. With whom will you discuss it before deciding to take it?
A. No one_____HI
B. Your parents_____VC
C. Your spouse or close friend_____HC
D. Experts about the place you are going to visit_____VI

54. Suppose you won a large sum at a lottery. Will you divide it among others or keep it all for yourself?
A. I will keep it all_____HI
B. I will share it with my closest friends_____HC
C. I will share it with my parents_____VC
D. I will organize a feast and invite everyone I know to eat, drink, and be merry _____VI

55. A famous photographer has offered you a very reasonable price for having a picture taken. Which picture would you chose? You with
A. your three best friends_____HC
B. a very important person (a person who is bound to get into history books) _____VI
C. no one else_____HI
D. many members of the community whom you are helping; it shows that you are sacrificing yourself for them_____VC

56. A friend who is in the advertising business has offered to let you "play around" writing advertising copy that may appear on national television. Which task appeals to you the most to write about? Advertise
A. rental of a place where people can meet with their friends_____HC
B. the need to provide community services_____VC
C. the availability of a place where people can "get away from it all"_____HI
D. a luxury car_____VI

57. Which one of these four books appears to you to be the most interesting?
A. How to make friends_____HC
B. How to succeed in business_____VI
C. How to enjoy yourself inexpensively_____HI
D. How to build a harmonious family_____VC

58. Which attribute of a job do you consider most important?
A. It links you with friends_____HC
B. It gives you prestige_____VI
C. It allows you to set your own goals_____HI
D. It helps your community_____VC

59. Suppose you won a large sum at a lottery, and to reduce your income tax rate, it is a good idea to give some of it away. How will you give it away?
A. Give it to those with the greatest needs_____HC
B. Give it in the most visible way, so your philanthropy will be mentioned by the national television news programs_____VI
C. Give it to whatever group will make you feel really good about yourself_____ HI
D. Give it to a person like Mother Teresa (Nobel prize for peace given to her for her work among the poor in India)_____VC

60. Which is the most important factor in an employee's promotion, assuming that all other factors such as tenure and performance are equal. Employee
A. is loyal to the corporation_____HC
B. has shown obedience to the instructions from management_____VC
C. is able to think for him/herself_____HI
D. has contributed to the corporation much in the past_____VI

61. When you buy clothing for a major social event you would be most satisfied if
A. you like it_____HI
B. your parents like it_____VC
C. your friends like it_____HC
D. it is so elegant that it will dazzle everyone_____VI

62. Which of the following activities is likely to be most satisfying to you?
A. thinking about yourself_____HI
B. doing things for others_____VC
C. linking with others_____HC
D. beating your competitors_____VI

63. There is conflict between management and union in your place of work. Which procedure would you find best to resolve the conflict?
A. Use a mediator_____HI
B. Present all the evidence to a judge and have him/her decide_____VI
C. Have each side negotiate until they reach a satisfactory solution_____HC
D. Have a respected member of the community who is satisfactory to both sides tell each side what they must do_____VC

Instrument 2

Are You an Individualist or a Collectivist?

Cultures differ in their emphases on collectivism and individualism. Collectivists place some collective (family, work group, country) in a central position regulating social life. Individualists place the individual in the center of things. For example, when there is a conflict between the goals of a collective and an individual, in collectivist cultures it is obvious that the collective *should* "win," whereas in individualist cultures it is obvious that the individual should "win."

In this questionnaire we wish to help you find out for yourself if you are a collectivist or an individualist by asking you to answer questions about your own circumstances and lifestyle.

We will help you find out where you stand on these tendencies by summing "points."

Under C (collectivism) and I (individualism) you should enter a rating on a 0 to 10 scale, following the instructions under each question.

For example, suppose we ask you: Do you feel a part of any group, so if you were expelled by that group you would feel that your life has ended? If the answer is "Yes, very definitely, absolutely true," you would enter 10 under C. On the other hand, if it is not at all true, you might use a zero.

We will ask you questions that either reflect individualism, so you should enter a number between 0 and 10 next to I = , or collectivism, so you should enter a number between 0 and 10 next to C = . After you answer all the questions, add all the points you have given to C and separately the points you have given to I. You will then get an idea of how high you are in these tendencies.

This activity is cooperative between you and the researchers. We will give you the theoretical rationale for each question, and then you will make a judgment concerning whether you are high in C or in I.

We suggest that you simply add the various influences in the collectivist and individualistic direction to get your total scores.

Please follow the instructions carefully and faithfully, so you will get an accurate estimate of your individualism and collectivism.

1. Individualists tend to be concerned with their personal success, even if that does not help their family. Collectivists often choose family over personal goals. On the whole how close do you feel to your family?
The closer you feel, the higher should be your collectivism rating.
To remind you: Enter numbers from 0 to 10.
   0 = no trace   5 = quite a bit   10 = the maximum possible
C =

2. There are probably other groups to which you feel very close. These might be co-workers, neighbors; people of your own religion, race, nationality, political orientation, civil rights views, personal rights views, environmental views, social standing, people with similar aesthetic standards, etc. Now select the three or four groups that you feel closest to and enter an average collectivism rating, indicating how close you feel to these groups.
C =

3. The younger people are, the more they like to explore new ideas and do things that do not necessarily fit what their groups want them to do. But that is not constant with age. Young children often want to do what their parents want them to do; in some cultures teenagers want to do what their friends want them to do; old people often want to do what their own children and grandchildren want them to do. *Now think how free you are from group influences.* If you feel *totally* free enter a 10. Otherwise use a lower number.
I =

4. Individuals who travel a lot or change residences frequently do not feel that they must necessarily do what their neighbors want them to do. How free do you feel from the influences of your neighbors? If you feel totally free enter a 10.
I =

5. The smaller the community in which you live, the more people (fellow villagers, neighbors) know what you are doing, and you may feel that you must pay attention to their ideas about your lifestyle. If you feel that you are paying maximum attention to the ideas that people in your community have about your lifestyle, enter a 10 below.
C =

6. You have probably picked up a lot of ideas about how you should live from your parents, and they from their parents. So it is likely that traditions that were in

the families of your grandparents are still very influential in your own life. If these traditions are maximally influential in your life use a 10.

C =

> To remind you: Enter numbers from 0 to 10.
> 0 = no trace   5 = quite a bit   10 = the maximum possible

7. Think of your grandparents and parents in terms of how much they have been influenced by individualistic cultures such as those of the United States, England, Canada, Australia, New Zealand or collectivist cultures such as those of Africa, East Asia, Latin America.

One clue is the kind of child rearing. When the child rearing you have experienced was warm-controlling, in other words, your parents adored you as long as you did what they told you to do, you are most likely to have become a collectivist; on the other hand, if the child rearing was warm-independent, that is, your parents adored you and encouraged you to be independent, self-reliant, exploratory, it was okay to get into trouble, and they would help you get out of trouble, you are likely to have become an individualist.

If your child rearing was cold and neglected, you would also be an individualist; if it was cold and controlling, you would be a collectivist, but these relationships are weaker, so do not give too many points in this rating.

Try to estimate how individualistic you are, taking into account who your parents and other important influences (e.g., relatives, teachers) were and also how influential each of them was while you were growing up. If you feel you were influenced so as to become an extreme individualist, enter a 10; if on the other hand, you were influenced not to be individualistic, enter a 0.

I =

8. Think of the people you socialized (e.g., close friends) with when you were growing up. In the previous question the influences from the different cultures were present, but they did not necessarily influence you directly. *Now we are talking about direct influence.* Did the people you socialized with come from different cultures and traditions? The more diverse they were, the more likely it is that you are an individualist. Rate yourself on I = by giving yourself a 10 if most of your friends and influential adults (e.g., teachers) when you were growing up were from different ethnic groups.

I =

9. How interdependent are you in your finances? Some people cannot make any decisions about how to spend their money without consulting others, either because they have too little money or because they have important financial obligations. If you can not spend even small amounts of money without considering what that will do to other people, give yourself a 10.

C =

10. How much education do you have? The more education you have, the more you can consider different points of view from different parts of the world, and you have to decide for yourself what is right and wrong, and so you become more of an individualist. Rate the maximum a 10.

I =

11. How much formal traditional education did you have? This is education about your ethnic group (e.g., Sunday School, language school) covering the language, religion, history, rituals, and traditions of your ethnic group. The more traditional education you have had, the higher you should rate yourself on C =.

C =

12. How much have you traveled alone abroad? If you have traveled that way a lot, enter I = 10 because you have seen many countries and met people from all over the world, and you had to decide for yourself what lifestyle is best for you, and so you must have become more of an individualist. If you traveled with your own group, you maintained your home culture while you were abroad, so you did not have to face the question of lifestyles. In that case, give few points or a 0.

I =

13. Did you live abroad for more than 6 months? The chances are that if you did, you had to decide for yourself whether the way of life of the host people was the kind of life you wanted for yourself, and so you would have become more individualistic. If you have not lived abroad enter a 0; if you lived in different countries every few years, enter I = 10.

I =

14. Are you married? Generally married people have to live in a way that pays attention to the needs of their spouse and that makes them more collectivist. How collectivist do you feel because of your marital status? If you are not married, enter a 0.

C =

15. Did you grow up in a large family, with many siblings and other relatives, in which you had to pay attention to the needs of others? In that case you may have become a collectivist. Rate yourself accordingly.

C =

16. Television, movies, and magazines often expound an individualistic viewpoint (e.g., boy meets girl, they fall in love and get married, though sometimes this upsets their family and friends). How much exposure to such media did you experience? The more exposure, the greater the I.

I =

17. Do you approve or disapprove of the stories in the media mentioned in the previous question? The more you disapprove, the more collectivist you may be. If you strongly condemn these stories, enter a 10 below.
C =

18. Are your jobs or most of your activities allowing you to do your own thing (e.g., you are writing novels as you see fit) or do you have to act so as to take into account the needs and views of others? The more you have to take into account other people the more collectivist you are likely to be.
C =

19. What percent of your time do you work alone? If you work alone almost all the time, you do not have to pay attention to the needs of others, thus enter a 10 under I.
I =

20. Do you enjoy doing fun things alone (e.g., taking a walk alone), or must you do things with others? The more you must have others with you in order to have fun, the more a collectivist you are. Rate yourself on that.
C =

21. Would you say that most of the time you do "your own thing," paying no attention to whether it fits customs and "proper" behavior? If you do your own thing all the time, enter a 10.
I =

22. How much do you value your privacy? If you value your privacy very much, enter a 10 below; if you think that privacy is unimportant, rate I = 0.
I =

23. Is your occupation or job such that you *can* make decisions while ignoring the needs and views of others?
The more you can do that, the larger should be the number below.
I =

24. Finally, in your occupation or job do you generally pay a lot of attention to the views and needs of others? The more you pay such attention, the higher the score.
C =

Self-Scoring

Now add all the C and I scores and look at your grand total. A score of 60 is average. The more you deviate from 60, the more (or less) of that quality you have.

ENTER HERE   C =   I =

References

Adamopoulos, J., & Bontempo, R. (1984). A note on the relationship between socialization practice and artistic preference. *Cross-Cultural Psychology Bulletin* 18, 4–7.

Adamopoulos, J., & Smith, C. M. (1990). The emergence of individualism and collectivism as cultural patterns of interpersonal behavior. Paper presented to the Individualism-Collectivism conference in Seoul, Korea, July 1990.

Adamopoulos, J., Smith, C. M., Shilling, C. J., & Stogiannidou, A. (submitted). Cross-cultural invariance in the perception of social environments: A rule-theoretic approach to situational classification.

Adams, K. A., & Hill, L. (1989). Protest anality in Japanese group-fantasies. *Journal of Psychohistory* 15, 113–145.

Adorno, T. W., Frenkel-Bruswik, E., Levinson, D. J., & Sanford, R. N. (1950). *The authoritarian personality.* New York: Harper & Row.

Albert, R. (1983). The intercultural sensitizer or culture assimilator: A cognitive approach. In D. Landis & R. W. Brislin (eds.). *Handbook of intercultural training,* vol. 2 (pp. 186–217). New York: Pergamon Press.

Argyle, M., Henderson, M., Bond, M., Iizuka, Y., & Contarello, A. (1986). Cultural variations in relationship rules. *International Journal of Psychology* 21, 287–315.

Aron, J. P. (1975). *Qu'est-que la culture Française?* Paris: Denoel/Gauthier.

Asch, S. F. (1956). Studies of independence and conformity: A minority of one against a unanimous majority. *Psychological Monographs* 70, no. 9 (Whole of no. 416).

Avrahami, A., & Dar, Y. (1993). Collectivistic and individualistic motives among kibbutz youth volunteering for community service. *Journal of Youth and Adolescence* 22, 697–714.

Bacon, M. K. (1973). Cross-cultural studies in drinking. In P. G. Bourne & R. Fox (eds.). *Alcoholism: Progress in research and treatment.* New York: Academic Press.

Bakan, D. (1966). *The duality of human existence.* Chicago: Rand McNally.

Bakare, C. (1974). The development of laterality and right-left discrimination in Nigerian children. In J. L. M. Dawson & W. J. Lonner (eds.). *Readings in cross-cultural psychology* (pp. 150–167). Hong Kong: University of Hong Kong Press.

Bandura, A. (1989). Perceived self-efficacy in the exercise of personal agency. *The Psychologist: Bulletin of the British Psychological Society* 10, 411–424.

Banfield, E. (1958). *The moral basis of a backward society.* Glencoe, Ill.: Free Press.

Barker, R. G. (1968). *Ecological psychology: Concepts and methods for studying the environment of human behavior.* Stanford: Stanford University Press.

Barlund, D. C. (1975). *Private and public self in Japan and the United States.* Tokyo: Simul Press.

Barry, H., Child, I., & Bacon, M. (1959). Relation of child training to subsistence economy. *American Anthropologist* 61, 51–63.

Baumrind, D. (1967). Child care practices anteceding three patterns of preschool behavior. *Genetic Psychology Monographs* 75, 43–88.

Baumrind, D. (1971). Current patterns of parental authority. *Developmental Psychology Monographs* 4, no. 1, pt. 2, 1–103.

Bellah, R. N., Madsen, R., Sullivan, W. M., Swidler, A., & Tipton, S. M. (1985). *Habits of the heart: Individualism and commitment in American life.* Berkeley: University of California Press.

Bellah, R. N., Madsen, R., Sullivan, W. M., Swidler, A., & Tipton, S. M. (1988). *Individualism and commitment in American life: Readings on the themes of habits of the heart.* New York: Harper & Row.

Bergeron, A. P., & Zanna, M. P. (1973). Group membership and belief similarity as determinants of interpersonal attraction in Peru. *Journal of Cross-Cultural Psychology* 4, 397–410.

Berry, J. W. (1980). Acculturation as varieties of adaptation. In A. Padilla (ed.). *Acculturation: Theory, models and some new findings* (pp. 9–25). Boulder, Colo.: Westview Press.

Berry, J. W. (1994). Ecology and individualism. In U. Kim, H. C. Triandis, C. Kagitcibasi, S-C. Choi, & G. Yoon. *Individualism and collectivism: Theory, method and applications* (pp. 77–84). Newbury Park, Calif.: Sage Press.

Berry, J. W., Poortinga, Y. H., Segall, M. H., & Dasen, P. R. (1992). *Cross cultural psychology.* Cambridge, England: Cambridge University Press.

Bettelheim, B., & Janowitz, J. (1950). *Dynamics of prejudice.* New York: Harper.

Bhawuk, D., & Brislin, R. W. (1992). The measurement of intercultural sensitivity using the concepts of individualism and collectivism. *International Journal of Intercultural Relations* 16, 413–436.

Bierbrauer, G., Meyer, H., & Wolfradt, U. (1994). Measurement of normative and evaluative aspects in individualistic and collectivistic orientations: The cultural orientation scale. In U. Kim, H. C. Triandis, C. Kagitcibasi, S-C. Choi, & G. Yoon. *Individualism and collectivism: Theory, method and applications* (pp. 189–199). Newbury Park, Calif.: Sage Press.

Billings, D. K. (1989). Individualism and group orientation. In D. M. Keats, D. Munro, & L. Mann (eds.). *Heterogeneity in cross-cultural psychology* (pp. 92–103). Lisse, The Netherlands: Swets & Zeitlinger.

Black, J. S., & Mendenhall, M. (1990). Cross-cultural training effectiveness: A review and theoretical framework for future research. *Academy of Management Review* 15, 113–136.

Blinco, P. M. A. (1992). Task persistence of young children in Japan and the United States: A cross-cultural study. In S. Iwawaki, Y. Kashima, & K. Leung (eds.). *Innovations in cross-cultural psychology* (pp. 331–348). Amsterdam/Lisse: Swets & Zeitlinger.

Blumberg, I., & Winch, R. F. (1972). Societal complexity and familial complexity: Evidence for a curvilinear hypothesis. *American Journal of Sociology* 77, 896–920.

Bochner, S. (1994). Culture shock. In W. J. Lonner & R. Malpass (eds.). *Psychology and culture* (pp. 245–252). Boston: Allyn & Bacon.

Bond, J., & Smith, P. B. (submitted). Conformity across cultures.

Bond, M. H. (1985). Teasing etics out of emics. The case of Chinese values. Paper given at the conference on culture and values, Nags Head, June. Published later under Chinese Cultural Connection authorship.

Bond, M. H. (1986). *The psychology of the Chinese people.* Hong Kong: Oxford University Press.

Bond, M. H. (1988). *The cross-cultural challenge to social psychology.* Newbury Park, Calif.: Sage.

Bond, M. H. (1989). Chinese values and health. Mimeo.

Bond, M. H. (1994). Continuing encounters with Hong Kong. In W. J. Lonner & R. Malpass (eds.). *Psychology and culture* (pp. 239–244). Boston: Allyn & Bacon.

Bond, M. H. (in preparation). Chinese values. In M. H. Bond (ed.). *Handbook of Chinese Psychology.*

Bontempo, R., & Rivero, J. C. (1992). Cultural variation in cognition: The role of self-concept in the attitude behavior link. Paper presented at the meetings of the American Academy of Management, Las Vegas, Nevada, August.

Bontempo, R., Lobel, S., & Triandis, H. (1990). Compliance and value internalization in Brazil and the U.S. *Journal of Cross-Cultural Psychology* 21, 200–213.

Brandt, V. S. (1974). Skiing cross-culturally. *Current Anthropology* 15, 64–66.

Breer, P. E., & Locke, E. A. (1965). *Task experience as a source of attitudes.* Homewood, Ill.: Dorsey Press.

Brewer, M. B. (1991). The social self: On being the same and different at the same time. *Personality and Social Psychology Bulletin* 17, 475–482.

Brewer, M. B., & Weber, J. G. (1994). Self-evaluation effects of interpersonal versus intergroup social comparison. *Journal of Personality and Social Psychology* 66, 268–275.

Brickman, P., Coates, D., & Janoff-Bulman, R. (1978). Lottery winners and accident victims: Is happiness relative? *Journal of Personality and Social Psychology* 36, 917–927.

Brislin, R. W. (1993a). Personal communication, Fall.

Brislin, R. W. (1993b). *Understanding culture's influence on behavior.* Fort Worth: Harcourt Brace Jovanovich.

Brislin, R. W. (1994). Preparing to live and work elsewhere. In W. J. Lonner & R. Malpass (eds.). *Psychology and culture* (pp. 239–244). Boston: Allyn & Bacon.

Brislin, R. W., & Yoshida, T. (1994). *An introduction to intercultural communication training.* Thousand Oaks, Calif.: Sage.

Brislin, R. W., Cushner, K., Cherrie, C., & Yong, M. (1986). *Intercultural interactions: A practice guide.* Beverly Hills, Calif.: Sage.

Brodbar, N., & Jay, Y. (1986). Divorce and group commitment: The case of the Jews. *Journal of Marriage and the Family* 48, 329–340.

Bronfenbrenner, U. (1970). *Two worlds of childhood.* New York: Russell Sage Foundation.

Brown, H. P. (1990). The counter revolution of our time. *Industrial Relations* 29, 1–15.

Buchanan, A. E. (1989). Assessing the communitarian critique of liberalism. *Ethics* 99, 852–882.

Burton, M. L., Moore, C. C., Whiting, J. W., & Romney, A. K. (1992). World cultural regions. Paper presented at the Santa Fe meetings of the Society for Cross-Cultural Research, February.

Buss, D. M., et al. (1990). International preferences in selecting mates. *Journal of Cross-Cultural Psychology* 21, 5–47.

Buss, D. M., & Schmitt, D. P. (1993). Sexual strategies theory: An evolutionary perspective on human mating. *Psychological Review* 100, 204–232.

Campbell, D. T. (1964). Distinguishing differences of perception from failures of communication in cross-cultural studies. In F. S. C. Northrop and H. H. Livingston (eds.). *Cross-cultural understanding: Epistemology in anthropology.* New York: Harper & Row.

Campbell, D. T. (1975). On the conflicts between biological and social evolution and between psychology and moral tradition. *American Psychologist* 30, 1103–1126.

Campbell, J. D. (1990). Self-esteem and clarity of the self-concept. *Journal of Personality and Social Psychology* 59, 538–549.

Campbell, J. K. (1964). *Honor, family and patronage.* Oxford, England: Clarendon Press.

Caplan, N., Whitmore, J. W., and Choy, M. H. (1989). *The boat people and achievement in America: A study of family life, hard work, and cultural values.* Ann Arbor: University of Michigan Press.

Cardem, A. (1993). Homesickness. Seminar given at the East-West Center in Hawaii, October.

Carter, H., & Glick, P. C. (1970). *Marriage and divorce: A social and economic study.* Cambridge, Mass.: Harvard University Press.

Caudill, W., & Scarr, H. (1962). Japanese value orientations and culture change. *Ethnology* 1, 53–91.

Cha, J-H. (1994). Aspects of individualism and collectivism in Korea. In U. Kim, H. C. Triandis, C. Kagitcibasi, S-C. Choi, & G. Yoon. *Individualism and collectivism: Theory, method and applications* (pp. 157–174). Newbury Park, Calif.: Sage Press.

Chan, D. K-S. (1991). Effects of concession pattern, relationship between negotiators, and culture on negotiation. Unpublished Master's Thesis, Department of Psychology, University of Illinois.

Chan, D. K-S. (1994). COLINDEX: A refinement of three collectivism measures. In U. Kim, H. C. Triandis, C. Kagitcibasi, S-C. Choi, & G. Yoon (eds.). *Individualism and collectivism: Theory, method and applications* (pp. 200–212). Newbury Park, Calif.: Sage Press.

Chao, C., & Seligman, M. (draft MS). Chinese optimism.

Cheek, J. M. (1989). Identity orientations and self-interpretation. In D. M. Buss & N. Cantor (eds.). *Personality psychology: Recent trends and emerging directions.* New York: Springer.

Chen, C. C., & Meindl, J. R. (submitted). Collectivism and the Chinese enterprise reform: A cultural adaptation perspective.

Chen, C. C., Meindl, J. R., and Hunt, R. G. (submitted). Tradition and change: Cultural adaptation in China.

Chency, D., Seyforth, R., & Smuts, B. (1986). Social relationships and social cognition in non-human primates. *Science* 234, 1361–1366.

Chinese Cultural Connection (1987). Chinese values and the search for culture-free dimensions of culture. *Journal of Cross-Cultural Psychology* 18, 143–164.

Chiu, C. Y. (1990). Normative expectations of social behavior and concern for members of the collective in Chinese society. *Journal of Psychology* 124, 103–111.

Christin, P., & Lefebvre, P. (1970). *Comprendre la France*. New York: Scribner's.

Church, T. A. (1987). Personality research in a non-Western culture: The Philippines. *Psychological Bulletin* 102, 272–292.

Clark, M., Ouellette, R., Powell, M. C., & Milberg, S. (1987). Recipient's mood, relationship type and helping. *Journal of Personality and Social Psychology* 53, 94–103.

Coats, T. J., Stall, R. D., & Hoff, C. C. (1988). *Changes in sexual behavior of homosexual and bisexual men since the beginning of the AIDS epidemic*. Washington, D.C.: Office of Technology Assessment, U.S. Congress.

Cohen, R. (1991). *Negotiating across cultures*. Washington, D.C.: United States Institute of Peace Press.

Committee on Law and Justice, Commission on Behavioral and Social Sciences and Education (1994). *Violence in urban America: Mobilizing a response*. Washington, D.C.: National Academy Press.

Confucius (1915). *The ethics of Confucius*. New York: Putnam.

Cooley, C. H. (1902). *Human nature and social order*. New York: Scribner's.

Cousins, S. D. (1989). Culture and self-perception in Japan and the United States. *Journal of Personality and Social Psychology* 56, 124–131.

Crandall, J. E. (1980). Adler's concept of self-interest: Theory, measurement and implications for adjustment. *Journal of Personality and Social Psychology* 39, 481–495.

Creighton, M. R. (1990). Revisiting shame and guilt cultures: A forty-year pilgrimage. *Ethos* 18, 279–307.

Cross, S., & Markus, H. (1993). Views of the self: Chinese and American perspectives. Paper presented at the Santa Barbara, California, meetings of the Society of Experimental Social Psychology, October.

Cushner, K. (1989). Assessing the impact of a culure-general assimilator. *International Journal of Intercultural Relations* 13, 125–146.

Daab, W. Z. (1991). Changing perspectives on individualism. Paper presented at the International Society for Political Psychology, University of Helsinki, July.

Dale, P. N. (1986). *The myth of Japanese uniqueness*. London: Croom Helm.

D'Andrade, R. G., & Strauss, C. (eds.) (1992). *Human motives and cultural models*. Cambridge, England: Cambridge University Press.

Dasenbrock, R. W. (1991). The multicultural West. *Dissent*, Fall, pp. 550–556.

Daun, A. (1991). Individualism and collectivity among Swedes. *Ethnos* 56, 165–172.

Daun, A. (1992). Modern and modest: Mentality and stereotypes among Swedes. In A. Sjoegren & L. Janson (eds.). *Culture and management*. Stockholm: Institute for International Business.

Davey, C. J. (1960). *Kagawa of Japan.* London: Epworth Press.

Davidson, A. R., Jaccard, J. J., Triandis, H. C., Morales, M. L., & Diaz-Guerrero, R. (1976). Cross-cultural model testing: Toward a solution of the etic-emic dilemma. *International Journal of Psychology* 11, 1–13.

Dawson, J. L. M. (1974). Ecology, cultural pressures toward conformity and left-handedness: A bio-social psychological approach. In J. L. M. Dawson & W. J. Lonner (eds.). *Readings in cross-cultural psychology* (pp. 124–150). Hong Kong: University of Hong Kong Press.

deBary, W. T. (1979). Sagehood as a secular and spiritual ideal in Tokugawa neo-Confucianism. In W. T. deBary & I. Bloom (eds.). *Principle and practicality: Essays in neo-Confucianism and practical learning.* New York: Columbia University Press.

deBary, W. T. (1991). *Learning for one's self.* New York: Columbia University Press.

deBary, W. T. (in preparation). Sources of Chinese tradition.

Deeken, A. (1992). The saliency of mortality: Western and Japanese philosophical perspectives. In H. Motoaki, J. Misumi, and B. Wilpert (eds.). *22nd International Congress of Applied Psychology: Proceedings* (vol. 4, pp. 234–235). Hillsdale, N.J.: Erlbaum Publishers.

Demick, J., Inoue, W., Wapner, S., Ishii, S., Minami, H., Nishiyama, S., & Yamamoto, T. (1992). Cultural differences in impact of government legislation. *Journal of Cross-Cultural Psychology* 23, 468–487.

Derber, C. (1979). *The pursuit of attention: Power and individualism in everyday life.* Cambridge, Mass.: Schenkman.

Deshpande, S. P., & Viswesvaran, C. (1992). Is cross-cultural training of expatriate managers effective? A meta-analysis. *International Journal of Intercultural Relations* 16, 295–310.

de Tocqueville, A. (1835, 1985). See Tocqueville.

Deutsch, M. (1949). An experimental study of the effects of cooperation and competition upon group process. *Human Relations* 2, 199–232.

Deutsch, M. (1962). Cooperation and trust: Some theoretical notes. In M. R. Jones (ed.). *Nebraska Symposium on Motivation* (pp. 275–319). Lincoln: University of Nebraska Press.

Dewey, J. (1930). *Individualism old and new.* New York: Minton, Balch.

Diaz-Guerrero, R. (1979). The development of coping style. *Human Development* 22, 320–331.

Diaz-Guerrero, R. (1991). Mexican ethnopsychology. Paper presented at the 20th meeting of the Society for Cross-Cultural Research, Puerto Rico, February.

Diaz-Guerrero, R., & Diaz-Loving, R. (1990). Interpretation in cross-cultural personality assessment. In C. R. Reynolds & R. W. Kampaus (eds.). *Handbook of psychological and educational assessment of children: Personality, behavior, and context* (pp. 491–523). New York: Guilford Press.

Diener, E., & Diener, M. (1993). Self-esteem, financial satisfaction, and family satisfaction as predictors of life satisfaction across 31 countries. Mimeo.

Diener, E., Diener, M., & Diener, C. (1993). Factors predicting the subjective well-being of nations. Mimeo.

Diener, E., Suh, M., & Shao, L. (in press). National and cultural differences in reported subjective well-being: Why do they occur? *Social Indicators Research.*

Dion, K. K., Pak, A. W., & Dion, K. (1990). Stereotyping and physical attractiveness. *Journal of Cross-Cultural Psychology* 21, 158–179.

Dionne, E. J., Jr. (1993). Summoning the spirit of togetherness. Review of Etzioni (1993) in the Book Section of the *Washington Post,* National Weekly Edition, April 26–May 2.

Doi, T. (1986). *The anatomy of conformity: The individual versus society.* Tokyo: Kadansha.

Dollard, J. (1937). *Caste and class in a Southern town.* New Haven: Yale University Press.

Domino, G. (1992). Cooperation and competition in Chinese and American children. *Journal of Cross-Cultural Psychology* 23, 456–467.

Donohue, W. A. (1990). *The new freedom: Individualism and collectivism in the social lives of Americans.* New Brunswick, N.J.: Transaction Publishers.

Doumanis, M. (1983). *Mothering in Greece: From collectivism to individualism.* New York: Academic Press.

Draguns, J. (1990). Normal and abnormal behavior in cross-cultural perspective: Specifying the nature of the relationship. In J. Berman (ed.). *Nebraska Symposium on Motivation, 1989* (pp. 235–278). Lincoln: University of Nebraska Press.

Duley, M. I., & Edwards, M. (eds.) (1986). *The cross-cultural study of women: A comprehensive guide.* New York: Feminist Press.

Dumont, L. (1986). *Essays on individualism.* Chicago: University of Chicago Press.

Durkheim, E. (orig. 1893; retransl. 1984). *The division of labour in society.* London: Macmillan.

Durkheim, E. (trans. 1949). *The division of labor in society.* Glencoe, Ill.: Free Press.

Dweck, C. S., & Leggett, E. L. (1988). A social cognitive approach to motivation and personality. *Psychological Review* 95, 256–273.

Earley, P. C. (1989). Social loafing and collectivism: A comparison of the U.S. and the People's Republic of China. *Administrative Science Quarterly* 34, 565–581.

Earley, P. C. (1993). East meets West meets Mideast: Further explorations of collectivistic and individualistic work groups. *Academy of Management Journal* 36, 319–348.

Earley, P. C. (1994). *Self or group? Cultural effects of training on self-efficacy and performance.* Irvine, Calif.: Graduate School of Management, Working Paper #OB94004.

Eaton, J., & Weil, R. (1955). *Culture and mental disorders.* New York: Free Press.

Eckensberger, L. H. (1994). Moral development and its measurement across cultures. In W. J. Lonner & R. Malpass (eds.). *Psychology and culture* (pp. 71–78). Boston: Allyn & Bacon.

Edgerton, R. B. (1985). *Rules, exceptions, and social order.* Berkeley: University of California Press.

Edgerton, R. B. (1992). *Sick societies: Challenging the myth of primitive harmony.* New York: Free Press.

Ekeh, P. P. (1974). *Social exchange theory: The two traditions.* Cambridge, Mass.: Harvard University Press.

Elias, N. (1991). *The society of individuals.* Oxford, England: Blackwell.

Eliot, C. W. (1910). *The conflict between individualism and collectivism in a democracy.* New York: Scribner's.

Ember, C. R., & Levinson, D. (1991). The substantive contributions of world-wide cross-cultural studies using secondary data. *Behavior Science Research* 25, 79–140.

Emmons, R. A. (1991). Personal strivings, daily life events, and psychological and physical well-being. *Journal of Personality* 59, 453–472.

Engel, J. W. (1988). Work values of American and Japanese men. *Journal of Social Behavior and Personality* 3, 191–200.

Erchak, G. M. (1992). *The anthropology of self and behavior.* New Brunswick, N.J.: Rutgers University Press.

Erez, M. (1994). Toward a model of cross-cultural industrial and organizational psychology. In H. C. Triandis, M. Dunnette, and L. Hough (eds.). *Handbook of industrial and organizational psychology* (2d ed., vol. 4, pp. 557–607). Palo Alto, Calif.: Consulting Psychologists Press.

Erez, M., & Earley, P. C. (1987). Comparative analysis of goal setting strategies across cultures. *Journal of Applied Psychology* 72, 658–665.

Erez, M., & Earley, P. C. (1993). *Culture, self-identity, and work.* New York: Oxford University Press.

Espinoza, J. A., & Garza, R. T. (1985). Social group salience and interethnic cooperation. *Journal of Experimental Social Psychology* 21, 380–392.

Etzioni, A. (1988). *The moral dimension: Toward a new economics.* New York: Free Press.

Etzioni, A. (1993). *Rights, responsibilities, and the communitarian agenda.* New York: Crown.

Evans-Pritchard, E. E. (1940). *The Nuer.* Oxford: Oxford University Press.

Feather, N. T. (1991). Human values, global self-esteem, and belief in a just world. *Journal of Personality* 59, 83–107.

Feather, N. T. (1992). Global self-esteem and the fall of high achievers: Australian and Japanese comparisons. Paper delivered at the 4th regional Congress of the International Association of Cross-cultural Psychology, Katmandu, Nepal, January.

Feather, N. T. (1994). Attitudes toward high achievers and reactions to their fall: Theory and research concerning tall poppies. In M. Zanna (ed.). *Advances in Experimental Social Psychology* (vol. 25, pp. 1–73). New York: Academic Press.

Feldman, S. S., & Rosenthal, D. A. (1991). Age expectations of behavioral autonomy in Hong Kong, Australia and American youth: The influence of family variables and adolescents' values. *International Journal of Psychology* 26, 1–23.

Fiedler, F. E., Mitchell, T., & Triandis, H. C. (1971). The culture assimilator: An approach to cross-cultural training. *Journal of Applied Psychology* 55, 95–102.

Fishbein, M., & Ajzen, I. (1975). *Belief, attitude, intention, and behavior: An introduction to theory and research.* Reading, Mass.: Addison-Wesley.

Fiske, A. P. (1990). *Structures of social life: The four elementary forms of human relations.* New York: Free Press.

Fiske, A. P. (1992). The four elementary forms of sociality: Framework for a unified theory of social relations. *Psychological Review* 99, 689–723.

Fiske, A. P. (1993). Social errors in four cultures: Evidence about universal forms of social relations. *Journal of Cross-Cultural Psychology* 24, 463–494.

Foa, U., & Foa, E. (1974). *Society structures of the mind.* Springfield, Ill.: Thomas.

Foster, G. (1965). Peasant society and the image of limited good. *American Anthropologist* 67, 293–315.

Fowers, B. J., & Tredinnick, M. (no date). Hidden ideology and psychotherapy: Examining individualist values in case conceptualizations. Mimeo.

Fox, M. M. (1993). Miscommunication when both culture and gender differ: A new cultural assimilator. Mimeo.

Fromm, E. (1941). *Escape from freedom.* New York: Farrar & Rinehart.

Fry, L. W., Kerr, S., & Lee, C. (1986). Effects of different leader behavior under different levels of task interdependence. *Human Relations* 39, 1067–1082.

Furnham, A., & Bochner, S. (1986). *Culture shock: Psychological reactions to unfamiliar environments.* London: Methuen.

Gallois, C., Barker, M., Jones, E., & Callan, V. (1992). Intercultural communication: Evaluations of lecturers by Australian and Chinese students. In S. Iwawaki, Y. Kashima, & K. Leung (eds.). *Innovations in cross-cultural psychology* (pp. 86–102). Amsterdam/Lisse: Swets & Zeitlinger.

Gallup, G. (1976). Human needs and satisfactions: A global survey. *Public Opinion Quarterly* 40, 459–467.

Galtung, J. (1979). On the last 2,500 years in Western history. In P. Burke (ed.). *The new Cambridge modern history comparison volume.* Cambridge, England: Cambridge University Press.

Geertz, C. (1963). *Peddlers and princes: Social change and economic modernization in two Indonesian towns.* Chicago: University of Chicago Press.

Geertz, C. (1983). *Peddlers and princes: Social change and economic modernization in two Indonesian towns* (2d ed.). Chicago: University of Chicago Press.

Gelfand, M., Triandis, H. C., & Chan, D. K-S. (submitted). Individualism versus collectivism or versus authoritarianism?

Georgas, J. (1986). *Social psychology.* Athens: University of Athens Press (in Greek).

Georgas, J. (1989). Changing family values in Greece: From collectivism to individualism. *Journal of Cross-Cultural Psychology* 20, 80–91.

Giddens, A. (1991). *Modernity and self-identity.* Stanford, Calif.: Stanford University Press.

Gorney, R., & Long, J. M. (1980). Cultural determinants of achievement, aggression and psychological distress. *Archives of General Psychiatry* 37, 452–459.

Gottfredson, M. R., & Hirschi, T. (1990). *A general theory of crime.* Stanford, Calif.: Stanford University Press.

Graen, G., & Wakabayashi, M. (1994). In H. C. Triandis, M. Dunnette, & L. Hough (eds.). *Handbook of industrial and organizational psychology* (pp. 415–446). Palo Alto, Calif.: Consulting Psychologists Press.

Gross, J. L., & Raynor, S. (1985). *Measuring culture.* New York: Columbia University Press.

Gould, J., & Kolb, W. I. (1964). *A dictionary of the social sciences.* Glencoe, Ill.: Free Press.

Gudykunst, W. B. (1983). *Intercultural communication theory*. Beverly Hills, Calif.: Sage.

Gudykunst, W. B. (1991). *Bridging differences*. Newbury Park, Calif.: Sage.

Gudykunst, W. B. (ed.) (1993). *Communication in Japan and the United States*. Albany: State University of New York Press.

Gudykunst, W. B. (in press). Anxiety/uncertainty management (AUM) theory: Current status. In R. L. Wiseman (ed.). *Intercultural communication theory*. Thousand Oaks, Calif.: Sage.

Gudykunst, W. B., & Nishida, T. (1994). *Bridging Japanese North American differences*. Thousand Oaks, Calif.: Sage.

Gudykunst, W. B., & San Antonio, P. (1993). Approaches to the study of communications in Japan and the United States. In W. B. Gudykunst (ed.). *Communication in Japan and the United States* (pp. 18–50). Albany: State University of New York Press.

Gudykunst, W. B., Gao, G., Nishida, T., Bond, M. H., Leung, K., Wang, G., & Barraclough, R. A. (1989). A cross-cultural study of self-monitoring. *Communication Research Reports* 6, 7–12.

Gudykunst, W. B., Gao, G., Nishida, T., Nadamitsu, Y., & Sakai, J. (1992). Self-monitoring in Japan and the United States. In S. Iwawaki, Y. Kashima, & K. Leung (eds.). *Innovations in cross-cultural psychology* (pp. 185–198). Amsterdam/Lisse: Swets & Zeitlinger.

Gudykunst, W. B., Matsumoto, Y., Ting-Toomey, S., Nishida, T., & Karimi, H. (1994). Measuring self construals across cultures: A derived etic analysis. Paper presented at the International Communication Association convention, Sydney, Australia, July.

Gudykunst, W. B., Yang, S. M., & Nishida, T. (1987). Cultural differences in self-consciousness and self-monitoring. *Communication Research* 14, 7–36.

Gudykunst, W. B., Yoon, Y., and Nishida, S. (1987). The influence of individualism-collectivism on perceptions of communication in ingroup and outgroup relationships. *Communication Monographs* 54, 295–306.

Guthrie, G. M. (1961). *The Filipino child and the Philippine society*. Manila: Philippine Normal College Press.

Hamaguchi, E. (1985). A contextual model of the Japanese. *Journal of Japanese Studies* 11, 283–321.

Hamilton, V. L., & Sanders, J. (1983). Universals in judging wrongdoing: Japanese and Americans compared. *American Sociological Review* 48, 199–211.

Hamilton, V. L., Blumenfeld, P. C., Akoah, H., & Miura, K. (1991). Group and gender in Japanese and American elementary classrooms. *Journal of Cross-Cultural Psychology* 22, 317–346.

Han, G., & Park, B. (1990). Children's choice in conflict: Application of the theory of individualism-collectivism. Paper presented at the Individualism-Collectivism Conference, Seoul, Korea, July.

Han, S., & Shavitt, S. (1994). Persuasion and culture: Advertising appeals in individualistic and collectivist cultures. *Journal of Experimental Social Psychology* 30, 326–350.

Hao, B. (1993). China's traditional culture and the process of modernization. Lecture given at the East-West Center, Honolulu, Hawaii, November 17.

Haruki, Y., & Shigehisa, T. (1983). Experimental analyses of the types of reinforcement. *Waseda Psychological Reports* 25, 63–93.

Haruki, Y., Shigehisa, T., Nedate, K., Wajima, M., & Ogawa, R. (1984). Effects of alien-reinforcement and its combined type of learning behavior and efficacy in relation to personality. *International Journal of Psychology* 19, 527–545.

Hatfield, E., & Rapson, R. L. (1993). Historical and cross-cultural perspectives on passionate love. In K. T. Strongman (ed.). *International Review of Emotion*, vol. 3. New York: Wiley.

Hayashi, C. (1992a). Belief systems and the Japanese way of thinking. In H. Motoaki, J. Misumi, & B. Wilpert (eds.). *22nd International Congress of Applied Psychology, Kyoto, Japan, Proceedings,* vol. 3. (pp. 3–28). Hove, U.K.: Erlbaum.

Hayashi, C. (1992b). Quantitative social research: Belief systems, the way of thinking, and sentiments of five nations. *Behaviormetrika* 19, 127–170.

Heelas P., & Lock, A. (eds.) (1981). *Indigenous psychologies: The anthropology of the self.* London: Academic Press.

Helgeson, V. S. (1993). Implications of agency and communion for patient and spouse adjustment to a first coronary event. *Journal of Personality and Social Psychology* 64, 807–816.

Helmreich, R. L., Beane, W. E., Lucker, G. W., & Spence, J. T. (1978). Achievement motivation and scientific attainment. *Personality and Social Psychology Bulletin* 4, 222–226.

Helson, H. (1964). *Adaptation level theory.* New York: Harper & Row.

Hillhouse, R. J. (1993). The individual revolution: The social basis of transition toward democracy? Ph.D. Dissertation, Department of Political Science, University of Michigan, Ann Arbor.

Hinkle, S., & Brown, R. J. (1993). Intergroup comparison and social identity: Some links and lacunae. In D. Abrams & M. Hogg (eds.). *Social identity: Constructive and critical advances* (pp. 48–70). New York: Harvester/Wheatsheaf.

Ho, D. Y. F., & Chiu, C-Y. (1994). Component ideas of individualism, collectivism and social organization: An application in the study of Chinese culture. In U. Kim, H. C. Triandis, C. Kagitcibasi, S-C. Choi, & G. Yoon. *Individualism and collectivism: Theory, method and applications* (pp. 137–156). Newbury Park, Calif.: Sage Press.

Hofstede, G. (1980). *Culture's consequences.* Beverly Hills: Sage.

Hofstede, G. (1982). *Cultural pitfalls for Dutch expatriates in Indonesia.* Maastricht, Netherlands: Institute for Research on Intercultural Cooperation.

Hofstede, G. (1991). *Cultures and organizations: Software of the mind.* London: McGraw-Hill.

Hofstede, G., & Bond, M. H. (1984). Hofstede's cultural dimensions: An independent validation using Rokeach's Value Survey. *Journal of Cross-Cultural Psychology* 15, 417–433.

Hofstede, G., Bond, M. H., & Luk, C-L. (1993). Individual perceptions of organizational cultures: A methodological treatise on levels of analysis. *Organizational Studies* 14, 483–503.

Hogan, R. (1975). Theoretical ethnocentrism and the problem of compliance. *American Psychologist* 30, 533–540.

Holtzman, W. H., Diaz-Guerrero, R., & Swartz, J. D. (1975). *Personality development in two cultures.* Austin: University of Texas Press.

Holzberg, C. S. (1981). Anthropology and industry: Reappraisal and new directions. *Annual Review of Anthropology* 10, 317–360.

Homans, G. (1961). *Social behavior: The elementary forms.* New York: Harcourt Brace Jovanovich.

House, J. S., Landis, K. R., & Umberson, D. (1988). Social relationships and health. *Science* 241, 540–545.

Howell, W. S. (1982). *The empathic communicator.* Belmont, Calif.: Wadsworth.

Hsu, F. L. K. (1981). *American and Chinese: Passage to differences.* Honolulu: University of Hawaii Press.

Hsu, F. L. K. (1983). *Rugged individualism reconsidered.* Knoxville: University of Tennessee Press.

Huelshoff, A. S., Markovits, A. S., & Reich, S. (eds.) (1993). *From Bundesrepublik to Deutschland.* Ann Arbor: University of Michigan Press.

Hughes, R. (1993). *Culture of complaint: The fraying of America.* New York: Oxford University Press.

Hui, C. H. (1984). Individualism-collectivism: Theory, measurement and its relationships to reward allocation. Unpublished doctoral dissertation, Department of Psychology, University of Illinois at Champaign-Urbana.

Hui, C. H. (1988). Measurement of individualism-collectivism. *Journal for Research in Personality* 22, 17–36.

Hui, C. H., & Triandis, H. C. (1986). Individualism and collectivism: A study of cross-cultural researchers. *Journal of Cross-Cultural Psychology* 17, 225–248.

Hui, C. H., & Triandis, H. C. (1989). Effects of culture and response format on extreme response style. *Journal of Cross-Cultural Psychology* 20, 296–309.

Hui, C. H., & Villareal, M. (1989). Individualism-collectivism and psychological needs: Their relationships in two cultures. *Journal of Cross-Cultural Psychology* 20, 310–323.

Hui, C. H., & Yee, C. (submitted). The shortened individualism-collectivism scale: Its relations with demographic and work-related variables.

Hui, C. H., Eastman, K. L., and Yee, C. (1990). Individualism-collectivism and job satisfaction. Paper presented at the conference on individualism and collectivism, Seoul, Korea, July.

Huntington, S. P. (1993). The clash of civilizations. *Foreign Affairs* 72, 22–49.

Hwang, K. (1987). Face and favor: The Chinese power game. *American Journal of Sociology* 92, 944–974.

Ichheiser, G. (1970). *Appearances and realities.* San Francisco: Jossey-Bass.

Ingelhart, R. (1990). *Culture shift in advanced industrial societies.* Princeton, N.J.: Princeton University Press.

Inkeles, A. (1983). The American character. *Center Magazine*, November/December, pp. 25–39.

Inkeles, A., & Smith, D. H. (1974). *Becoming modern.* Cambridge, Mass.: Harvard University Press.

Iwao, S. (1993). *The Japanese woman: Traditional image and changing reality.* New York: Free Press.

Iwao, S., & Triandis, H. C. (1993). Validity of auto- and hetero-stereotypes among Japanese and American students. *Journal of Cross-Cultural Psychology* 24, 428–444.

Iwata, O. (1992). Comparative study of person perception and friendly/altruistic behavior intentions between Canadian and Japanese undergraduates. In S. Iwawaki, Y. Kashima, & K. Leung (eds.). *Innovations in cross-cultural psychology* (pp. 173–183). Amsterdam/Lisse: Swets & Zeitlinger.

Jackson, S. E., and Associates. *Diversity in the workplace.* New York: Guilford Press.

James K., & Cropanzano, R. (in press). Dispositional group loyalty and individual action for the benefit of an ingroup: Experimental and correlational evidence. *Organizational Behavior and Human Decision Processes.*

Jing, Q. (1994). Implications of China's one-child policy. Lecture given at the University of Illinois, January 13.

John, O. P., & Robins, R. W. (1994). Accuracy of bias in self-perception: Individual differences in self-enhancement and the role of narcissism. *Journal of Personality and Social Psychology* 66, 206–219.

Johnson, D. W., & Norem-Hebeison, A. A. (1979). A measure of cooperative, competitive and individualistic attitudes. *Journal of Social Psychology* 109, 251–261.

Johnson, R. T., & Johnson, D. W. (1981). Building friendships with handicapped and non-handicapped students: Effects of cooperative and individualistic instruction. *American Educational Research Journal* 18, 415–423.

Johnson, R. T., & Johnson, D. W. (1982). Effects of cooperative and competitive learning experiences on interpersonal attraction between handicapped and non-handicapped students. *Journal of Social Psychology* 116, 211–219.

Jones, A. P., Rozelle, R. M., & Chang, W. C. (1990). Perceived punishment and reward value of supervisor actions in a Chinese sample. *Psychological Studies* 35, 1–10.

Josephs, R. A., Markus, H. R., & Tafardodi, R. W. (1992). Gender and self-esteem. *Journal of Personality and Social Psychology* 63, 391–402.

Kagitcibasi, C. (1990). Family and socialization in cross-cultural perspective: A model of change. In *Nebraska Symposium on Motivation, 1989,* vol. 37 (pp. 135–200). Lincoln: University of Nebraska Press.

Kagitcibasi, C. (1994). A critical appraisal of individualism-collectivism: Toward a new formulation. In U. Kim, H. C. Triandis, C. Kagitcibasi, S-C. Choi, & G. Yoon. *Individualism and collectivism: Theory, method and applications* (pp. 52–65). Newbury Park, Calif.: Sage Press.

Kaiser, R. G. (1984). *Russia: The people and the power.* New York: Washington Square Press.

Kanfer, F. (1979). Personal control, social control, and altruism: Can society survive the age of ego-centrism? *American Psychologist* 34, 231–239.

Kashima, E. (1989). Determinants of perceived group heterogeneity. Unpublished doctoral dissertation. Champaign, University of Illinois Department of Psychology.

Kashima, E., & Kashima, Y. (1993). Perceptions of general variability of social groups. *Social Cognition* 11, 1–21.

Kashima, Y., & Callan, V. J. (1994). The Japanese workgroup. In H. C. Triandis, M. Dunnette, and L. Hough (eds.). *Handbook of industrial and organizational psychology* (2d ed., vol. 4, pp. 609–646). Palo Alto, Calif.: Consulting Psychologists Press.

Kashima, Y., & Triandis, H. C. (1986). The self-serving bias in attribution as coping strategy: A cross-cultural study. *Journal of Cross-Cultural Psychology* 17, 83–98.

Kashima, Y., Siegel, M., Tanaka, K., & Kashima, E. S. (1992). Do people believe behaviors are consistent with attitudes? Toward a cultural psychology of attribution processes. *British Journal of Social Psychology* 331, 111–124.

Kasser, T., & Ryan, R. M. (1993). A dark side of the American dream: Correlates of financial success as a central life aspiration. *Journal of Personality and Social Psychology* 65, 410–422.

Katakis, C. D. (1984). *The three identities of the Greek family*. Athens: Kevros (in Greek).

Kateb, G. (1992). *The inner ocean: Individualism and democratic culture*. Ithaca, N.Y.: Cornell University Press.

Kato, H., & Kato, J. (1992). *Understanding and working with the Japanese business world*. Englewood Cliffs, N.J.: Prentice Hall.

Katz, L. G. (1993). Reading, writing, and narcissism. *New York Times*, July 15.

Kausikan. B. (1993). Human rights must adjust to Asian power. *New Perspectives Quarterly* 10, 62–63.

Kernis, M. H., Grannermann, B. D., Richie, T., & Hart, J. (1988). The role of contextual factors in the relationship between physical activity and self-awareness. *British Journal of Social Psychology* 27, 265–273.

Kidder, L. H. (1992). Requirements for being "Japanese": Stories of returnees. *International Journal of Intercultural Relations* 16, 383–394.

Kilham, W., & Mann, L. (1974). Level of destructive obedience as a function of transmitter and executant roles in the Milgram obedience paradigm. *Journal of Personality and Social Psychology* 29, 696–702.

Kim, M-S., Sharkey, W. F., & Singelis, T. M. (1994). Relationship between individuals' self-construals and perceived importance of interactive constraints. *International Journal of Intercultural Relations* 18, 117–140.

Kim, U. (1993). The self in different contexts. Lecture given at the East-West Center in Honolulu, November.

Kim, U. (1994a). Introduction. In U. Kim, H. C. Triandis, C. Kagitcibasi, S-C. Choi, & G. Yoon. *Individualism and collectivism: Theory, method and applications*. Newbury Park, Calif.: Sage.

Kim, U. (1994b). Significance of paternalism and communalism in the occupational welfare system of Korean firms: A national survey. In U. Kim, H. C. Triandis, C. Kagitcibasi, S-C. Choi, & G. Yoon (eds.). *Individualism and collectivism: Theory, method, and applications*. Newbury Park, Calif.: Sage.

Kim, U., & Berry, J. W. (1983). *Indigenous psychologies*. Thousand Oaks, Calif.: Sage.

Kim, U., & Lee, S. (1992). Culture and self: Comparative analysis of liberal and Confucian moral philosophy. Paper presented at the International Congress of the International Association of Cross-Cultural Psychology, Liege, Belgium, July.

Kim, U., Triandis, H. C., Kagitcibasi, C., Choi, S-C., & Yoon, G. (1994). *Individualism and collectivism: Theory, method and applications.* Newbury Park, Calif.: Sage.

Kirkbridge, P. S., Tang, S. F. Y., & Westwood, R. I. (1991). Chinese conflict preferences and negotiation behavior: Cultural and psychological influences. *Organization Studies* 12, 365–386.

Kitayama, S. (1992). Some thoughts on the cognitive-psychodynamics self from a cultural perspective. *Psychological Inquiry* 3, 41–44.

Kitayama, S. (1993). Culture, self, and emotion: The nature and functions of "good moods/feelings" in Japan and the United States. Mimeo. Also lecture given at East-West Center, Honolulu, Hawaii, October 21.

Kitayama, S., & Markus, H. (in press a). Construal of the self as cultural frame: Implications for internationalizing psychology. In H. K. Jacobson (ed.). *Internationalization of higher education.*

Kitayama, S., & Markus, H. (in press b). Culture, self, and emotion: A cultural perspective to "self-conscious" emotions. In J. P. Tangney & K. W. Fisher (eds.). *Shame, guilt, embarrassment, and pride: Empirical studies of self-conscious emotions.* New York: Guilford.

Kluckhohn, C. (1956). Toward a comparision of value emphasis in different cultures. In L. D. White (ed.). *The state of the social sciences* (pp. 116–132). Chicago: University of Chicago Press.

Kluckhohn, F., & Strodtbeck, F. (1961). *Variations in value orientations.* Evanston, Ill.: Row, Peterson.

Klugel, J. R., & Smith, E. R. (1986). *Beliefs about inequality: Americans' views of what is and what ought to be.* Chicago: Aldine.

Knight, G. P. (1981). Behavioral and sociometric methods of identifying cooperators, competitors, and individualists: Support for the validity of the social orientation construct. *Developmental Psychology* 17, 430–433.

Kohlberg, L. (1981). *Essays on moral development.* New York: Harper & Row.

Kohn, M. L. (1969). *Class and conformity.* Homewood, Ill.: Dorsey Press.

Kohn, M. L. (1987). Cross-national research as an analytic strategy. Presidential address to the American Sociological Association, August.

Korte, C. (1984). The helpfulness of urban villagers. In E. Staub, D. Bar-tal, J. Karylowski, & J. Reykowski (eds.). *Development and maintenance of prosocial behavior* (pp. 323–334). New York: Plenum.

Kotkin, J. (1993). *Tribes: How race, religion, and identity determine success in the global economy.* New York: Random House.

Kuechler, M. (1993). Political attitudes and behavior in Germany: The making of a democratic society. In A. S. Huelshoff, A. S. Markovits, & S. Reich (eds.). *From Bundesrepublik to Deutschland* (pp. 33–58). Ann Arbor: University of Michigan Press.

Kuhn, M. H., & McPartland, R. (1954). An empirical investigation of self attitudes. *American Sociological Review* 19, 68–76.

Kurowski, L. L. (1993). A study of norms. Mimeographed paper.

Kymlicka, W. (1989). Liberal individualism and liberal neutrality. *Ethos* 99, 889–905.

Lalonde, R. N., & Cameron, J. E. (1993). An intergroup perspective on immigrant acculturation with a focus on collective strategies. *International Journal of Psychology* 28, 57–74.

Lalonde, R. N., & Silverman, R. A. (1994). Behavioral preferences in response to social injustice: The effects of group permeability and social identity salience. *Journal of Personality and Social Psychology* 66, 78–85.

Landis, D., & Brislin, R. W. (eds.) (1983). *Handbook of intercultural training* (3 volumes). New York: Pergamon Press.

Langer, E. (1983). *The psychology of control.* Beverly Hills, Calif.: Sage.

Lasch, C. (1978). *The culture of narcissism: American life in an age of diminishing expectations.* New York: Norton.

Lau, S. (1989). Religious schema and values. *International Journal of Psychology* 24, 137–156.

Lebra, T. (1976). *Japanese patterns of behavior.* Honolulu: University of Hawaii Press.

Lebra, T. (1984). *Japanese women: Constrain and fulfillment.* Honolulu: University of Hawaii Press.

Lee, D. (1976). *Valuing the self: What can we learn from other cultures?* Englewood Cliffs, N.J.: Prentice Hall.

Lee, Y-T., & Ottati, V. (1993). Determinants of ingroup and outgroup perceptions of heterogeneity. *Journal of Cross-Cultural Psychology* 24, 298–318.

Lester, D. (1988). National character and rates of personal violence (suicide and homicide). *Personality and Individual Differences* 9, 423.

Leung, K. (1987). Some determinants of reactions to procedural models of conflict resolution: A cross-national study. *Journal of Personality and Social Psychology* 53, 898–908.

Leung, K., & Bond, M. H. (1989). On the empirical identification of dimensions of cross-cultural comparison. *Journal of Cross-Cultural Psychology* 20, 296–309.

Levine, R. V. (1941). Love and marriage in seven cultures. Mimeo.

Levine, R. V. (1992). Personal communication.

Levine, R. V., & Bartlett, K. (1984). Pace of life, punctuality, and coronary heart disease in six countries. *Journal of Cross-Cultural Psychology* 15, 233–255.

Lew, W. J. F. (in preparation). Values and personality.

Li, M. C. (1992). The patterns of ingroup favoritism in a collectivist and individualistic society. *International Journal of Psychology* 27, 558.

Lincoln, J. R. (1989). Employee work attitudes and management practices in the U.S. and Japan: Evidence from a large comparative survey. *California Management Review* 32, 89–106.

Lipset, S. M. (1990). *Continental divide.* New York: Routledge.

Lonner, W. (1980). The search for psychological universals. In H. C. Triandis & W. W. Lambert (eds.). *Handbook of Cross-Cultural Psychology* (vol. 1, pp. 143–204). Boston: Allyn and Bacon.

Lortie-Lussier, M., & Fellers, G. L. (1991). Self-ingroup relationships: Their variations among Canadian pre-adolescents of English, French, and Italian origin. *Journal of Cross-Cultural Psychology* 22, 458–471.

Lukes, S. (1973). *Individualism.* Oxford, England: Basil Blackwell.

Lykes, M. B. (1985). Gender and individualistic vs. collectivist bases for notions about the self. *Journal of Personality* 53, 356–383.

Ma, H. K. (1988). The Chinese perspective on moral judgment and development. *International Journal of Psychology* 23, 201–227.

Macfarlane, A. (1978). *The origins of English individualism: The family, property and social transition.* New York: Cambridge University Press.

Malinowski, B. (1922, 1960). *Argonauts of the Western Pacific.* London School of Economics and Political Science, No. 65, also London: Routledge.

Marin, G., & Triandis, H. C. (1985). Allocentrism as an important characteristic of the behavior of Latin Americans and Hispanics. In R. Diaz-Guerrero (ed.). *Cross-cultural and national studies in social psychology* (pp. 85–104). Amsterdam: North Holland.

Marjoribanks, K. (1991). Sex composition of family sibships and family learning environments. *Psychological Reports* 69, 97–98.

Markus, H. R., & Kitayama, S. (1991a). Cultural variation in the self-concept. In J. Strauss & G. R. Goethals (eds.). *The self: Interdisciplinary approaches* (pp. 18–48). New York: Springer Verlag.

Markus, H. R., & Kitayama, S. (1991b). Culture and self: Implications for cognition, emotion and motivation. *Psychological Review* 98, 224–253.

Marmot, M. G., & Syme, S. L. (1976). Acculturation and coronary heart disease in Japanese Americans. *American Journal of Epidemiology* 104, 225–247.

Marsella, A. J. (1993). Counseling and psychotherapy with Japanese Americans. *American Journal of Orthopsychiatry* 63, 200–208.

Massimini, F., & Calegari, P. (1979). *Il contesto normativo sociale.* Milan: Angeli.

Matsui, T., Kakuyama, T., & Onglatco, M. L. (1987). Effects of goals and feedback on performance in groups. *Journal of Applied Psychology* 72, 407–415.

Matsumoto, D. (1989). Cultural differences in the perception of emotion. *Journal of Cross-Cultural Psychology* 20, 92–105.

Matsumoto, D. (1991). Cultural influences on facial expressions of emotions. *Southern Journal of Communication* 56, 128–137.

Matsumoto, D., & Fletcher, D. (1993). Cultural influences on disease. Mimeo.

Mboga, M. M. (1986). Black adolescents: A descriptive study of their self-concepts and academic achievement. *Adolescence* 21, 689–696.

Mead, M. (1967). *Cooperation and competition among primitive peoples.* Boston: Beacon Press.

Milgram, S.(1974). *Obedience to authority.* New York: Harper & Row.

Miller, J. G. (1984). Culture and the development of everyday social explanation. *Journal of Personality and Social Psychology* 46, 961–978.

Miller, J. G. (1994). Cultural diversity in the morality of caring: Individually-oriented versus duty-oriented interpersonal codes. *Cross-Cultural Research* 28, 3–39.

Mills, J., & Clark, M. S. (1982). Exchange and communal relationships. In L. Wheeler (ed.). *Review of personality and social psychology* (vol. 3, pp. 121–144). Beverly Hills, Calif.: Sage.

Minturn, L., & Lambert, W. W. (1964). *Mothers of six cultures.* New York: Wiley.

Misumi, J. (1985). *The behavioral science of leadership: An interdisciplinary Japanese research program.* Ann Arbor: University of Michigan Press.

Mitchell, T. R., & Silver, W. S. (1990). Individual and group goals when workers are interdependent: Effects on task strategies and performance. *Journal of Applied Psychology* 75, 185–193.

Moghaddam, F. M., Taylor, D. M., & Wright, S. C. (1993). *Social psychology in cross-cultural perspective.* New York: Freeman.

Mordkowitz, E. R., & Ginsburg, H. P. (1987). The academic socialization of successful Asian American college students. *Quarterly Journal of Laboratory of Comparative Human Cognition* 9, 85–91.

Morris, M. W., & Peng, K. (submitted). Culture and cause.

Morsbach, H. (1980). Major psychological factors influencing Japanese interpersonal relations. In N. Warren (ed.). *Studies in cross-cultural psychology* (vol. 2, pp. 33–50). London: Academic Press.

Moskowitz, D. S., Suh, E. J., & Desaulniers, J. (1994). Situational influences on gender differences in agency and communion. *Journal of Personality and Social Psychology* 66, 753–761.

Moynihan, D. P. (1993). *Pandaemonium.* New York: Oxford.

Munroe, R. H., & Munroe, R. L. (1994). Behavior across cultures: Results from observational studies. In W. J. Lonner & R. Malpass (eds.). *Psychology and culture* (pp. 239–244). Boston: Allyn & Bacon.

Nader, L. (1975). Anthropological perspectives. In M. J. Lerner (ed.). The justice motive in social behavior. *Journal of Social Issues* 31, 151–170.

Naidoo, J. C., & Davis, J. C. (1988). Canadian South Asian women in transition: A dualistic view of life. *Journal of Comparative Studies* 19, 311–327.

Naito, T. (1994). A survey of research on moral development in Japan. *Cross-Cultural Research* 28, 40–57.

Naoi, M., & Schooler, C. (1990). Psychological consequences of occupational conditions among Japanese wives. *Social Psychology Quarterly* 53, 100–116.

Naroll, R. (1983). *The moral order.* Beverly Hills, Calif.: Sage.

Newman, L. S. (1993). How individualists interpret behavior: Idiocentrism and spontaneous trait inference. *Social Cognition* 11, 243–269.

Nisbett, R. E. (1990). Evolutionary psychology, biology and cultural evolution. *Motivation and Emotion* 14, 255–263.

Noesjirwan, J., Gault, U., & Crawford, J. (1983). Beliefs about memory in the aged. *Journal of Cross-Cultural Psychology* 14, 455–468.

Norem-Habeisen, A. A., & Johnson, D. W. (1981). The relationship between cooperative, competitive, and individualistic attitudes and different aspects of self-esteem. *Journal of Personality* 49, 415–426.

Noricks, J. S., Agler, L. H., Bartholomew, M., Howard-Smith, S., Martin, D., Pyles, S., & Shapiro, W. (1987). Age, abstract thinking, and the American concept of person. *American Anthropologist* 89, 667–675.

Oberg, K. (1954). *Culture shock.* Bobb-Merrill Reprint Series, No. A–329.

Oberg, K. (1960). Culture shock: Adjustment to new cultural environments. *Practical Anthropology* 7, 177–182.

Oettingen, G. (1994). Cross-cultural perspectives on self-efficacy beliefs. In A. Bandura (ed.). *Self efficacy in changing societies.* New York: Cambridge University Press.

Ohbuchi, K., & Takahashi, Y. (1994). Cultural styles of conflict management in Japanese and Americans: Passivity, covertness, and effectiveness of strategies. *Journal of Applied Social Psychology* 24, 1345–1366.

O'Neill, J. (ed.) (1976). *Modes of individualism and collectivism.* London: Heinemann Educational.

Otrocska, K., Jarymowicz, M., & Kwiatowska, A. (1991). Group attributive components of social identity in national ingroup favoritism. Paper presented at the conference of the International Association of Cross Cultural Psychology, in Debrecen, Hungary, July.

Oyama, N. (1990). Some recent trends in Japanese values. Beyond individual-collective dimension. Paper presented at the International Congress of Sociology, Barcelona, Spain, July.

Oyserman, D. (1993). The lens of personhood: Viewing the self and others in a multicultural society. *Journal of Personality & Social Psychology* 65, 993–1009.

Pandey, J. (1986). Socio-cultural perspectives on ingratiation. In B. A. Maher and W. B. Maher (eds.). *Progress in Experimental Personality Research* 14, Orlando, Fla.: Academic Press.

Pandey, J., Sinha, Y., Prakash, A., & Tripathi, R. C. (1982). Right-left political ideologies and attribution of the causes of poverty. *European Journal of Social Psychology* 12, 327–331.

Pareek, U. (1968). A motivational paradigm of development. *Journal of Social Issues* 24, 115–122.

Parsons, T. (1949). *The structure of social action.* Glencoe, Ill.: Free Press.

Pearson, L. (1990). *Children of glasnost.* Seattle: University of Washington Press.

Pedersen, P. (1994). "Cross-Cultural Counseling." Talk to American Psychological Association conference, Los Angeles, August.

Pelto, P. J. (1968). The difference between "tight" and "loose" societies. *Transaction,* April, 37–40.

Pettigrew, T. (1959). The demography of desegregation. *Journal of Social Issues* 15, 61–71.

Phillips, H. P. (1965). *Thai peasant personality: The patterning of interpersonal behavior in the village of Bang Chan.* Berkeley: University of California Press.

Pilisuk, M., & Parks, S. (1985). *The healing web.* Hanover, N.H.: University Press of New England.

Quattrone, G. A. (1986). On the perception of group variability. In S. Worchel & W. G. Austin (eds.). *The psychology of intergroup relations* (pp. 25–48). Chicago: Nelson-Hall.

Radcliffe-Brown, A. R. (1913). Three tribes of Western Australia. *Journal of the Royal Anthropological Institute* 43, 143–170.

Radford, M., Mann, L., Ohta, Y., & Nakone, Y. (1993). Differences between Australian and Japanese students in decisional self-esteem, decision stress, and coping styles. *Journal of Cross-Cultural Psychology* 24, 284–297.

Rakoff, W. (1978). The illusion of detachment. *Adolescent Psychiatry* 6, 119–129.

Razran, G. (1940). Conditioned response changes in rating and appraising socio-political slogans. *Psychological Bulletin* 37, 481.

Redding, S. G., Norman, A., Schlander, A. (1994). The nature of individual attachement to the organization: A review of East Asian variations. In H. C. Triandis, M. Dunnette, and L. Hough (eds.). *Handbook of industrial and organizational psychology* (2d ed., vol. 4, pp. 557–607). Palo Alto, Calif.: Consulting Psychologists Press.

Redfield, R. (1956). *Peasant society and culture: An anthropological approach to civilization.* Chicago: University of Chicago Press.

Reykowski, J. (1994). Collectivism and individualism as dimensions of social change. In U. Kim, H. C. Triandis, C. Kagitcibasi, S-C. Choi, & G. Yoon (eds.). *Individualism and collectivism: Theory, method, and applications* (pp. 276–292). Newbury Park, Calif.: Sage.

Riesman, D., Glazer, N., & Denney, R. (1961). *The lonely crowd: A study of the changing American character.* New Haven: Yale University Press.

Robarchek, K., & Robarchek, C. J. (1992). Cultures of war and peace: A comparative study of Waorani and Semai. In J. Silverberg & J. P. Gray (eds.). *Aggression and peacefulness in humans and other primates* (pp. 189–213). New York: Oxford University Press.

Robbins, M. C., de Walt, B. R., & Pelto, P. J. (1972). Climate and behavior: A biocultural study. *Journal of Cross-Cultural Psychology* 3, 331–344.

Rodnick, D. (1955). *The Norwegians.* Washington, D.C.: Public Affairs Press.

Rohner, R. P. (1986). *The warmth dimension: Foundations of parental acceptance-rejection theory.* Newbury Park, Calif.: Sage.

Rokeach, M. (1960). *The open and closed mind.* New York: Basic Books.

Rokeach, M. (1973). *The nature of human values.* New York: Basic Books.

Rokeach, M., & Rothman, G. (1965). The principle of belief congruence and the congruity principle as models of cognitive interaction. *Psychological Review* 72, 128–142.

Ronen, S. (1994). An understanding of motivational need taxonomies: A cross-cultural confirmation. In H. C. Triandis, M. Dunnete, and L. Hough (eds.). *Handbook of industrial and organizational psychology* (2d ed., vol. 4, pp. 241–270). Palo Alto, Calif.: Consulting Psychologists Press.

Rosenthal, D., & Bornholt, I. (1988). Expectations about development in Greek and Anglo-Australian families. *Journal of Cross-Cultural Psychology* 19, 19–34.

Ross, L., & Nisbett, R. E. (1991). *The person and the situation.* New York: McGraw-Hill.

Rotenburg, M. (1977). Alienating individualism and reciprocal individualism: A cross-cultural conceptualization. *Journal of Humanistic Psychology* 17, 3–17.

Sakamoto, N. M. (1982). *Polite fictions: Why Japanese and Americans seem rude to each other.* Tokyo, Japan: Kinseido.

Sampson, E. E. (1977). Psychology and the American ideal. *Journal of Personality and Social Psychology* 35, 767–782.

Sandel, M. (1982). *Liberalism and the limits of justice.* Cambridge, England: Cambridge University Press.

Sanger, D. E. (1993). Student's killing displays dark side of Japan schools. *New York Times,* October 15.

Scheper-Hughes, N. (1985). Culture, scarcity, and maternal thinking: Maternal detachment and infant survival in a Brazilian shantytown. *Ethos* 13, 291–317.

Schmidt, N., & Sermat, V. (1983). Measuring loneliness in different relationships. *Journal of Personality and Social Psychology* 44, 1038–1047.

Schmitz, P. G. (1990). Individualism-collectivism and acculturation modes. Paper presented at the individualism-collectivism conference in Seoul, Korea, July.

Schooler, C. (1990a). Individualism and historical and social structural determinants of people's concerns over self-directedness and efficiency. In J. Rudin, C. Schooler, & K. W. Schaie (eds.). *Self-directedness.* Hillsdale, N.J.: Erlbaum.

Schooler, C. (1990b). The individual in Japanese history: Parallels to and divergences from the European experience. *Sociological Forum* 5, December.

Schwartz, B. (1986). *The battle of human nature: Science, morality, and modern life.* New York: Norton.

Schwartz, S. H. (1990). Individualism-collectivism. Critique and proposed refinements. *Journal of Cross-Cultural Psychology* 21, 139–157.

Schwartz, S. H. (1992). Universals in the content and structure of values: Theoretical advances and empirical tests in 20 countries. In M. Zanna (ed.). *Advances in Experimental Social Psychology* (vol. 25, pp. 1–66). New York: Academic Press.

Schwartz, S. H. (1994). Beyond individualism and collectivism: New cultural dimensions of values. In U. Kim, H. C. Triandis, C. Kagitcibasi, S-C. Choi, & G. Yoon (eds.). *Individualism and collectivism: Theory, method, and applications* (pp. 85–122). Newbury Park, Calif.: Sage.

Schwartz, S. H., & Bilsky, W. (1987). Toward a universal psychological structure of human values. *Journal of Personality and Social Psychology* 53, 550–562.

Schwartz, S. H., & Bilsky, W. (1990). Toward a theory of the universal content and structure of values: Extensions and cross-cultural replications. *Journal of Personality and Social Psychology* 58, 878–891.

Sears, D. (1988). Symbolic racism. In P. A. Katz & D. A. Taylor (eds.). *Eliminating racism.* New York: Plenum.

Segal, R. A. (1987). *Joseph Campbell: An introduction.* New York: Garland Publishing.

Selznick, P. (1992). *The moral commonwealth.* Berkeley: University of California Press.

Semin, G. R., & Rubini, M. (1990). Unfolding the concept of persona by verbal abuse. *European Journal of Social Psychology* 20, 463–474.

Setiadi, B. N. (1984). Schooling, age, and culture as moderators of role perceptions. Unpublished Doctoral Dissertation, University of Illinois, Champaign-Urbana.

Shannon, P. (1986). Hidden within the pages: A study of social perspective in young children's favorite books. *Reading Teacher* 39, 656–663.

Shouval, R., Kav, V. S., Bronfenbrenner, U., Devereux, E. C., & Kiely, E. (1975). Anomalous reactions to social pressure of Israeli and Soviet children raised in family vs. collective settings. *Journal of Personality and Social Psychology* 32, 477–489.

Shweder, R. A., & Bourne, E. J. (1982). Does the concept of person vary cross-culturally? In A. J. Marsella & G. M. White (eds.). *Cultural conceptions of mental health and therapy* (pp. 130–204). London: Reidel.

Shweder, R. A., Mahapatra, M., & Miller, J. G. (1990). Culture and moral development. In J. W. Stigler, R. A. Shweder, & G. Herdt (eds.). *Cultural psychology* (pp.
130–204). New York: Cambridge University Press.

Sigmon, B. A. (1993). Physical anthropology in socialist Europe. *American Scientist*
81, 130–139.

Simon, B. (1993). On the asymmetry in the cognitive construal of ingroup and
outgroup: A model of egocentric social categorization. *European Journal of Social Psychology* 23, 131–147.

Singelis, T. M. (1992). Collectivist communication and interdependent self-
construals: An individual-level analysis. Master of Arts Thesis. Honolulu: University of Hawaii.

Singelis, T. M. (1994). The measurement of independent and interdependent self-
construals. *Personality and Social Psychology Bulletin* 20, 580–591.

Singelis, T. M., & Brown, W. J. (submitted). Culture, self, and collectivist communication: Linking culture to individual behavior.

Singelis, T. M., & Sharkey, W. F. (in press). Embarrassability, ethnicity and self-
construals. *Journal of Cross Cultural Psychology.*

Singelis, T. M., Triandis, H. C., Bhawuk, D. S., & Gelfand, M. (in press). Horizontal
and vertical dimensions of individualism and collectivism: A theoretical and measurement refinement. *Cross-Cultural Research.*

Singh, R. (1981). Prediction of performance from motivation and ability: An appraisal of the cultural difference hypothesis. In J. Pandey (ed.). *Perspectives on
Experimental Social Psychology in India* (pp. 21–53). New Delhi: Concept.

Sinha, D. (1988). The family scenario in a developing country and its implications
for mental health: The case of India. In P. Dasen, J. Berry, & N. Sartorius (eds.).
Health and cross-cultural psychology (pp. 48–70). Newbury Park, Calif.: Sage.

Sinha, J. B. P. (1980). *The nurturant task leader.* New Delhi: Concept.

Sinha, J. B. P. (1982). The Hindu (Indian) identity. *Dynamische Psychiatrie* 15,
148–160.

Sinha, J. B. P. (1994). Cultural embeddedness and the developmental role of industrial organizations in India. In H. C. Triandis, M. Dunnette, and L. Hough (eds.).
Handbook of industrial and organizational psychology (2d ed., vol. 4, pp. 727–
764). Palo Alto, Calif.: Consulting Psychologists Press.

Sinha, J. B. P., & Verma, J. (1990). Social support as a moderator of the relationship
between allocentrism and psychological well-being. Paper presented at the individualism-collectivism conference, Seoul, Korea, July.

Skinner, B. F. (1981). Selection by consequences. *Science* 213, 501–504.

Smith, H. (1991). *The new Russians.* New York: Random House.

Smith, K., Johnson, D. W., & Johnson, R. T. (1982). Effects of cooperative and individualistic instruction on achievement of handicapped, regular, and gifted students. *Journal of Social Psychology* 116, 277–283.

Smith, M. B. (1978). Perspectives on selfhood. *American Psychologist* 33, 1053–
1063.

Smith, P. B., & Bond, M. H. (1994). *Social psychology across cultures.* Boston: Allyn
and Bacon.

Snyder, M. (1974). Self-monitoring of expressive behavior. *Journal of Personality
and Social Psychology* 30, 526–537.

Spence, J. T. (1985). Achievement American style: The rewards and cost of individualism. *American Psychologist* 40, 1285–1295.

Spranger, E. (1928). *Types of men.* Halle, Germany: Max Niemeyer Verlag.

Springwood, C. F. (1992). Space, time, and hardware individualism in Japanese baseball: Non-Western dimensions of personhood. *Play and Culture* 5, 280–294.

Stevens, S. S. (1966). Matching functions between loudness and ten other continua. *Perception and Psychophysics* 1, 5–8.

Stewart, E. (1966). The simulation of cultural differences. *Journal of Communication* 16, 291–304.

Stewart, R. A. C. (1971). *Cultural dimensions.* New Haven: Human Relations Area Files.

Strodtbeck, F. (1958). Family interaction, values, and achievement. In D. McClelland (ed.). *Talent and society* (pp. 135–195). New York: Van Nostrand.

Suh, E. M. (1994). Emotion norms, value, familiarity and subjective well-being: A cross-cultural examination. M.A. Thesis. University of Illinois, Champaign. Department of Psychology.

Tajfel, H. (1982). *Social identity and intergroup relations.* New York: Cambridge University Press.

Tallman, I., Marotz-Baden, R., & Pindas, P. (1983). *Adolescent socialization in cross-cultural perspective.* New York: Academic Press.

Tanaka, Y. (1978). The analysis of subjective political culture. *Gakushin Review of Law and Politics* 13, 1–93.

Tanaka, Y. (1983). Personal communication.

Tata, S. P., & Leong, F. T. L. (in press). Individualism-collectivism, network orientation, and acculturation as predictors of attitudes towards seeking professional psychological help among Chinese Americans. *Journal of Counseling Psychology.*

Taylor, C. (1985). *Philosophy and human sciences: Philosophical paper.* New York: Cambridge University Press.

Taylor, C. (1989). *Sources of the self: The making of modern identity.* Cambridge, Mass.: Harvard University Press.

Tetlock, P. E., Peterson, R. S., & Berry, J. M. (1993). Flattering and unflattering personality portraits of integrative simple and complex managers. *Journal of Personality and Social Psychology* 64, 500–511.

Thomson, I. T. (1989). The transformation of the social bond: Images of individualism in the 1920s and 1970s. *Social Forces* 67, 851–870.

Ting-Toomey, S. (1988). Intercultural conflict styles: A face-negotiation theory. In Y. Y. Kim and W. B. Gudykunst (eds.). *Theory of intercultural communication.* Newbury Park, Calif.: Sage.

Ting-Toomey, S. (1993). Communicative resourcefulness: An identity negotiation perspective. In R. Wiseman & J. Koester (eds.). *Intercultural communication competence.* Newbury Park, Calif.: Sage.

Ting-Toomey, S. (1994a). Managing intercultural conflicts effectively. In L. Samovar & R. Porter (eds.). *Intercultural communication: A reader* (7th ed.). Belmont, Calif.: Wadsworth.

Ting-Toomey, S. (1994b). Managing intimate conflict in intercultural personal relationships. In D. D. Cahn (ed.). *Intimate conflict in personal relationships.* Hillsdale, N.J.: Erlbaum.

Ting-Toomey, S., Gao, G., Trubisky, P., Yang, Z., Kim, H. S., Lin, S-L., & Nishida, T. (1991). Culture, face maintenance, and styles of handling interpersonal conflict: A study in five cultures. *International Journal of Conflict Resolution* 2, 275–296.

Tocqueville, A. de (1985 [reprint], vol. 1, trans. 1835; vol. 2, trans. 1840). *Democracy in America.* New York: Alfred Knopf.

Todd, E. (1983). *La troisieme planète.* Paris: Editions du Seuil.

Todd, E. (1987). *The causes of progress.* Oxford: Basil Blackwell.

Toennies, F. (1957). *Community and society,* trans. C. P. Loomis. East Lansing: Michigan State University Press.

Trafimow, D., Triandis, H. C., & Goto, S. (1991). Some tests of the distinction between private self and collective self. *Journal of Personality and Social Psychology* 60, 649–655.

Triandis, H. C. (1967). Interpersonal relationships in international organizations. *Journal of Organizational Behavior and Human Performance* 2, 26–55.

Triandis, H. C. (ed.) (1972). *The analysis of subjective culture.* New York: Wiley.

Triandis, H. C. (1975). Cultural training, cognitive complexity, and interpersonal attitudes. In R. W. Brislin, S. Bochner, and W. J. Lonner (eds.). *Cross cultural perspectives on learning.* Beverly Hills, Calif.: Sage.

Triandis, H. C. (1977). *Interpersonal behavior.* Monterey, Calif.: Brooks/Cole.

Triandis, H. C. (1978). Some universals of social behavior. *Personality and Social Psychology Bulletin* 4, 1–16.

Triandis, H. C. (1980). Values, attitudes, and interpersonal behavior. In H. E. Howe & M. M. Page (eds.). *Nebraska Symposium on Motivation, 1979.* Lincoln: University of Nebraska Press.

Triandis, H. C. (1988). Collectivism v. individualism: A reconceptualization of a basic concept in cross-cultural social psychology. In G. K. Verma & C. Bagley (eds.). *Cross-cultural studies of personality, attitudes and cognition* (pp. 60–95). London: Macmillan.

Triandis, H. C. (1989). The self and social behavior in differing cultural contexts. *Psychological Review* 96, 506–520.

Triandis, H. C. (1990). Cross-cultural studies of individualism and collectivism. In J. Berman (ed.). *Nebraska Symposium on Motivation, 1989* (pp. 41–133). Lincoln: University of Nebraska Press.

Triandis, H. C. (1993). Collectivism and individualism as cultural syndromes. *Cross-Cultural Research* 27, 155–180.

Triandis, H. C. (1994). *Culture and social behavior.* New York: McGraw-Hill.

Triandis, H. C., & Singelis, T. (submitted). Training to discriminate collectivists and individualists within culture.

Triandis, H. C., & Vassiliou, V. (1972). A comparative analysis of subjective culture. In H. C. Triandis (ed.). *The analysis of subjective culture* (pp. 299–338). New York: Wiley.

Triandis, H. C., Bontempo, R., Betancourt, H., Bond, M., Leung, K., Brenes, A., Georgas, J., Hui, C. H., Marin, G., Setiadi, B., Sinha, J. B. P., Verma, J., Spangenberg, J., Touzard, H., & de Montmollin, G. (1986). The measurement of etic aspects of individualism and collectivism across cultures. *Australian Journal of Psychology* 38, 257–267.

Triandis, H. C., Bontempo, R., Leung, K., & Hui, C. H. (1990). A method for determining cultural, demographic, and personal constructs. *Journal of Cross-Cultural Psychology* 21, 302–318.

Triandis, H. C., Bontempo, R., Villareal, M. J., Asai, M., & Lucca, N. (1988). Individualism and collectivism: Cross-cultural perspectives on self-ingroup relationships. *Journal of Personality and Social Psychology* 54, 323–338.

Triandis, H. C., Brislin, R., & Hui, C. H. (1988). Cross-cultural training across the individualism-collectivism divide. *International Journal of Intercultural Relations* 12, 269–289.

Triandis, H. C., Chan, D. K-S., Bhawuk, D., Iwao, S., & Sinha, J. B. P. (in press). Multimethod probes of allocentrism and idiocentrism. *International Journal of Psychology.*

Triandis, H. C., Kashima, Y., Shimada, E., & Villareal, M. (1986). Acculturation indices as a means of confirming cultural differences. *International Journal of Psychology* 21, 43–79.

Triandis, H. C., Leung, K., Villareal, M., & Clack, F. L. (1985). Allocentric vs. idiocentric tendencies: Convergent and discriminant validation. *Journal of Research in Personality* 19, 395–415.

Triandis, H. C., McCusker, C., & Hui, C. H. (1990). Multimethod probes of individualism and collectivism. *Journal of Personality and Social Psychology* 59, 1006–1020.

Triandis, H. C., McCusker, C., Betancourt, H., Iwao, S., Leung, K., Salazar, J. M., Setiadi, B., Sinha, J. B. P., Touzard, H., & Zaleski, Z. (1993). An etic-emic analysis of individualism and collectivism. *Journal of Cross-Cultural Psychology* 24, 366–383.

Triandis, H. C., Marin, G., Hui, C. H., Lisansky, J., & Ottati, V. (1984). Role perceptions of Hispanic young adults. *Journal of Cross-Cultural Psychology* 15, 297–320.

Triandis, H. C., Marin, G., Lisansky, J., & Betancourt, H. (1984). *Simpatia* as a cultural script of Hispanics. *Journal of Personality and Social Psychology* 47, 1363–1374.

Trilling, L. (1972). *Sincerity and authenticity.* London: Oxford University Press.

Trimble, J. E. (1994). Cultural variations in use of alcohol and drugs. In W. J. Lonner & R. Malpass (eds.). *Psychology and culture* (pp. 239–244). Boston: Allyn & Bacon.

Trubisky, P., Ting-Toomey, S., & Lin, S. (1991). The influence of individualism-collectivism and self-monitoring on conflict styles. *International Journal of Intercultural Relations* 15, 65–84.

Tu, W-M. (1985). Selfhood and otherness in Confucian thought. In A. J. Marsella, G. deVos, and F. L. K. Hsu (eds.). *Culture and self.* New York: Tavistock Publications.

Turnbull, C. M. *The mountain people.* New York: Simon & Schuster.

Turner, B. L., II, Clark, W. C., Kates, R. W., Richards, J. F., Mathews, J. T., & Meyer, W. B. (eds.) (1990). *The earth as transformed by human action: Global and regional changes in the biosphere over the past 300 years.* Cambridge, England: Cambridge University Press with Clark University.

Ueda, K. (1974). *Sixteen ways to avoid saying "No" in Japan: Patterns of communication in and out of Japan.* Tokyo: ICU Communication Department.

Ulaszek, W. R. (1990). Cultural differences in the perception of stress. Honors Bachelor of Science thesis. University of Illinois, Champaign.

Umpleby, S. A. (1990). Comparing conceptual systems: A strategy for changing values as well as institutions. Paper presented to the European Conference on Cybernetics and Systems Research, Vienna, Austria, April.

Vassiliou, G., & Vassiliou, V. (1966). Social values as a psychodynamic variable: Preliminary explorations of the semantics of philotimo. *Acta Neurologica et Psychiatrica Hellenika* 5, 121–135.

Verma, J. (1992). Allocentrism and relational orientation. In S. Iwawaki, Y. Kashima, & K. Leung (eds.). *Innovations in cross-cultural psychology* (pp. 152–163). Amsterdam/Lisse: Swets & Zeitlinger.

Vijayakumar, V. S. R. (1991). On the exercise on individualism and collectivism. Mimeo.

Wagner, J. A., III (1992). Individualism-collectivism and free riding: A study of main and moderator effects. Paper presented at the Las Vegas, Nevada, meetings of the Academy of Management, August.

Wagner, J. A., III, & Moch, M. K. (1986). Individualism-collectivism: Concept and measurement. *Group and Organizational Studies* 11, 280–304.

Walzer, M. (1990). The communitarian critique of liberalism. *Political Theory* 18, 6–23.

Wang, Z-M. (1994). Culture, economic reform and the role of industrial/organizational psychology in China. In H. C. Triandis, M. Dunnette, and L. Hough (eds.). *Handbook of industrial and organizational psychology* (pp. 689–726). Palo Alto, Calif.: Consulting Psychologists Press.

Waterman, A. S. (1981). Individualism and interdependence. *American Psychologist* 36, 762–773.

Waterman, A. S. (1984). *The psychology of individualism.* New York: Praeger.

Weber, M. (1930, 1958). *The protestant ethic and the spirit of capitalism,* trans. T. Parsons. New York: Scribner's.

Weber, M. (1947, 1957). *The theory of social and economic organization.* Glencoe, Ill.: Free Press.

Weiss, C., Courty, M. A., Wetterstrom, W., Guichard, F., Senior, L., Meadow, R., & Curnow, A. (1993). The genesis and collapse of third millennium North Mesopotamia civilization. *Science* 261, 995–1004.

Weissman, M., Matsumoto, D., Brown, B., & Preston, K. (1993). Measuring culture. Paper presented at the meetings of the American Psychological Association in Toronto, August.

Weldon, E. (1984). Deindividuation, interpersonal affect, and productivity in laboratory task groups. *Journal of Applied Social Psychology* 14, 469–485.

Westcott, M. R. (1988). *The psychology of human freedom.* New York: Springer.

Westie, F. R., & Westie, M. L. (1957). The social distance pyramid: Relationships between caste and class. *American Journal of Sociology* 63, 190–196.

Wheeler, L., Reis, H. T., & Bond, M. H. (1989). Collectivism-individualism in everyday social life: The Middle Kingdom and the melting pot. *Journal of Personality and Social Psychology* 57, 79–86.

Whiting, B. B., & Whiting, J. W. M. (1975). *Children of six cultures.* Cambridge, Mass.: Harvard University Press.

Wichiarajote, W. (1975). A theory of the affiliative society vs. the achieving society. Mimeo.

Wiggins, J. S. (1991). Agency and communion as conceptual coordinates for the understanding and measurement of interpersonal behavior. In W. M. Grove and D. Cicchetti (eds.). *Thinking clearly about psychology* (pp. 89–113). Minneapolis: University of Minnesota Press.

Williams, J., & Best, D. (1982). *Measuring sex stereotypes: A thirty-nation study.* Beverly Hills, Calif.: Sage.

Williams, J., & Best, D. (1990). *Self and psyche: Gender and sex viewed cross-culturally.* Newbury Park, Calif.: Sage.

Williams, J., & Best, D. (1994). Cross-cultural views of women and men. In W. J. Lonner & R. Malpass (eds.). *Psychology and culture* (pp. 239–244). Boston: Allyn & Bacon.

Wink, P. (1992). Three narcissism scales for the California Q-set. *Journal of Personality Assessment* 58, 51–66.

Witkin, H., & Berry, J. W. (1975). Psychological differentiation in cross-cultural perspective. *Journal of Cross-Cultural Psychology* 6, 4–87.

Wooddell, V. (1989, mimeo). Individualism and collectivism: The effect of race and family structure.

Wu, D. Y. H. (1985). Child training in Chinese culture. In D. Y. H. Wu & W. Tseng (eds.). *Chinese culture and mental health* (pp. 113–134). New York: Academic Press.

Yamagishi, T. (1988). Exit from the group as an individualistic solution to the free rider problem in the United States and Japan. *Journal of Experimental Social Psychology* 24, 530–542.

Yamaguchi, S. (1993). Recent research on collectivism (Lecture, University of Illinois, September 9).

Yamaguchi, S. (1994). Empirical evidence on collectivism among the Japanese. In U. Kim, H. C. Triandis, C. Kagitcibasi, S-C. Choi, & G. Yoon (eds.). *Individualism and collectivism: Theory, method, and applications* (pp. 175–188). Newbury Park, Calif.: Sage.

Yang, K. (1988). Will societal modernization eventually eliminate cross-cultural psychological differences? In M. Bond (ed.). *The cross-cultural challenge to social psychology* (pp. 67–85). Newbury Park, Calif.: Sage.

Yergin, D. (1992). *The prize: The epic quest for oil, money, and power.* New York: Touchstone Books.

Yu, A-B., & Yang, K-S. (1994). The nature of achievement motivation in collectivist societies. In U. Kim, H. C. Triandis, C. Kagitcibasi, S-C. Choi, & G. Yoon (eds.). *Individualism and collectivism: Theory, method, and applications* (pp. 239–250). Newbury Park, Calif.: Sage.

Yum, J. O. (1988). The impact of Confucianism on interpersonal relationships and communication patterns in East Asia. *Communication Monographs* 55, 374–388.

Zahrly, J., & Tosi, H. (1989). The differential effect of organizational induction process on early work role adjustment. *Journal of Organizational Behavior* 10, 59–74.

Zern, D. S. (1982). The impact of values on development in a cross-cultural sample. *Genetic Psychology Monographs* 106, 179–197.

Zern, D. S. (1983). The relationship of certain group-oriented and individualistically oriented child-rearing dimensions of cultural complexity in a cross-cultural sample. *Genetic Psychology Monographs* 108, 3–20.

Ziller, R. C. (1965). Toward a theory of open and closed groups. *Psychological Bulletin* 64, 164–182.

Zucker, G. S., & Weiner, B. (1993). Conservatism and perceptions of poverty: An attributional analysis. *Journal of Applied Social Psychology* 23, 925–943.

About the Book and Author

IN THIS, his latest book, Harry Triandis explores the constructs of collectivism and individualism. Collectivists are closely linked individuals who view themselves primarily as parts of a whole, be it a family, a network of co-workers, a tribe, or a nation. Such people are mainly motivated by the norms and duties imposed by the collective entity. Individualists are motivated by their own preferences, needs, and rights, giving priority to personal rather than to group goals.

Reviewing relevant literature in philosophy, political science, anthropology, sociology, and psychology, Triandis shows how culture shapes the way we think. He also explores the wide-ranging implications of individualism and collectivism for political, social, religious, and economic life. He makes compelling arguments for the appreciation of both perspectives, drawing on examples from Japan, Sweden, China, Greece, Russia, the United States, and other countries.

Triandis challenges the view that psychology is universal, offering evidence for culture-specific influences on thought and action. We learn that the cultural patterns represented by individualism and collectivism lead people to view their worlds through different lenses, attaching different meanings to life events. Triandis explains how these variations in meaning can help us better understand why crime rates, divorce rates, levels of self-esteem, feelings of well-being, and indeed overall behavioral patterns can be so different from one society to another.

HARRY C. TRIANDIS is professor of psychology at the University of Illinois at Urbana-Champaign.

Index